HONG KONG MOVERS
AND STAYERS

STUDIES OF
WORLD MIGRATIONS

Series Editors
Donna R. Gabaccia
Leslie Page Moch

*A list of books in the series appears
at the end of the book.*

HONG KONG
MOVERS AND STAYERS

Narratives of
Family Migration

JANET W. SALAFF,
SIU-LUN WONG, AND ARENT GREVE

UNIVERSITY OF ILLINOIS PRESS

Urbana and Chicago

Manufactured in the United States of America
1 2 3 4 5 C P 5 4 3 2 1
∞ This book is printed on acid-free paper.

Library of Congress Cataloging-in-Publication Data
Salaff, Janet W.
Hong Kong movers and stayers : narratives of family migration /
Janet W. Salaff, Siu-lun Wong, and Arent Greve.
p.   cm. — (Studies of world migrations)
Includes bibliographical references and index.
ISBN 978-0-252-03518-0 (cloth : alk. paper) —
ISBN 978-0-252-07704-3 (paper : alk. paper)
1. Hong Kong (China)—Emigration and immigration—
Social aspects. 2. Hong Kong (China)—Social conditions.
3. Families—China—Hong Kong. 4. Chinese—Migrations.
5. Immigrants—China—Hong Kong—Family relationships.
6. Immigrants—China—Hong Kong—Biography.
7. Hong Kong (China)—Biography.
I. Wong, Siu-lun. II. Greve, Arent. III. Title.
JV8758.S25   2010
304.8095125—dc22   2009027064

CONTENTS

PREFACE

This book evolved from the jostling of diverse interpretations of the international furor in Hong Kong in 1991 over the colony's pending reversion to the People's Republic of China (PRC). Migration is an integral part of our lives. But as the number of emigrants swelled in response to the great pressure of those events, it was hard for observers and participants to assess how migration was structured. By looking at the lives of nine Hong Kong families over time within a neo-institutional framework, this book shows how social structures at different levels underlie emigration and how these change over time.

In 1995, *Fortune Magazine* pundits pronounced "The Death of Hong Kong" (Kraar 1995). Between the inking of the agreement between Britain and China in 1984 to the actual reversion in 1997, many Hong Kong residents applied for foreign papers and an estimated 500,000 left. Then, several years before the handover itself, many returned. Wasn't the source of this popular movement obvious? Voting with their feet, people left Hong Kong due to political anxieties ascribed to the impending handover, and when fears receded, they returned.

But what everyone thought they knew was challenged when we began this study. "We didn't emigrate because of 1997," Uncle Chou (chapter 4) proclaimed, when we met in 1992. But Francis Kwong insisted (chapter 5) around the same time, "I want my son to live in a liberal land!" This book emerged as our answer to what motivates people to consider migration and what contributes to its realization.

Ten years after the handover there has been surprisingly little evaluation of the exceptionally large movements of people leading up to Hong Kong's reversion to China. In this book we evaluate the diverse migration stories of nine Hong Kong families whom we have known since the early 1990s, some having left for Canada and others staying in Hong Kong. Over this significant period, these families responded in different ways to the immense sea change of the reversion of Hong Kong to China. Their migration experiences give us a window into their shared and distinct responses to institutional changes.

We learned that the social structures around them strongly influence whether families can or want to leave Hong Kong. We analyze their diverse responses using a multilevel neo-institutional framework that helps us understand the experiences of families remaining in Hong Kong, migrating, settling, or returning. At the broadest level, globalization and large-scale legal and economic forces underlay their moves, successes, and failures. At the intermediate level, social relationships spark motivation to emigrate. Finally, people develop interpretative schemas around these structures that prompt or discourage leaving.

Studying how the position of these families in relation to migration changes over a significant period of time brings into relief even more the key social structures in the migration process. We find that institutional structures affect those with the same kinds of resources in a relatively similar manner. But each family creatively interprets what moving or staying means to them. The materials in this book provide a rich source of understanding how families make, change, or avoid decisions to emigrate.

ACKNOWLEDGMENTS

In researching and writing this book over fifteen years, we owe much to many. The Research Grants Council of Hong Kong funded the initial survey from which this sample was drawn, as well as our two follow-up waves of interviews.[1] The Hong Kong Culture and Society Programme at the University of Hong Kong and the Social Science and Humanities Research Council of Canada gave us support for the last waves of follow-up discussions with respondents and their children. The Centre of Asian Studies, University of Hong Kong, housed this project throughout, and we thank the staff for their support.

Our research assistants who followed us along to homes and teahouses were crucial in recording, interpreting, and empathizing with our respondents. We wholeheartedly thank Franklin Au, Anita Chan, Chang Chuen Man, Jonathan Cheng, Nellie Cheng, Connie Chiu Chuk Yi, Fung Mei Ling, Stephen C. K. Law, Tammy Leung, Fannie Leung, Lily Lap Li, Lydia Li, Li Tao, Hilary Mar, Candy Tsang, Jenny Wong, Louisa Yan, Diana Yeung, and Daniel Young. We especially appreciate the comments on earlier drafts from many people: Jacqueline Adams, Colin Day, Ruth Dixon, Steve Gold, Nancy Howell, Sharon Lee, Ellen Judd, Maggi Leung, Patricia Landolt, Constance Lever-Tracy, Peter Li, Myrla Magness, Guida Man, Frank Pieke, Caroline Pluss, Shana Salaff, Shelby Sampson, Angela Shik, Elizabeth Sinn, Metta Spencer, and Lillian Weitzner. Linn Clark, Allyson Skene, and Alan Sutterfield were valuable editors to earlier drafts. We wish to thank the University of Illinois Press, its series' editors, outside readers, and editor Terri Hudoba for their talented work to transform a manuscript into a book.

Above all, we are grateful to the families in our project for sharing their lives with us. We thank them all, and accept responsibility for our erratic memory and interpretations.

CHAPTER ONE

Institutional Theory
and Family Migration

At midnight on June 30, 1997, the red flag was raised over Hong Kong as Britain's most profitable colony was returned to China, marking the end of 156 years of Colonial rule. Hong Kong, long renowned as a great trade and financial center, was a gateway linking the West to China. In search of business and jobs, Hong Kong's cosmopolitan populace had become the leading edge of the Chinese diaspora, which settled in the major cities of the world (Skeldon 2003; Wang 1989). Hong Kong's hardworking people, its traveling managers, trained professionals, family firms, and capital-generating financial institutions had spearheaded China's emergence into the market economy. The handover to China marked the political integration of this global city with the world's largest developing Communist nation, a nation long isolated by the Western world. The joining of two more contrasting places was hard for many to imagine. Yet for others, reunification was their chance to reclaim their Chinese roots.

During the extended period leading up to reversion, substantial numbers of Hong Kongers left—mostly business people and professionals. The exit of so many elite families at once had an immense impact on Hong Kong and resounded beyond its borders as well. In their choice of destinations, Hong Kongers followed a pattern, forming large ethnic settlements and changing the face of major Western cities (Li 1992; Li et al. 1998; Ray et al. 1997). Canada received over half of these newcomers, an estimated 314,792 people between 1984 and 1996 (see Table 1). The flow rose from 16,170 in 1987, peaking at 44,169 in 1995 (Chiang 2001, 126). But within several years, half of them returned to Hong Kong (Aydemir and Robinson 2006, 44). Despite this return migration, Hong Kongers did not yield their presence in the West, with many (mostly husbands) becoming transnational migrants. The local term for them was astronauts, because they spent so much time flying between their Hong Kong jobs and families abroad.[1] The many transnational migrants challenged Western assumptions that citizenship meant not only the right of abode, but actual residence, and called for understanding their moves in structural as well as human terms (Castles 2003).

Perspectives on Migration

During our study period, perspectives on migration have become multivaried accounts, rooted in structures. However, when we began this study in 1991, most explanations of migration were monocausal and ethnocentric. Observers were sure that one single factor, political anxieties, a version of the push-pull model of migration, had created the flight from Hong Kong. The push-pull paradigm reflects modernization theory. This posits that pulled by money or values, after weighing their choices, people leave a poor economic or political situation toward a better life—usually in the West. Arrival in the receiving country is considered to be the end of the migration process. People settle, and their norms, behaviors, and attitudes become similar over time to those of the locals.

This simplistic account of migration is not only ethnocentric (the West is best), it is premised on the outdated view that the migrants rationally weigh alternatives. Moreover, the role of gender in migration is undertheorized. Typically, women are seen as "tied" migrants (Lee 1966). If husbands move for better economic opportunities, their family members, tied to them, follow. In emphasizing the receiving society's perspectives at the expense of the migrants,' writers expect immigrants, presumed to be uprooted from their culture, to assimilate to local ways of life. If they do not, they are accused of being traditional. Key features of immigrant life, from living with extended

Table 1. Hong Kong Immigrants in Major Receiving Countries

	Population[a] 1991	Population[a] 1996	Population[a] 2001	Inflows[b] 1991-2001	Percent remaining
Australia	58,995	68,430	67,124	56,817	61.6
Canada	163,400	249,175	240,045	207,670	66.5
USA			239,000[c]	82,363[d]	
UK			96,445	29,509	
Total				376,359	

Source: Migration Information Source, database, various years.
[a]Population born in Hong Kong
[b]Last place of residence is Hong Kong
[c]1990
[d]1990–2000

family members to marriage choice to forming identities, are regarded as caused by cultural preferences, disregarding underlying structural variations (Wong 2008).

Reviewing the main migration theories in 1993, Massey et al. (1993) found that push-pull theory dominated four of them. Classical economists posited that international wage differences stimulate flows of labor from nations with low-paid labor; after assessing the costs and benefits of the move, people travel toward a net gain in income. Somewhat revising this perspective, neoclassical economists argue that families often make migration decisions for their members and are motivated by other factors than income. Finally, in dual labor market and world systems theories, structural inequalities and global markets induce moves. Despite different assumptions, people are still pushed and pulled by economic forces. A theory of migration should explain why some people migrate while others stay despite being in similar economic or social conditions. Most people do not migrate, but some areas have more migration than similar others. This is one of the most serious shortcomings of the push-pull theory.

Other explanations of population movements are still monocausal and ethnocentric, although they veer from rational, economic-based explanations. Drawing on modernization theory, some propose that large-scale forces of a postmodernist global society weaken traditional social structures, norms, and values. As people's imaginings about who they can become and where they can go are set free, migration takes off (Giddens 1990).

In contrast, recent conceptual frameworks have emphasized social-structural factors in shaping family life (McLoyd et al. 2000). Network theorists locate features of many network characteristics in immigrant life (Lubbers et al. 2007). Segmented assimilation theory explains youths' identification with their own or another ethnicity by the structure of group contacts (Zhou 1997). These perspectives introduce complex, historically rooted processes, in which migration is rooted in structures and cognitive meanings. Multiple research methods have furthered complex theorizing. An example is the Mexican migration project of Massey et al. (1987; Palloni, et al. 2001) that surveyed and interviewed respondents and obtained their personal and community migration network histories.

Finally, given the large numbers of Hong Kong migrants, there are idiosyncratic cultural explanations for the flood of leavers. These posit that Hong Kong has long been a city of migrants. Hong Kong people under Colonialism were supposedly migration prone, living in a "borrowed place, [on] borrowed time," their moves contributing to the Chinese diaspora (Baker 1993; Hughes 1958). However, even in a city renowned for its population

mobility, particular social structures shape migration. Hong Kong's reversion to China meant different things to different people, and these meanings
were rooted in people's experiences and embedded in structures. People in
diverse structural positions experience situations that prompt migration
and encounter other circumstances that confound their plans. Their origins
also continue to define their way of life, even in a cosmopolitan setting
(Lin 2002). These are not simple pushes and pulls. Nor do they result from
structural breakdown or lack of norms. Strongly relational, Hong Kongers
contemplate migration with the family group in mind.

To uncover underlying continuities and distinguish people's migration
projects as they relate to social structure, we apply neo-institutional concepts
to the migration trajectories of Hong Kong families. We drew our families
from a two-tiered study consisting of a 1991 random population survey
(n=1,552) and a qualitative panel study of a subsample of families (n=30).
From these thirty, we chose nine for inclusion in this book (see "Meeting
Our Families" later in this chapter).

A word is in order here about our use of the term *emigrants,* which we
define as people who officially applied to immigrate to one of the major
receiving nations, whether or not they were accepted, or even left. Our
definition of emigrants as applicants emphasizes intent and actions taken
rather than the ultimate place of residence. Migration is not a single act of
leaving one place and arriving at another where migrants stay permanently.
It is a process, a continuum, and many people go back and forth (Levitt and
Nyberg-Sørensen 2004). Our focus on behavior further distinguishes those
who were motivated enough to develop migration projects from the rest,
even if their applications failed. Indeed, the reasons for success or failure
are central to our analysis. We compare people with four different migration statuses: (1) those who applied to immigrate to a Western country and
who settled there; (2) those whose applications were successful but do not
live abroad; (3) those who applied to immigrate but were rejected; and (4)
those who never applied to immigrate. In this way, we can better understand
structures that motivate migration and those that inhibit it, and we can
learn how migration fits into people's lives.

We focus on families because family-related migration is the dominant
mode of legal entry in many nations, not only in family reunification but
also in the human capital categories (Bailey and Boyle 2004; Kofman 2004).
Globally, people consider migration with the family group in mind, even
when their moves appear to bend the family contours by straining these
relations. The family is particularly important for the Chinese, especially

those in the diaspora. In spotlighting the family, we focus on the choices of each family, what they do, and how they feel about migration. At the same time, we take into account the family's structural position at several levels of social institutions, some promoting and others blocking migration (Shuval and Leshem 1998). Since institutions originate beyond household walls, members have various roles and interests inside and outside the family. The family (especially when taking into account the extended family) is not a unified entity; its members can be diverse in occupations and status, gender, and life-course positions. Although we discuss what happens in a family unit, we heed the varied voices of its members regarding migration and take into account their differing institutional positions.

The neo-institutional framework provides us with tools to understand action within the settings in which it occurs. Neo-institutional studies are often comparative, showing how structures matter in different ways to diverse populations. Creative applications include comparisons in Brinton (2001) of married Taiwanese and Japanese women, which reveal how disparate structures shape women's work. Alba and Nee (2003) study two periods of immigrant settlement in the United States, showing how similar structures integrate diverse peoples, while revealing the importance of historicity. Our neo-institutional study is comparative in a qualitative way, observing shifts in the migration plans and comparing how institutional structures shape the emergence and realization of these plans of families of different class backgrounds. In addition, the conclusion takes up the possibility of comparisons with migration processes in other global locations.

In the rest of this chapter we develop our institutional framework for understanding family migration and describe how we did our research. Readers may choose to go directly to chapter 2 for the historical background of Hong Kong institutions, or to chapter 3 for the first example of family life.

The Institutional Perspective: Scope and Mechanisms

The stories that follow describe how migration activities of families are embedded in institutional structures as guidelines for social behavior. Institutions give stability and meaning to social life, and persist over time, in formal and informal, public and private forms. Following Scott (2001), we group institutions into large-scale structures, often with regulative powers; social and professional relationships surrounded by norms and regulations; and individuals' personalization of taken-for-granted cultural-cognitive elements.[2] Through regulations, norms about relationships, and cognitive schemes people make sense of their social reality. These institutional group-ings are deeply stratified and families from diverse backgrounds face dif-ferent opportunities and limits.

Large-Scale Institutions and Migration

Large-scale institutional structures underlie both who tries to emigrate and who succeeds. The large-scale factors that most affect those we study de-termine who is eligible to emigrate. These factors are international market relations, state border controls, the spread of the British empire, professional regulations imposed on immigrants' right to work, and political shifts in the relationship between the state and its citizens.

Global institutions integrate parts of the world through their social con-nections and international markets, giving rise to population movements between countries. As large corporations invest in Asia, their flow of capital, products, work sites, and transportation integrate the region with Europe and North America economically and socially (Goss and Lindquist 1995). As a British colony, Hong Kong was internationalized as a place where raw materials were exchanged for finished goods. Today, many of its firms have intercity connections within the global system (Taylor et al. 2002). Continuous contact between global nodes makes it easier for Hong Kong's people to live elsewhere, particularly for those in close contact with global structures (i.e., people with the most resources) (Chan 1997).

Nation-state institutions patrol their own borders and control who may enter. Although the role of the nation-state in restricting international mi-gration has changed through time (Gabaccia et al. 2004), state regulative institutions are important in the Chinese diaspora (Waldinger and Fitzgerald 2004). Historically, government sanctions in receiving countries discrimi-nated against Chinese immigrant workers, thus determining the social and demographic composition of the Chinese diaspora (Harris and Ryan 1988). During their early industrialization, settler countries (including Canada, the United States, Australia, and New Zealand) brought in unskilled male Asian laborers to build railroads and work mines, but excluded their families. Eventually legislation blocked Chinese migrants entirely until the Second World War. Even after rescinding the exclusionary legislation, the major set-tler states limited the entry of those of non-Northern European ethnicity.[3]

Laws continue to regulate who may immigrate, with mature industrial nations shifting their policies to balance their demographic composition, fill skilled positions, promote investment, meet humanitarian goals, and allow residents to reunite with their families. At the time of the handover, countries competed for the Hong Kong middle class—prized immigrant contenders. Canada relaxed its immigration policies, becoming the most liberal Western settler nation.[4] Private immigration consultants helped Hong Kong entrepreneurs set up businesses and recruited professional workers (Hardie 1994). The proportion entering through family migration, the main avenue for the poor, shrank as the Canadian government favored the economic classes (Citizenship and Immigration Canada 2006, 2).[5]

Shared membership in the British empire eased Hong Kongers' access to Canada. English-language schooling, Commonwealth scholarships, and acceptance of some of their professional degrees privileged the better off. Canadian churches, schools, and clubs extended their spheres of influence to Hong Kong (Waters 2000). A former vice principal of a prestigious Toronto private school recalled marketing their boarding facilities to Hong Kong parents in the mid-1990s.[6] The number of pre-1997 migrants swelled along with the number of institutions connecting Canada and Hong Kong (Massey 1990).

However upon arrival, immigrants face major settlement problems, starting with local regulations that restrict their incorporation (Collins 1979). Institutional theorists commend Canada's policies for generously funding multicultural institutions aimed at integrating immigrants into the political system (Bloemraad 2006). Nevertheless, although the settler nations pursue professionals from Hong Kong, Mainland China, India, and elsewhere, they do not monitor the immigrants' access to the economic sphere. Canada is slow to curtail the power of the professions to control the qualifications that doctors, engineers, and others need to practice (Bambrah 2006; Boyd 2000). The numerous expatriates surely influenced professionals and business people to migrate (Skeldon 1997, 269). But many qualified Hong Kong immigrants were unaware of discrepancies in the rules of local professions under the umbrella of the British empire that excluded them (Findlay and Li 1998). This was a dilemma for the business people and professionals in our study.

Transformations in the state's relationship to its citizens, crucial in our study period, forcefully trigger migration. When the prospect of large-scale structural change threatens a way of life, emigration is a common response for those with resources to lose. Hirschman (1970) proposed that citizens react to the deterioration in the state's performance by exiting if they can or protesting if they cannot. For example, during the German Democratic Republic's final months of 1989 as living conditions became progressively worse people with human capital left, signaling discontent to others who could not leave (Pfaff and Kim 2003). Mass protests along with the loss of talent accelerated the regime's decline. In Hong Kong, massive emigration, which accelerated in 1987 and peaked in 1995 (revealing widespread feelings of uncertainty), had an impact. In an effort to stem the flow, the Colonial and PRC governments provided guarantees of minimal institutional change, dubbing the post-handover decades as "fifty years without change."

We now turn to these institutional selection mechanisms that work through people's relationships.

Social Relations, Social Norms, and Migration

It is well known that people turn to their social relations for help in getting what they need, from finding jobs to migration. But people have markedly different relations that they can mobilize. Thus, although many in our study population thought of moving, they were drawn by different contacts depending on their social class and organization memberships. These differences in the structure of social relations will become important in our study families. But first it is useful to introduce several concepts.

The connections between people are their social networks. People share ways of seeing the world around them and imitate the behavior of those with whom they interact. For example, engineers are indirectly connected to each other through their specialized education and professional memberships, which cement an occupational identity and similar outlooks.

We term these wider structures in which networks are embedded "social fields." This concept is associated with Lewin's work on social identification that Bourdieu drew on to explain how class position was linked to reputation (Lewin 1935; Bourdieu 1986). Networks of people in similar positions resemble each other. Thus, school graduates are often linked to professional associations and other connected organizations (DiMaggio and Powell 1983). Social fields contain social relations that offer different social and economic opportunities and help people identify how to pursue their goals (Scott 2007, 54–55). Social fields have their own norms and expectations, signaling one's social identity to others. Since similarity in social position creates trust, people perceive that others in social fields like theirs hold the same goals, even if they have never met.

Social fields figure in all stages of migration: anticipating and planning, leaving, arriving and settling (Levitt and Schiller 2004). When they settle in a new country, workers seek out jobs from people they know. Professionals need help in reestablishing their careers. They also want reliable information about good neighborhoods and schools from those who are socially similar to them.

Migration also is a way of resolving concerns that are felt by others. Since people in the same social fields tend to behave in a like manner, social fields can create a "bandwagon" effect (Feldman-Savelsberg et al. 2005). People who are not personally acquainted imitate each other in migration, a pull that is especially strong during anxious political periods (Pfaff and Kim 2003). Thus, before the handover, many professionals feared that under Mainland rule they would lose autonomy; they followed those in their social fields who were leaving. Furthermore, in the international city of Hong Kong, local employees in multinational firms could compare themselves with expatriates and consider whether to go abroad for training or jobs. In other words, their social fields become migration channels (Findlay and Li 1998).

We can study how social fields are geographically delimited and where networks cross institutional boundaries. Family and personal networks are likely to accompany migrants (Salaff and Greve 2004). In contrast, professional and business contacts that are closely linked to formal institutions are examples of networks that do not travel with migration. When the professional positions they attained in the home country are poorly understood abroad, problems are created for immigrants trying to integrate into their field in a new country.

A related conceptual distinction is between strong and weak ties. The strongest bonds are between people who share several roles because norms and rules spill over from one interaction to another—that is, they have multiplex relations. Massey et al. (1987) reveal how the strong social network ties of the Mexican working class prompt migration and provide the means to carry out this action. Pooling resources, people imitate the behavior of others and their overlapping, multiplex relations build migration chains. Direct contact through letters, photos, reunions, and recounting of life in distant places encourages journeys and helps voyagers find housing and jobs on arrival. Strong feelings of "ought to help" characterize these networks, although they may fail to deliver (Gold 2005; see also chapters 8 and 10 in this text).

In contrast, middle-class people with sufficient resources of their own build personal networks with acquaintances based on loosely structured, weak ties. These ties influence journeys through feedback more than through reciprocal help (Johnston et al. 2006).

We can view assimilation as the incorporation of immigrants into local social fields (Alba and Nee 2003). To get good jobs, professionals need to connect with others who are well placed in their line of work. This poses less of a problem at home, where they graduated from known universities, climbed career ladders in recognized companies, and received help from their colleagues. Once abroad however, the networks of first-generation immigrants rarely connect professionals to the types of firms they aim for.

Professional associations define appropriate skills and certification, often blocking access of the foreign educated (Boyd and Thomas 2001). With their careers ending abruptly, some immigrants remigrate rather than take jobs that threaten their professional identity (Mak 1997).

Entrepreneurs' social fields are composed of business-related networks. Lack of access to them means it may not be easy to open profitable firms (Greve and Salaff 2003). Ong (1999) studied successful wealthy immigrant entrepreneurs. However, more people attempt than succeed. Trying to replicate what worked at home, they find such enterprises work differently in the new country or that local firms already offer their products (Chu 1996; Leicht et al. 2005). Lacking social fields to provide good information on how to make their business profitable, the immigrants start new types of enterprises, enter marginalized ethnic markets, or return to their home country as transnational migrants.[7] Although they may become citizens of the new country, their migration projects, intended to support their families, fail (see chapter 4 for examples).

In many ways women and men have different social fields. Although they are in the same family unit, their worlds are separate, their problems not apparent to each other. As Pessar and Mahler emphasize, transnationality brings together in new spaces unfamiliar combinations of social roles and needs (Foner 1986; Pessar and Mahler 2003). It is often hard for husbands to fathom wives' objections to migration, because husbands and wives are integrated in their own social fields. Women's work is constructed differently than back home and entails new tasks, while at the same time, resources are harder to obtain (McLaren and Dyck 2004; Moon 2003). Their unpaid family care work is also invisible (Luxton 1980). On their part, male professionals have trouble identifying the many reasons that they cannot restart their careers since they cannot see social fields. Although both men and women find it hard to get the resources they need to meet the expectations of their cultural milieu and the host society, migration journeys are gender specific.

Sharing social fields brings husband/wife relations closer together and helps in problem solving (Bott 1957; Leung 2002; Komarovsky 1971). Even in difficult times, family support systems matter. In the following chapters, we explore how diverse couples devote their conjugal, kin, and collegial resources to attain family goals, such as migration.

Migration as a Cognitive-Cultural Response

People perceive their institutional environment through cognitive frames that cast issues in a particular light by suggesting ways that people should interpret and respond to their reality (Scott 2007, 57, 141–42, 187). Frames arise through interaction and are specific to social fields. Frames establish the meaning of events enabling people to respond appropriately (Goffman 1974). Framing and interpreting do not rubber-stamp actions; people evaluate alternatives. Four kinds of variation in the frames are especially important in migration as a cognitive response: historically rooted cultural alternatives; "family scripts"; professional identities; and *habitus,* the logic of appropriateness (March 1994).

On the cusp of Hong Kong's reversion to China, many observers interpreted the emigration swell as a form of cultural resistance to protect a way of life. Colonialism was founded on the notion of the European colonizers' cultural superiority. The introduction of European institutions gave the colonized a new sense of belonging. Their pride in the cosmopolitan culture that Colonialism created on their soil came at the expense of their traditional culture (Carroll 2005; Fanon 1970). Colonialism thus distorted the identities of its subjects, tainting them with what author Kiran Desai (2006) evocatively terms "the inheritance of loss." This culture was continually reconstructed and epitomized the climate of their generation (Ma 1999). On the cusp of reversion, seeing their familiar way of life at risk, many Hong Kongers sought to migrate to the source culture (Donkor 2005). (See, for example, Francis Kwong, chapter 5.)

Systems of cultural responses are "tool kits" (Swidler 1986). Those people we study have choices of cultural frames, not all prompting emigration. For some, reversion mobilized feelings of cultural patriotism (Anderson 1983; Bellah 1970). Mr. Ong, (chapter 7) takes pride in resilient China, never formally colonized, with its culture fast gaining international appreciation. Because multiple frames with their component tool kits coexist, people can appropriate new evidence and reorient their frames. This eventually occurred, as will be seen in the many who adjusted to the post-1997 era (Mathews et al. 2008).

"Family scripts" refer to cognitive frames that families develop as part of their shared way of life as they adapt to other institutions. Families construct perspectives about how they were in the past, how they are now, and where they are headed. Their accounts of family life define its core ingredients and the desirable ways to achieve their ideals (Ng et al. 2009; Wong 2008). Scripts are agendas for action, with normative power that enjoins members to comply. We saw several distinctive family scripts. Families who lost property during the Chinese revolution handed on to the next generation a script enjoining resistance to living under Communism (Bertaux 1997; Elazar 2002). In another example, diasporic families whose members have become scattered committed to reunite (Bertaux-Wiame 1981; Hondagneu-

Sotelo and Avila 1997). Because family scripts are least supported by other institutional structures, families must work hard to comply. Some family elders recount emotionally evocative stories, passing on explicit family goals that demand members' actions.

The threatened loss of a deeply held identity also spurs an exit (Hughes 1958). Many professionals anticipated that the Special Administrative Region (SAR) government would centralize power over their occupations, as on the Mainland. Such prospects deeply challenged educated professionals' cultural identities, threatening their normative framework, and many considered exiting.

Social structures powerfully shape how people frame events and what they consider as appropriate responses. Bourdieu (1981) introduced the concept of *habitus* or personal identity to explain how identities are constructed and how they change. Although frames are socially derived people personalize them as dispositions or habitus. By mediating structural and cultural forces habitus shapes individual choice or agency. A person who alters a typical response sends a signal to others in their social fields about new ways of framing a situation. When people embark on a new adventure, their actions become appropriate for people in similar social fields (March and Olsen 1989).

In these ways, shared cognitive views can encourage migration. But there is not a single frame—people can realign their views to incorporate new information and the changing opinions of others in their social fields. To act, families must work out the multiple views they hold. We now turn to the ways the Chinese family formulates and carries out migration goals.

The Chinese Family: An Institution That Prompts Migration

As the main group in which people live, invest their energies, refer to, and care about, and a standard against which their behavior is judged, the family joins regulative, normative, and cultural levels. The anthropologist Santos (2006) urges those who study Chinese family behavior to take into account interaction patterns as well as kinship structure, both of which shape action.

The Chinese family mobilizes members to improve family well-being and family unity, which often leads to migration (Hamilton 2006). The family structure is patrilineal and hierarchically organized, with authority vested in the most senior male and family membership inherited from the father. The family practices partible inheritance; each son receives an equal share of the estate at their father's death. Members engage in patrilocal residence; at marriage a woman moves to her husband's household (Baker 1979). This regulative structure sets normative relations whose central bond is between generations, not the married couple. The senior male has lifetime authority over his sons and married-in females, who are expected to contribute to the patrilineal group. Daughters, who do not inherit or contribute to their natal families after they marry out, have low status. The family as a group prefers to rely upon kinship, work and live together, and establish networks based on personal relationships (Das Gupta 1999).

In such a setting, family ties and a sense of reciprocal obligations underpin many migration projects, and these differ with the family resource base. For business families, migration is often seen as an avenue to prosperity. Firms are family centered, organized around kin and quasi-kin relationships (Omohundro 1981). Entrepreneurs expand their assets by starting small- and medium-sized family firms linked together through personal relationships. Compared to large firms, small enterprises more easily remain intact when they are divided among sons after the father's death (Hamilton and Kao 1990). Such firms can easily be started in dispersed locales, and thus entrepreneurship contributes to migration. (Chapters 4 and 8 introduce merchant families who form migration chains that respect the joint family system.)

Families without property also send sons and daughters afar to pursue new opportunities. By underwriting migration, members are expected to remit money so that the whole household benefits (Davin 2005a). Although they physically divide in migration, households often maintain a common economy (Cohen 1976).

Family ideologies extol children's contributions to the long-term betterment of the group, which often prompts members to migrate for the family good. Yet this patrilineal structure fosters internal divisions. Brothers have incentives to both cooperate to better the family economy, but also to compete for their father's favor. Sisters-in-laws argue over their small family's interests (Watson 2004). These fissures are reflected in migration projects (see chapter 8 for an example).

Recent writers take women's standpoint and explore the means through which women assert their influence in everyday behavior, in migration, and other realms of family action, unheralded by the patrilineal structure. Margery Wolf (1972) identified an informal female-centered kinship group (the "uterine family") without a juridical structure or ideology, built on relationships and loyalties within the patrilocal household, through which they exert influence. In her study of rural Szechwan women, Gates (2004) found that although young women are still subordinated to larger family decisions in education, work, and marriage, senior women hold the purse strings, deciding which child migrates. Most women draw on social networks, migrating only short distances to find jobs, a practice overlooked by those who focus on men's more dramatic long-distance moves. Davin (2005b) places migrant women's interaction within the more general study of kinship, marriage, and social change. She notes that rural parents often marry their daughters into well-off families some distance away. Such brides experience a profound break with natal kin (Judd 2008).

Chinese family structures such as patrilineal co-residence, inheritance rules, and provision of economic and social support help explain Hong Kong family migration. Apart from kinship structures, families pay attention to family care, reciprocity, mutual assistance through transnational kinship, and morality (Morgan 2001). At the same time, those with fewer resources are less able to fulfill family role obligations (Wong 2008). In these realms, Chinese families work at their migration projects.

Meeting Our Families

The 1991 survey conducted in Hong Kong (from which we chose our families) explored key issues that interest us in this book: family migration and attitudes about 1997.[8] Interviewees were asked whether they or their families planned to emigrate before the handover, and information was gathered on the stages of their applications. The researchers believed that the palpable political concerns of the time motivated the populace to exit and devoted a battery of questions to this topic. Beyond important statistical information about who was leaving and who was not, the survey checklist revealed little about the structures that underlie emigration or its meaning to families.

As a more sensitive means to understand family migration trajectories, we contacted thirty people from diverse backgrounds from the survey roster, a dual methodology (Bourdieu 1981; Fawcett and Arnold 1987). With a topical questionnaire in hand, we talked with them and their families repeatedly from 1992 through 1998. Of these, twenty-eight were married and two were single men. They comprised ten working-class, ten lower-middle-class, and ten affluent respondent households. When first interviewed in 1992, their ages ranged from twenty-eight to seventy-eight years. We assessed their class position by their education and occupational status when surveyed. Over time, two young couples (the Gungs, chapter 6; the Szetos, chapter 9) upgraded their occupational status, while other livelihoods worsened (Brian Wan, chapter 8; the Hungs, chapter 10). We continued discussions through 2005 with half of these, from whom we picked the nine focal families chosen for this book. We elaborate the varied effects of institutional structures on their migration projects and their responses.

During our long panel study period, Hong Kong's institutional structures and people's personal dynamics naturally underwent changes that affected migration. Those who had anticipated a downturn in their profession and a loss of status and autonomy tested their fears against reality during this period (Mathews et al. 2008). When the worst did not materialize, many decided against leaving. Others who had emigrated, returned. Some had transnational family networks who had pushed for reunion abroad; with the passage of time they withdrew their efforts. A rejection by the immigration gatekeepers or the profession in the host country forced others to revise their family emigration plans. We would have liked to have followed working-class applicants' adaptation to the host society. However, powerful institutions limited their courses of action and none actually emigrated, underscoring the ways that institutional context shapes migration.

Our repeated encounters created special personal dynamics for all participants (McCracken 1988; Saldaña 2003). Janet Salaff joined the interviews throughout; her ongoing association built rapport for continued talks. Chats were enriched by eating together and sharing many leisure activities such as outings to Lamma Island and other family pleasure spots. Salaff also lived with two families for some time.

Observations in a natural setting unobtrusively added to what we learned through our conversations. We met brothers, sisters, and other kin and friends, allowing a fuller understanding of our participants' social circles that contributed to—or blocked—the migration impulse. We had occasion to hear the varied voices of women and men and older and younger family members with regard to their migration plans. Our talks were not one way. Our respondents were as curious about our life changes over time as we were about theirs. We became part of the discourse as we bounced ideas off each other.

We were privileged to partake of these family lives, and chose to analyze their trajectories over time. The sociology of the individual in society is a long tradition, although one mainly attempted in novels (Mills 1959). We engage this method to explain why some people exit while others do not. Our aim is distinguishing between actors, to link a family's way of life to its migration outcomes, and to provide a compass to guide us in understanding which families make the dramatic international moves when they do. By so doing, we can pay attention to migrants' diverse paths, especially that of return migration (Glick-Schiller et al. 1992).

Narratives gave us insights into the meanings of events to these families. Repeated topics in people's recountings opened windows to their views of where their lives were going and their sense of identities. Young Ruby

Luk (chapter 3) stated in 2005 "I always knew that I was going to go to school abroad." In reality, this knowledge surely developed as an awareness over time. Still, her emphasis underscores the importance of her family's planned emigration project in their lives, which was being passed on to her to carry out.

Interviews are people's reconstructions of what they did and thought about. Over time, as families and institutions evolve, people reassess their opportunities. What was important at one time recedes, and recollections often change. There are contradictions in their remembered accounts. For example, in 1991 our survey recorded that Mr. Cheng and his sister, both security officers, had applied for the British Right of Abode. In our 1994 interview with him, he told us that his application had been turned down, but his sister's had been approved. When we met again in 2003, in an apparent resolution of his disappointment at being rejected, Cheng protested that he had never applied to immigrate to Great Britain. Festinger (1962) explains that people reconstruct their memories to bring them in line with what happened to them. As Nobel-prizewinning author Halldór Laxness (2005, xv) evocatively states, "Don't forget that few people are likely to tell more than a small part of the truth: no one tells much of the truth, let alone the whole truth. . . . When people talk they reveal themselves, whether they're lying or telling the truth." A longitudinal study provides a unique occasion to interpret the changing meanings of migration to families.

The Nine Families

The chapters in this book follow the evolution of each family's life and migration projects, presented over time. Six of these families applied to immigrate to a Western country, while three did not. Of the six families, only three actually made the foray abroad—all to Canada. Among these three, none remained intact as a family there, with the husbands all becoming transnational migrants (or astronauts) for a period of time. Immigration authorities turned down applications from the other three families.

The accounts of three well-to-do migrant families begin the book (chapters 3 to 6). Through them we learn how large-scale institutions encouraged the migration projects of those with money and professional training. These families also reveal the powerful effect of poor settlement on those with resources and the creation of the astronaut phenomenon. Their children in turn face decisions about where to reside; migration is an ongoing process.

Stories of three medium-earning families follow in chapters 6 to 8. With modest resources, they displayed mixed motivations to emigrate and encountered uneven success. By the time we met them, two of these families were unsuccessful applicants: one for the British Right of Abode and one for business-class immigration to Canada, while the third family had no inclination to emigrate at all. These families reveal diverse modes of building a family economy and caring for kin, yet all depend in many respects on personal ties, which determined their migration intent. Since all three families remain in Hong Kong, we are able to follow the differing adaptation of failed emigrants and nonemigrants to institutional changes following the reunification with China.

Working-class families depend most on kin and other personal ties, and these relations strongly influence migration projects. This is seen in the accounts of three laboring families: two nonapplicants and one rejected immigrant-applicant (see chapters 9 through 11). They weather social and economic uncertainty primarily with the help of kin and others close to them. These familiar ties prompt actions, whether encouraging families to reunite with kin abroad or to remain in Hong Kong embraced in their close circles. Yet if laboring families chose to emigrate, they were subject to decisions of official gatekeepers, apt to reject immigration of the poor. Without exit, all three families survived in the ever-changing Hong Kong society by continuing to devote their energy to family and personal ties.

Chapter 12 retraces the institutional mechanisms that contribute to migration intent and outcomes in these nine family scenarios. It draws out the underlying structures that place migration at the center of everyday action for some Hong Kong families (but not for others) and how, over time, institutions shape and reshape migration projects. Family stories themselves are presented chronologically according to their social-class positions. The unfolding of family migration tales over time reveals a complex interplay of factors that shaped peoples' fortunes as movers or stayers, contributing to their eventual outcomes.

CHAPTER TWO

Hong Kong's Institutional Background

This chapter provides background to our Hong Kong families' migration stories. Growing up in Colonial Hong Kong a local identity emerged, grounded in shared basic institutions and historic events. Many structures were linked to the world beyond Hong Kong giving all contact with the broader scene. At the same time, wealth, age, gender, and other social resources differentiated them, shaping diverse life experiences and emigration intents.

Development of Social and Economic Structures

From its beginning, Hong Kong had strong ties both to China and to the major Western powers. This status contributed to the internationalization and cosmopolitan character of its institutions while still maintaining Hong Kong as part of the Chinese cultural area. Through gunboat diplomacy (the First and Second Opium Wars, 1839–42 and 1856–60), Britain colonized Hong Kong, the Kowloon Peninsula, and the New Territories. As an integral part of the Pearl River Delta, disruptions across the border historically have had a great impact on Hong Kong's populace. Britain stabilized Hong Kong's institutional environment by introducing legal, financial, educational, and other formal organizations, and easing exchanges of goods, information, and people between Hong Kong, the Chinese hinterland, the wider Asian region, and England. These orderly structures became the colony's source of strength in finance and trade (Faure 2003).

The separation of Hong Kong from China was gradual and incomplete. The populations went back and forth in cross-border trade and commerce and households divided with members working on both sides of the border. Still, Hong Kong's population grew—from 750,000 in 1931, its population tripled as people fled from China during the chaotic years of the Civil War (1945–49) and their aftermath (Skeldon 1994).

Following the Chinese revolution and the Korean War, the West cut China off, creating the conditions for Hong Kong's economy and society to develop apart from its hinterland, and eventually for a sense of identity to emerge among its populace (Ku 2004). With its borders closed, Hong Kong was unable to maintain its entrepôt economy. During the last years of the Civil War, Shanghai industrialists diverted their textile machinery, capital, and skills to Hong Kong, thereby shifting its economic direction to labor-intensive consumer goods manufacturing for Western markets (Wong 1988).

Migrants from China were the colony's manual labor resource who worked in a variety of occupations, in highly insecure environments, in manufacturing and construction industries, unlicensed trades and outwork. They struggled to find even subcontracting work and were often unemployed. Rising prices for public goods triggered major demonstrations in 1966, factory strikes in 1967, followed by violence that echoed the Cultural Revolution in China. These actions revealed the deep sense of alienation the exploited workforce experienced (Carroll 2007). Even as late as the 1981 census, only 3 percent of the population considered Hong Kong their home, with the vast majority citing roots in China (Lin 2002, 68–69).

After the economy moved into manufacturing the fundamental nature of Hong Kong society changed. To improve human resources, develop the economy, and commit the populace to the Colonial order, Lord Crawford Murray MacLehose, Hong Kong's first populist governor (1971–82), launched social services. Public housing, medical services, and compulsory education laid the foundations of contemporary Hong Kong's social institutions. A series of changes to governance structures cumulatively began to open channels for communication and grapple with corruption in government ranks. Educated Chinese were recruited to the civil service, referred to as localization. The civil service came to symbolize efficiency, stability, and prosperity through its guidelines of impartiality and rules.

Six-year free compulsory education was introduced in 1971, and extended to nine years in 1978. Without a centralized system, there were several political, religious, and economic streams to choose from, with foreign NGOs having an important role in funding and managing this sector. Pupils with resources went on to full secondary schooling, increasingly choosing the English language stream. Companies sought highly educated employees for complex projects: between 1962 and 1976, substantial numbers of Hong Kong overseas graduates returned to take on highly skilled positions, reflecting the importance of return migration in development (Bray and Koo 2005).

Although still poor, families were able to move from squatter shacks or subdivided rooms in tenement flats (meshed with bars for security, they were called cages [Cheung 2000]) and into large public housing estates (Castells et al. 1988; Smart 2006). The Housing Authority has now become the largest landlord in the world—today over half the population lives at a fraction of market costs. Some remain as renters throughout their life cycle, while others chart their improved livelihood by buying subsidized apartments of their own (Lee and Yip 2006).

The provision of rudimentary social services to the needy has become policy, setting the standard against which families measure their well-being. By 1995–96, the government was spending 47 percent of its public money on social services, nearly the same as its Colonial parent that year. This considerable expenditure was not termed welfare (Bell 1998, 16). The government is strongly opposed to implementing comprehensive social services that would give the people the notion that they were citizens with rights (Ku and Pun 2006). To keep wages low, the government has not guaranteed minimum wages or working hours. Fearing to weaken the family, it has not offered family supports such as child care to help working parents (Youngson 1983).

During the manufacturing era, the features of work life shaped the contingent everyday experiences of Hong Kong people. Social position and resources fluctuated. Workers saved money to put into small, often short-lived businesses, and entrepreneurship was a career stage. These conditions positioned Hong Kong as a place of both upward and downward class mobility (Chiu et al. 2005; Wong 1999). However, for most of the 1970s–1990s, the Hong Kong poor could expect their children to do better than their parents. Accustomed to constant instability, people rarely organized for concerted social change (Lau 1982).

Restructuring Hong Kong to Support China

Reunification with China was announced in 1984, to take place when the British lease on Hong Kong island expired in 1997. Enhanced economic interaction between Hong Kong and China foreshadowed this merger. In 1978 China opened its economy to private investment, marking a turning point in Hong Kong's economy as well. Hong Kong restructured toward a service economy geared to the region, becoming the conduit for raising international capital and managing investment in China (Sung 1991).

Proximity to the Shenzhen Special Economic Zone, cultural and linguistic commonalities, and personal ties allowed Hong Kong entrepreneurs to take advantage of cheaper land and labor in Guangdong Province (Smart 2002). Hong Kong manufacturers moved their factories to China to seek low-cost labor directly. By 1991, there were 25,000 Hong Kong-owned factories in

China, with 3 million employees, and by 1997, Hong Kong's direct investment in China reached USD 100 billion (Bell 1998, 21–22; Hong Kong Federation of Industries 1993). China's opening to the West freed peasants from the land, and within five years, 400,000 people entered Hong Kong, but with less need for low-cost labor, the Hong Kong government repatriated illegal immigrants. Over the years, Hong Kong, the Pearl River Delta, Guangzhou, its satellite towns, and Zhuhai and Macau have become integrated into a vast urban region. Development of the South China region took off.

The Middle Class Becomes an Economic Force

The move of its manufacturing base to China had a great impact on Hong Kong, prompting its economic restructuring in which the middle class had a greater role. Expansion of education enlarged their ranks. New universities produced more white-collar workers, engineers, accountants, and architects as well as managers in banking, real estate, and manufacturing. In this push for credentials, both women and men improved their educational levels. In 1981, 36.3 percent of adult women and 45.6 percent of adult men had attained secondary education and above. By 2002, those numbers had risen to 68.5 percent of adult women, and 75.9 percent of adult men (Lau et al. 2006, 93; Post and Pong 1998). As education became the channel for social mobility, competition for local elite schools intensified, as did the exodus for international education (Waters 2005).

The middle class was differentiated by the jobs its members held. In our 1992 survey those in professional, administrative, and managerial occupations comprised 13.6 percent of the employed population. Many had trained in the UK, Canada, and Australia, and on their return developed guidelines for professional conduct, licensing, accreditation, qualification, and registration and control of their members. They earned high salaries. There were also high-level civil servants; by the time of the handover, Hong Kong Chinese accounted for nearly half the 180,000 administrative civil servants (Tsang 2003). Civil service department heads gained the power to influence policy, took pride in their work and in adhering to rule of law, and were eager to protect their profession (So 1999). As people with a lot to lose if capitalism were to fail and their status taken away, professionals and high-level civil servants were especially anxious over the impending unification.

Social workers, teachers, nurses, journalists, lower levels of civil service, and other semi-professionals—members of the ordinary middle class—were recruited in large numbers to state and nongovernmental organizations. Many came from working-class backgrounds, lived in public housing, and were educated locally. Holding egalitarian social views, they lobbied for more services for the poor. Less likely to emigrate, they became a voice for broadened electoral democratization in the 1990s (Scott 1989).

Overall, the restructured Hong Kong economy prospered. Per capita GDP increased from USD 3,760 (1979) to USD 10,350 (1989) to USD 21,650 (1994). However, not all enjoyed prosperity, and income was related to occupation. Manufacturing fell from almost 920,000 employees in 1985 to 570,000 employees in 1994 (Skeldon 1997, 265–66). The new entrepôt industries linked to China created spinoff employment for some. Truck drivers, factory managers, technicians, supervisors, and construction engineers regularly crossed the border to supervise or service enterprises. However, not all laid-off factory workers entered growth areas. As Hong Kong's manufacturing sector was hollowed out, many were pushed into low-paid industries.

Inequalities polarize the Hong Kong population. The proportion of those living below the poverty line grew from over 900,000 in 1991 to nearly 1.3 million in 2001. Hong Kong's Gini coefficient rose sharply from 0.476 in 1991 to 0.525 in 2001, the most unequal ratio in a developed society (Ng 2005; Parwani 2007). The poor include the new migrants from China, as well as the second generation of those marginalized in the new economy. Inheritance of poverty is a new phenomenon in Hong Kong. With its great division between low-paid workers and the affluent middle class, Hong Kong has begun to resemble other global cities noted for their economically polarized populations (Sassen-Koob 1987).

Women's Employment

Hong Kong's consumer-based manufacturing industry relied on women. Most worked before starting a family. Married women also made a substantial contribution to their family economy as outworkers (Salaff 1981; Lui 1994).

As the demand for education and skill increased, women were bifurcated into the haves and have-nots. When restructuring cost blue-collar women their economic base, some found manufacturing jobs as finishers on products imported from China on their way to foreign destinations. Most worked in the service-sector in fast-food restaurants, as dim sum trolley-pushers or as hotel cleaners (Wong 1999). Many middle-aged women withdrew to the home for family work. Nevertheless, their daughters, able to access education in the newer universities, could get low paying white-collar jobs, thereby fulfilling their families' dreams for their children to leave manual labor.

Our 1991 survey data (n=1,552) describes the general employment conditions at the time we started our qualitative interviews. We found that working women held primarily lower-status jobs and were underrepresented as managers and administrators, professionals, semiprofessionals, and skilled workers. They were overrepresented as clerks and in unskilled occupations. Women earned less than men: whereas males' monthly income averaged HKD 9,957 (with a maximum of HKD 100,000), women's monthly income averaged only HKD 6,446 (with a maximum of HKD 40,000).[1]

Not all women in the survey worked, but those who did had long hours. It was hard for working parents to handle child care, senior care, and other family work. There are few publicly funded support services for working parents, and the schedules of schools and other social services do not mesh with family routines. Hong Kong women have to employ personal "circuits of care" for their children. They turn to their female kin or hire servants, responses that differ by social class (Vincent et al. 2008). Middle- and even lower-middle-class households contract low-waged Filipina, Thai, and other Asian women as domestic servants. Foreign contract labor has become a backup to ease the time bind and strains associated with raising a family and earning a living wage (Constable 1997). Over 10 percent of Hong Kong households have live-in foreign domestic workers (Chan and Wong 2005). Past their household role is another social effect: foreign domestic laborers lower the floor of acceptable wages and take jobs that working-class women might have held. Past their labor market impact, servants shape identity politics involved in the employer-domestic worker relation, fossilizing gender roles and dulling the clamor for social service reforms (Lee 2002). This is another instance of the wider repercussions of migration in the form of imported low-waged labor to Hong Kong from the region.

Political Structure and Views

One of the most dramatic changes in recent years has been the emergence of a politicized populace. The Colonial regime did not prepare the Hong Kong people for independence. The government was run top down and channels of political participation were late in coming. The executive-led Colonial government ruled, with the appointed governor (and later his appointed successor, the SAR chief executive) at its head. The executive made policy in consultation with the representatives of large British companies and wealthy Chinese. Civil servants, responsible for daily operations, were credited with Hong Kong's economic and social achievements (Goodstadt 2005). Most appreciated Britain's orderly, if authoritarian, Colonial governance; few in Hong Kong had ever lived in a democracy. They expected civil law and legal infrastructure to settle their affairs and accepted a submissive political role in return for a solid economy to support their families (Faure 2003; Tsang 2003).

By the 1980s, the population was better educated. Many employed in knowledge sector jobs and many who had studied in the West came to expect a say in their governance. Professionals, teachers, journalists, lawyers, and social workers led the call for fuller civic representation (So 1999). Talks between Britain and China from 1982 to 1984 over the terms of Hong Kong's repatriation concluded with the mode of popular representation still unsettled (Scott 1989). In elections held in following years, the executive granted a greater, indirect representation of professional people in legislation. The ambiguous political arena clouded the transition to the new regime (Pepper 2008). It was darkened further with the June 4, 1989, Tiananmen protests and crackdown, which alerted people to what could happen in an undemocratic Hong Kong after reversion. Over a million people turned out to demonstrate on June 5, converging on the Hong Kong racetrack to support the Beijing students' call for democracy and express opposition to the reunification (Bernstein 1989). At this point, many chose to exit, while others grappled with what life would be like under the new regime.

The Basic Law adopted in April 1990 would go into effect as the governing constitution of Hong Kong SAR on July 1, 1997. Although the document ensured China's absolute sovereignty, it also committed to a high degree of local autonomy and respect for the Hong Kong way of life for half a century after reversion. The slogan "no change for fifty years" was widely used to quell fears associated with the handover. At the same time, Colonial Governor Chris Patten unilaterally mounted "a fairly systematic, wide-ranging and speedy decolonization process on many fronts" (Chan 2003, 507). Political parties contended for votes and young elected politicians with legal training pushed the limits of legislation (Loh 2004). Ordinary people were given somewhat wider franchise in the historic first election to the Legislative Council in 1991. By unilaterally proposing popular representation to Hong Kong residents, Patten precipitated a political tug of war with the PRC leadership, deepening the crisis over retrocession.

Still, opinion over reversion was divided, as documented in our 1991 survey. While the majority—lacking confidence in the Chinese government—feared the handover, others, albeit a small minority, looked forward to reunification and had confidence that pre-handover conflicts would be resolved satisfactorily. Yet others were indifferent.[2] Lacking a voice in the proceedings, many chose to emigrate if they could. Others who were not eligible could only acquiesce and take the promise of no change at face value. Overall, whether the people worried about the handover (as did the majority surveyed) or looked forward to reunification with the Mainland, Hong Kongers expressed their opinions. They had become a civic people (Ku 2006).

Postretrocession

The Colonial government had ruled in a minimalist fashion, and after the transfer of sovereignty, the new regime lacked the institutional mechanisms needed for orderly regulation of the increasingly competing financial and popular interests (Lui and Chiu 2006). In the first six years of the new regime a series of devastating crises occurred (the Asian financial crisis of 1997–98, Hong Kong's economic recession, the avian flu, and the spread of severe acute respiratory syndrome [SARS] in 2003). The government's responses were criticized as slow and inadequate. Hong Kong's people had come to expect their government to be proactive and held the leadership accountable for its actions and promises. There was a new awareness of issues and a close correlation between levels of confidence and major events of the day (Public Opinion Programme 2009).

To shore up support, the SAR Chief Executive restructured the political system to make it more accountable to China. Top-tier administrative officers became political appointees (Lau 2003). Executive officers waged a campaign against what they called a bloated and overpaid civil service, reducing numbers and wages, which further weakened the civil service system (Scott 2003).[3]

In the years since reversion, Beijing has intervened a number of times in Hong Kong government decisions, creating constitutional crises. The proposed Security Bill 23 electrified the people, peaking in the first large antigovernment protest march held on July 1, 2003, against interference with freedom of speech. As a result of increasing criticism within Hong Kong and having lost the confidence of the populace and the central government, Tung Chee-hwa, the first SAR chief executive, resigned on March 12, 2005 (Cheng 2005). Politics was moving from the margins to the center of the stage, and this theme now entered Hong Kongers' sense of identity.

Hong Kong Belongers: Culture and Identity

Since the mid-1960s, Hong Kong society built a strong collective identity that was articulated in cultural terms; many viewed reversion to China through this lens (Mathews et al. 2008). Students of culture provide tools that help us understand how symbolism surrounding things contributes to identity formation. They point out that as people engage in transactions over possessions, they invest things with the properties of social relations (Appadurai 2006; Swidler 1986). People in the same social space who share goods that those in other locales cannot obtain appropriate these cultural products as special symbols of their identity. Since the poor and better off use different products, there are both class-specific and more general forms of culture and identity. Hence, class and power are embedded in goods and services in Hong Kong, further segmenting the populace (Bourdieu 1984). As well, cultural differences loomed so great between Hong Kong and Mainland China that they became enshrined in the Basic Law's guarantee: "no change for fifty years."

Hong Kongers became self-identified as a people with strongly differentiated culture based on resources that money can buy. Government actions were crucial in helping the vast majority develop an identity different from those on the other side of the border. In the colony's formative period, those educated and wealthy Chinese who had been co-opted into the government and British mercantile institutions developed class-specific structures that contributed to their separate elite identity (Carroll 2005). Sealing the border, begun in the 1950s but completed in 1980, was also fundamental to identity formation (Ku 2004). By then, most Hong Kongers, having grown up in Hong Kong, had seen a rapid improvement of the living standard based on provision of public goods—education, public housing, mass transit (Ma 2007). A sense of belonging developed.

Schools are an institutional system where youths developed peer ties that gave them social capital and mentors for careers (Bray and Koo 2005; Turner 1995). Schools extolled Hong Kong's liberalism and economic success and mixed in Christianity. This Colonial-derived ideology, in opposition to China's communism, taught pupils to consider themselves distinct from China's unsophisticated masses. English-language education reinforced class lines. A defining feature of the successful Hong Kong person, it could be gained only by those with the resources to attend the right schools long enough (Lin 2000; Lee 2006). Attending Christian or international schools, some of which eased emigration, fostered another division.

Most Hong Kong adults from a wide range of backgrounds have lived in public housing. Tenure security and physical features of the resettlement estates created close neighborhoods, which many recall nostalgically. There are diverse rental and purchasing options based on location, size, mode of administration, and monthly income. Family housing experience varies given the stage of family cycle when they moved in and the era of their occupancy, so public housing also contributes to a stratified sense of being a Hong Konger (Lee and Ip 2003).

Public transit became a geographical and cultural unifier after the Mass Transit Railway (MTR) opened in 1979. Public transit is also a common subject about which the public voices dissatisfactions in the media, an activity that has intensified with the development of a partially representative government (Lang 1994). However, inequality in transportation use is seen in our study (Lau 1998). Working-class families in public housing in outlying areas of Tuen Mun cannot easily travel to distant schools or workplaces, whereas the better off can drive to distant workplaces or take the MTR to jobs in the Central District. This creates another status distinction in the use of public goods.

Migration—the ability to enter and leave—is a constitutive element of the Hong Kong identity, yet Hong Kongers with more resources and social capital move most easily. Many youngsters from well-to-do families attend schools that prepare them for higher education overseas and thus take for granted migration as a way of life (Waters 2000; Baker 1983).

Consumerism is that part of the Hong Kong identity most clearly shaped by class (Mathews and Lui 2003). The affluent frequent the city's many high-end shops and restaurants and train their children to distinguish major foreign brands. The working class primarily rely on less costly outlets, from traditional, open-air markets and eateries to local chain stores, and consume made-in-China goods (Tam 1997; Smart 2004; Lui 1997).

The media has played a great role as unifier of Hong Kongers' identity. For decades, of the three authoritarian societies of Hong Kong, the PRC, and Taiwan, only Hong Kong enjoyed a fairly open cultural discourse, and this "window to the outside" became a pillar of its identity. The loose hand of censorship enables the Hong Kong people to access the media broadly, even to develop their own hedonistic versions of ads, TV shows and, more recently, blogs (Mathews et al. 2008). By the late 1970s, television sets were becoming an affordable commodity and could be found in most Hong Kong households. Dramas about Hong Kong life, such as the show 72 *Kinds of Jobs*, accompanied by theme songs with Cantonese lyrics expressed Hong Kong's values and sentiments (Ma 1999). In the late 1970s, the music industry and its superstars became a major commercial enterprise in Hong Kong, spawning a genre of music dubbed "Cantopop." As scholar of the genre, J. S. Wong wrote, "Hong Kong's freedom of expression, well captured by the songs, created for audiences on both sides of the China Strait a 'psychological window.'" Mainland audiences—even those who did not understand the dialect but loved the music—bought Cantopop records to make contact with the world outside (Wong 2003; Witzleben 1999). In this manner, music personified Hong Kongers' identity as a special kind of Chinese.

Hong Kong identity was, like many civic ideologies, amorphous, yet people felt they were Hong Kong belongers. Some held an oppositional identity of "us" versus "them." Worry over whether the Hong Kong persona would survive reversion to China contributed to their anxiety in the 1990s, which pushed many to emigrate. As the Hong Kong identity has continued to evolve, political themes are voiced. Threats to cherished cultural values such as freedom of speech precipitate large popular outbursts. The right to hold political demonstrations is itself central to this identity.

At the same time, life activities increasingly drew people into contact with Mainland people and institutions. As people experience cross-border integration in their daily living, a pan-Chinese cultural nationalism has emerged, giving rise to a sense of pride in being Chinese. Many see their identity in dual terms, holding both a local and a national Chinese identity (Fung 2004; Ma 2007). This allows some to celebrate the reversion to China, while holding the view that Hong Kongers should still maintain their own way of life. The civil identity that has emerged from unifying institutions and from everyday life sponsors action as emigration, protest, and sentiment.

Roots of Modern Emigration

Hong Kong was created as a mobile society, with cross-border traffic for employment, split families, and migration abroad. At the same time, migration has long been a contentious issue, with bitter struggles waged over who is allowed to enter and over their acceptance, as well as its people who moved abroad.

Migration was a colony-wide experience. In the past, labor recruiters developed Hong Kong as a location from which to organize the transshipment of laborers to the West, until anti-Asian immigration laws were put into place after the First World War (Sinn 2004). Mainlander elites crossed over to Hong Kong to obtain higher education and engage in revolutionary and economic activities that were illegal in China. For their part, the Hong Kong Chinese elite traveled to China and farther abroad for school, work, culture, and holidays. In doing so, they built connections to global institutions, developed social ties to these places, and assumed an identity marked by ease of travel (Carroll 2005).

Mainland laborers entered Hong Kong to work and escape China's poverty and political struggles until the border closed. Until 1980, Hong Kong granted sanctuary to illegal immigrants. Its "touch-base" policy permitted anyone to stay who had made it to Hong Kong by swimming, on a boat, or by other means (Ku 2004). Several of our respondent families were part of this passage (see chapter 11). By 1980, as many as 1,000 Mainlanders entered Hong Kong daily (as well as 1,000 Vietnamese refugees, who were not permitted to remain). The touch-base policy was ended in an effort to stem the flow of poorly educated male border-crossers. After this, slim quotas negotiated between the PRC and the British Colonial authorities strictly regulated Hong Kong border crossings. Seeking a political status quo through control over population movements, they paid little attention to families' trans-border social fields. After 1983, the one-way permit quota system enabled split families to reunite in Hong Kong (Leung 2006). This policy allowed seventy-five Mainlander dependents (the number has since risen), primarily women and children, to settle in Hong Kong every day.

Out-migration chains to the West formed over the years. As Hong Kong lost its New Territories farmland to industry, rural youths sought livelihoods as seamen. Jumping ship, they started new migration chains and industries such as the Chinese takeout food industry in the UK—a prized destination for Hong Kongers (Benton 2007; Watson 1975). Coincidentally, at the same time the Commonwealth Immigrants Acts (1962, 1968) denied Commonwealth residents easy entry, the major settler countries dropped racial quotas that had been in place since early in the century. The growing bilingual Hong Kong middle class, tied intellectually to Western nations, sent their children to North America to study. Finding jobs, they remained and formed new migration chains whose links prompted more people to emigrate, especially during the pre-handover years (Cheung 2004; Skeldon 1991).

Split families have long been a solution to the need to earn a living and raise a family when both cannot be accomplished in the same place (Glenn 1983; Landolt and Da 2005). In the past, married village men crossed into Hong Kong, often leaving their families behind. This separation posed little problem until the political border solidified in the early 1950s, and the commuters who lived in China and worked in Hong Kong could not return home. Also stuck behind Hong Kong's closed borders were poor, unmarried men who had "touched base" and whose presence in Hong Kong created social and demographic imbalances. Later, returning to their Mainland villages to seek brides, they created cross-border marriages (So 2003). With the emergence of China as a workplace, Hong Kong men working over the border began taking partners yet were prevented from bringing them back to Hong Kong (Lang and Smart 2002). Despite high levels of socioeconomic integration, the border still sharply restricts movement from China to Hong Kong. Hence, claiming the right of abode in Hong Kong is a key political issue that affects an estimated 1.67 million people (Smart 2003). It is an issue our subject families have experienced.

In this book we also meet the split families that developed among the affluent who emigrated and then found few suitable jobs abroad. They left their families in their foreign homes to obtain access to good housing and schools and returned to work in Hong Kong (Mak 1997). In this they resembled many others in distant countries (Pe-pua et al. 1996).

As an international city, Hong Kong attracts diverse peoples. The building of the Asian economies brought highly skilled international sojourners. In 1993, there were five hundred registered foreign engineers in high-ranking positions in multinational firms (Skeldon 1991).[4] In 1996, the year before retrocession, foreign nationals comprised an estimated 10 percent of the population. Expatriates work with local professionals and have goals and values in common. Side-by-side proximity in work builds common social fields, creating a cultural mix in which career migration is natural. These contacts built links to international destinations for Hong Kong professionals (Findlay et al. 1996).

Half of all pretransition emigrants from Hong Kong are estimated to have returned, another form of transnational migration (Aydemir and Robinson 2006, 41). Return migrant inflows in the post-handover period have brought home the parachute children who had been sent abroad for tertiary education by astronaut parents (Salaff et al. 2008).

In these many ways migration flows reflect and build on Hong Kong institutions. Historian Elizabeth Sinn (2008) draws out the implications of these migrations for Hong Kong's character when she notes how over the years Hong Kong forged many external links. As layers of overlapping regional and global networks converged, the city became a center of transnational social and business space.

Who Leaves? Who Stays? Survey Data

When we began our research, there was a high level of interest in exiting Hong Kong, strongest among those with money and those with kin abroad. The 1991 survey asked a series of questions about decisions to emigrate before reunification. One question asked whether people planned to apply for emigration before 1997: responses showed that 11.7 percent planned to apply to immigrate to a Western nation, while 5.1 percent had not yet decided. Few had actually applied (6.6 percent of the survey respondents). Their social position was decisive. More of those who were better off—who were realistically more acceptable to authorities abroad—had applied. Of those in our survey with middle-class occupations, 16.9 percent had applied compared with under 3.15 percent of those with working-class occupations.[5]

Hong Kong is densely networked internationally, which greatly influences emigration. Most know people who have left or have planned to leave. In the 1991 sample, 5 percent of those surveyed had lived abroad, and as many as 44 percent had relatives abroad. Their networks impel them to follow suit; having family abroad distinguished potential emigrants from the rest. Of those who had kin abroad, 11.5 percent had applied to immigrate to a Western country whereas only 2.7 percent of those without kin abroad applied to immigrate. Again, there were class differences. Although middle-class respondents were most likely to have kin abroad, this did not bear on whether they themselves had applied to immigrate, suggesting that having kin abroad was not their most important consideration in this decision. In contrast, the working class displayed a high correlation between having kin abroad and applying themselves, suggesting that overseas kin were powerful magnets for emigration (Salaff et al. 1999).

As an indirect measure of cognitive elements, poor confidence in the political future prompted thoughts of emigration. Of those in our 1991 survey, 65 percent lacked confidence in the Chinese government, and one third of these considered applying to immigrate to a Western nation (Wong 1995).

When we extrapolate to the wider population, the implications of our findings loom large. In 1991, the Hong Kong population was 5,674,000. Based on the 6.6 percent of respondents who stated they had applied to immigrate to a Western nation, we estimate that a total of 374,500 Hong Kong people had applied. Those in our study who applied had a mean family size of 2.96; assuming that this proportion could also be found in the population at large, the number of potential emigrants was a substantial 1.1 million people or 20 percent of the Hong Kong population.[6]

It is clear that the population had mixed views about emigrating from Hong Kong and that these views relate to their social-class resources. We now turn to our qualitative interviews with people from a range of positions to discover the complex ways that social institutions which regulate and control what people do interlace with normative social relations and cultural attitudes to shape emigration from Hong Kong.

PART ONE
COSMOPOLITAN EMIGRANTS

The next three chapters present the stories of three professional and business families that were highly motivated to emigrate. They applied for several countries and, with little problem at the regulative level, easily qualified under the human- and financial capital-based migration systems. Like many around them, these three families chose Canada. In these pages we meet the engineer Luk and his family (chapter 3); the Chou family and their kin the Leungs (chapter 4), both entrepreneurs; and the Kwongs (chapter 5), a professional manager's family. The three represent common emigration patterns of the well-off. The Luks, emigrant planners, sought to carry out the family mandate as well as improve their daughter's education (Waters 2005). The Chous were flexible emigrants who applied to engage in business abroad as the means to have a better lifestyle (Ong 1999). The Kwongs were ideological emigrants, who wished to continue their familiar Anglo-British way of life.

Each family's problems began in the economic and professional realms after migration. Although they commanded top opportunities in Hong Kong, their social relations reaching into Canada were not embedded into the social fields they needed to integrate into the new society. They could not access the structures in which careers like theirs are embedded. Given these unanticipated blocks to social integration, each family has imaginatively reshaped their emigration project.

CHAPTER THREE

The Luk Family

Exit and Return of Emigrant Planners

Cheung-Kwok, an engineer, and Ching, a homemaker, started planning their family emigration to Canada a few years after negotiations for Hong Kong's retrocession to China ended. Emigration was their family script. For decades their family migration plan was integral to the organization of their family economy, their relations with others, and their identity. However, Ching and Cheung-Kwok ultimately retreated from migration. Instead, they focused their emigration plans on their daughter, giving her all the cultural opportunities possible, building toward her education abroad. Their ultimate hope for Ruby is that with her foreign education she will be more able to compete in the job market at home in Hong Kong.

Our long time frame takes us through the twists and turns of the Luks' emigration project. We assess the overall structures that matter for their project, and how time transforms them. We also learn of the dramatic change in what they hope to gain for their family from the project as they adapt to the circumstances in which they find themselves.

The Origins of the Luk Family Emigration Project

The Luks' migration journey began before Cheung-Kwok and Ching even met, with devastating blows dealt to their families when the Communists consolidated power in China. Both Cheung-Kwok's parents, the Luks, and Ching's parents, the Ngais, were well-to-do Guangzhou families whose property was seized during the Communist revolution. (In 1952, when Cheung-Kwok was just four years old, his parents' goldsmith shop, shipping firm, cinema, and garment factory were seized. The family fled to Hong Kong. Expecting the Communist takeover to be brief, they left behind an elder son in Guangzhou to wait out the regime change.) The resulting fragmentation of families and fortunes led both to a sense of temporariness toward life in Hong Kong and a fear of communism, which strongly influenced Cheung-Kwok's reaction to retrocession.

We often heard tragic sagas of family displacement like theirs. Of this forced migration, Cheung-Kwok bitterly recalls the stories that resonated through his life: "My father had his lands and his property taken away. For years, he didn't take a job. Because of that, I didn't go to school until I was ten. Then when I finished, I had to go to work and give half my earnings to my younger brothers to go to school. I never had a chance to finish college." After his late start in school, he studied building trades in Hong Kong Poly-technic three evenings a week while clerking in a property firm. Combining a full time job and coursework was challenging, but he stayed with it: "It was hard to get in, so people thought their place was very precious. Twenty of my class of thirty stuck it out." Hard work paid off; nearing the peak of his career, he was highly sought after as a site engineer.

The family often vocalized collective memories about their losses, and early experiences with the Communist regime are a theme in their family identity. Cheung-Kwok recounted: "Mother packed boxes in a factory and father scraped rust from ships. I didn't know the meaning of breakfast or dinner. We'd wait until Father or Mother returned from work and eat what they brought. Usually it was a bun. I slept in the hallway of our Lei Cheng Uk housing estate room on a rattan mat. When people left for work early in the morning, I also had to get up or they'd walk on me." Cheung-Kwok's elder sister remembered water shortages, adding, "It was my job in the afternoon when my brother was at school to carry buckets of water up five floors to our room."

Cheung-Kwok deeply and resentfully feels his family's misfortunes, despite managing to do very well for himself professionally in his chosen trade of engineering. A company Christmas dinner in 2005 caused him to think of this past again. The employees participated in a game: "Our colleagues all brought childhood photos that we put together on the table. We'd get HKD 1,000 if someone recognized us. I was the only one that no one recognized. So thin!"

Their stories powered the family script—recoup family losses and do not live again under Communism—and underlaid Cheung-Kwok's response to retrocession. Emigration became Cheung-Kwok's family duty. This meant saving the family lineage by creating a safe place to reunite them all if needed.

Ching's family also fled after the Communists seized their textile factory in 1953. They left three sons to be raised by a relative. Her father's partner, his brother, remained behind as well. Ching explained: "We expected to regain the family business and had to leave someone in China to manage it." The sons later moved to Hong Kong, but this separation caused a family rift that never healed. Father Ngai managed a small garment factory in Hong Kong, while Mother Ngai gave birth to three daughters there. Ching, the capable second daughter (born in 1958), would eventually become leader in family affairs.

Ching's family's flight from political upheaval made her aware of the damage done to her family by their forced migration. She has become the member who ensures that her family continues to exist and remains connected. She fostered this role even more after her marriage.

Family Survival First

Ching came of age at a time when her family struggled economically after taking refuge in Hong Kong. Common at this difficult time, she put family survival before building a career of her own (Salaff 1981). This dutiful daughter continues this role after marriage, providing support to Cheung-Kwok's kin and working to ensure that their daughter becomes their success story.

Ching helped her father in the factory while she completed secondary school. She took secretarial courses and after graduating held a series of white-collar jobs. Her first, in a Japanese travel company in 1978, sparked her interest in North American life. "I worked for two years, and saved just enough for a ticket. Hardly any money to spend. I survived because my classmate in Calgary had opened a luncheon counter. I worked there for two weeks and earned CAD 200 so I could travel more. I got a Greyhound ticket and went everywhere. I met a professor in Cincinnati, and this person was so curious and friendly, still we keep in touch. I can always stay with that person if I go back to North America."

Fulfilling her family responsibilities while making her own way as a self-sufficient person entailed compromises. She learned when she was young to craft solutions that met both the family's and her own goals at the same time. By traveling to North America on a shoestring, she withheld only a small amount of funds from her family and then was able to earn more abroad while exploring a new culture. Ching called it letting one activity accomplish two ends, which has become her life theme. Although the twenty-year-old Ching was not yet committed to emigration, this early taste of life abroad marks the beginning of her job as emigrant planner after marriage to Cheung-Kwok.

A Foot In Two Doors: Early Planning

Ching and Cheung-Kwok met in 1980 while both worked in the same engineering firm. Cheung-Kwok was already well on his way to becoming established in the construction industry. Ching was attracted to this self-made professional: they had family backgrounds in common and shared an outlook toward the future. They married in 1986. Ching soon took on Cheung-Kwok's calling and became the organizer of the Luks' emigration mission.

The signing of the Sino-British Joint Declaration prompted the Luks to plan their escape from Hong Kong, fearing that they would lose their achievements. With little confidence in the Chinese government, Cheung-Kwok worried about political governance after retrocession. He believes in a government based on law rather than the Chinese-style state grounded on individual whims: "It's very unstable for one person or a small group to lead such a large country." He expressed the hope that a strong person (such as then-patriarch Deng Xiaoping) would maintain his influence as long as possible to prevent the chaos that occurred with the dissolution of the USSR.

Pessimistic, Cheung-Kwok even predicted a recession in 1997 due to the Chinese government's disregard for professional standards: "The Chinese government may ask our firm to take 100 of their workers, who don't have the training, and we won't be able to refuse!" His experiences foretold the worst-case scenario: "Once I visited a site in Shanghai, where we're building a large hotel, and talked to the engineer about his training. He told me he was trained as a chemist and assigned to this architectural job!" Teaming up with subcontractors to construct a three-star hotel in Shenzhen, their slipshod work again bedeviled him:

> The government requires us to hire Chinese personnel for security and engineering. I even gave them extra money to improve their fire protection. When I saw it was still not up to standard, I reproached the supervisor. He said, "Since I'm the inspector, I'll pass it." So I got angry and said, "That's why there are so many fires in China! I gave you more money to improve it, but you pocketed it." The man in charge of the dining room offered, "We have more room than the kitchen, why not put all the exits in here!" Of course if there is a fire in the kitchen that won't do. So I redesigned it and put in more exits. In Hong Kong, everything is checked and double checked. Same in your country, but in China they profit from it.

With these considerations about the future of his profession and his family script in the background, Cheung-Kwok's exit plans coalesced.

In 1992 when we first met the Luks, we noticed how they organized their family home around migration. They balanced their ability to buy comfortable material goods with a reluctance to encumber their ultimate exit. The modest 450–square-foot flat in a remote location suited contact with nearby kin. The apartment displayed a purposeful minimalism. Cheung-Kwok fitted the walls of their tiny flat with cupboards, and stocked the shelves with puzzles and other learning toys for their daughter, while leaving other furnishings diminutive. He directed our glance to a scroll in English, "The Ten Commandments of Poverty, Ten Commandments of Riches," posted in Ruby's room. Its message of hard work and determination symbolized planning their future life goals.

Cheung-Kwok held high professional standards, liked situations that tested his abilities, and proudly spoke of the projects he worked on: Telford Gardens, Kornhill, and Pacific Place. The Discovery Bay housing and airport projects on remote Lantau Island were pioneering efforts: "There was no water supply, no electricity, no roads. When there was a typhoon, we were usually the last group of workers to leave the island!" For Cheung-Kwok, retrocession risked the professional status that he worked so hard to achieve, directly challenging his work identity (Hughes 1958).

Weighing the Costs of Emigration

The Luks were both concerned over reversion, but their issues diverged with their family roles. For Cheung-Kwok, family economics were crucial. He weighed the costs of staying against leaving, largely considering formal employment. His belief that in Hong Kong, Communist excesses threatened his profession, was a political concern about change at the regulatory level. As in most of our Hong Kong families and other Asian businessmen studied (Chee 2005; Mak 1997) Cheung-Kwok assumed the formal role associated with his family's migration. Concerned with earning a living for their nuclear and broader families, he stood a lot to lose if his predictions were borne out.

Cheung-Kwok initially thought he could carry off his heavy financial responsibilities abroad. So to build economic stability and ensure his acceptance, he invested in Canada even before he applied. His colleagues who had already emigrated suggested investments in projects similar to theirs in Hong Kong. But without contacts to their Canadian counterparts (the engineers and businessmen familiar with Canadian markets), Luk and his colleagues were marginalized. Their contacts did not reach into the appropriate social fields, and their investments advice suffered from unfamiliarity with local conditions.

For example, while still in Hong Kong, Cheung-Kwok and his colleagues invested in a house maintenance service company in Montreal. It soon lost money. The next year, the Luks bought a Vancouver condominium expecting to make a profit. Ching carefully debated its location ("Near a golf course, that gives it good feng shui," she thought). They arranged the purchase through agents in Hong Kong who specialized in immigrants' investments, a link in the transnational institutions that foster migration for the affluent. But the Luks did not know about the typical problems of Vancouver's quickly built condos. After spending more on the condo repairing leaks and other maintenance than they received from rent, they cut their losses and sold it. In these investments, Cheung-Kwok's Hong Kong know-how turned out inapplicable in Canada: "In Hong Kong it's always better to buy an apartment, you never lose out. At least you'll earn it back and have a free place to live. In North America, it's different!"

Peer relations were crucial in their migration journey. They had no close kin in Toronto, but this was not their field of reference. At the time, emigration was the all-around hot topic among their social networks, fueling their desire to go. They tried to learn which way the migration wind was blowing from their contacts. As the person dedicated to manage the family emigration project, Ching drew on every opportunity to figure out what their life would be like abroad. Even we (the authors) became part of their migration network. Whenever we met, Ching queried our research project to obtain insights into Canadian life, asking, "Any feedback from your respondents about life in the West?" As the practical worker and emotional supporter in several family units, Ching worried about maintaining the kin fabric. She felt her responsibilities as strong normative-level issues that made emigration risky as well as necessary.

During most of the 1980s, the Luks held emigration as an eventual goal. Cheung-Kwok aimed to retire early and linked retirement (which he thought should occur around age forty-five, or in 1994) with emigration. He hoped to complete college abroad. And to him and others with demanding jobs, Canada appeared to be the ideal retirement home (Ley and Kobayashi 2005). Ching wanted to have a child and to educate her in Canada, "where the environment is better." Although they had intended to delay this until they emigrated, in 1989, Ching became pregnant.

Until this point, they still hadn't formally applied to immigrate to Canada. Still, they assumed they could decide later, and they kept that goal on the horizon. However, the events in Tiananmen Square impelled them to action. Expressing their beliefs, a pregnant Ching and her husband marched against the Tiananmen crackdown. After years of planning, the violence of this event by the government that was to rule Hong Kong combined with the fact that Ching was pregnant with their first child spurred them to apply. This process did not happen overnight. Emigration unfolded slowly over the next five years, which, as it turned out, provided ample time for the Luks to change their minds.

Waiting in Hong Kong

The Luks' reaction to Tiananmen was by no means unique. These events renewed urgency to emigrate for those, like the Luks, whose families had lost property decades earlier (Bertaux 1997). As a result, the Canadian Consulate was bogged down with so many applications that it was not until 1994 that the Luks had their immigration interview, and not until 1995 that they got landed status in Canada.

Meanwhile, life in Hong Kong continued. In 1990, Ching gave birth to their only child and, from that time, the Luks continued to plan for migration while raising their daughter, working, and maintaining their family relations. During their extended waiting period, we see their family roles developed against the background of their migration project.

A Family in Waiting

The three cosmopolitan families we meet in part I have "his" and "her" family work. Fathers work long hours to support the family. Wives, committed to their family roles, hold no other demanding jobs while their children grow up. Together, these activities prepare the family for emigration.

Family economics was Cheung-Kwok's strong point, and during the waiting period, he devoted himself to his migration plan. Educating their child overseas, which was part of their migration design, needed savings. Cheung-Kwok saved USD 1,250 every year in foreign currency for Ruby's educational fund, an amount that he increased as she got older. He left Ruby's training to Ching. He expressed his devotion to his child by taking her to children's gaming galleries and to fast-food joints, a proud smile lighting up his face. As Ruby grew a bit older, father and daughter time together was directed toward her training in sports. They dissected her wins or losses in windsurfing races together, mulling over wind velocity and direction. Past these, Cheung-Kwok's primary contribution was monetary. He would give more thought to Ruby's development as she grew older.

Intensive mothering is a pillar of the identity of the middle-class mother who aims to secure better education for her children (Hays 1996). Ching inherited an ideology in which the mother becomes a child-rearing expert in order to recognize what her child requires, and she is the chief caretaker who shapes the child in the right direction. To achieve this ideal, whether or not her family intends to emigrate, a Hong Kong middle-class mother spends a good deal of time and money developing the child's cultural capital to fit the family's social position. Ching encouraged Ruby in sports, music, art, and other activities. In this, Ching's mothering resonates with North American middle-class parenting (Sayer et al. 2004).

The Hong Kong institutional context intensifies the mother's child-raising tasks (McLaren et al. 2004). The school system, organized around highly competitive rote exams, demands parents' involvement in children's learning. Classrooms are large, teachers overextended. Helping their children progress takes time (Shek 2005).

Yet Ching did more than react to this setting. Beginning in Ruby's childhood and on through to adolescence, we noticed that Ching raises her daughter quite differently than the working-class parents we will meet in later chapters. Everybody wants their children to do better than they have done. The workers put it in terms of avoiding manual toil. Ching's mothering centered on grooming Ruby for a future professional life like her father's, which was denied this capable woman. In this case, the education was to be in Canada.

Many wonder whether it is families' money or their class culture that creates differences in styles of child rearing (Kotchick and Forehand 2002). It is true that Ching has the money and time she needs to devote to her sole daughter and chart her future (Chin and Phillips 2004). Yet by watching Ching and Ruby together and discussing Ching's ambitions for Ruby, we see that her mothering style is formed by social fields that poorer mothers cannot claim (Lareau 2003). The structures around her, which take for granted certain goals and assumes methods of achieving them, shape an approach to parenting and an identity as a mother. These factors come together in her distinct parenting style. And so, much earlier than thinking about a suitable career, Ching thought hard about how her daughter should learn to reason and about her own supportive role in expanding her young daughter's all-around learning (Devine 2004). There were lessons, parental direction, and goal-directed travel to achieve these aims.

Ching applied two principles to whatever she did: each activity should accomplish two things, and one should find the most economical means to do it—"In Hong Kong, you learn to be practical." As an example, theorizing that drawing develops the balance and spatial perspective in a child, Ching enrolled Ruby in art classes at an early age. These Saturday lessons were near Ruby's grandmother's home so that Ching could give her kin networks a regular part in Ruby's activities. Ching's sister met their MTR train, took Ruby to drawing class, and picked Ruby up to bring her to Grandmother, who spent a few hours with her. In the evening, the Luks joined the grandparents for the evening meal and brought Ruby home.

The mother in an emigrant family must also develop a child adapted to schools abroad (McLaren and Dyck 2004). Past the issue of English fluency, to Ching, producing an overseas student included building in her daughter an independence of mind and spirit. Ching's approach was to train Ruby to be self-reliant and depend little on her in daily activities (Lam 2007). To this end, Ching stressed reasoned explanations, putting her daughter in charge of the answer and turning what had to be done into a learning game (McBride-Chang and Chang 1998; Leung 2006). She asked her daughter, "What is the right way to do things? Is this way right? Or is it not?" Ruby easily chose the desired response, "It's right!" One afternoon, trudging home up the steep hill from the MTR with a four-year-old Ruby, Ching engaged in this form of learning play: "How many steps up the hill? Count! 1, 2, 3 . . . !" thereby teaching and diverting the tired tyke at the same time.

Ching did not mother alone. Chinese culture views children as members of the broader family, and kin share the family work (Lam 2007). Young mothers also expect their husbands' support, although professional men like Cheung-Kwok have little time to follow through their vows to share family tasks (Hyun et al. 2002). Most middle-class Hong Kong mothers hire a domestic helper to release them from routine housework (Chan and Wong 2005). Still, Hong Kong women have a lot of mothering work to do, and these various sources of help did not allow Ching to do demanding wage work for modest pay (Chan 2006).

Ching did not really face a choice of intensive mothering or paid work since her ability to land a good job was limited due to past practices. When she was matriculating, the school system had a small number of tertiary-level places. Parents demurred at paying steep fees for daughters' schooling (Post and Pong 1998). Coming of age in a difficult period, she dutifully sacrificed personal achievement to help support her family. Ching's modest educational level deterred her from getting a good professional job. She accepted this. "In Hong Kong you work night and day. I can't, I take care of the family."

In fact, Ching has held a series of white-collar service jobs, meshing with her family cycle (Lau et al. 2006). In the early years, when Ching was keen on contributing financially to the family emigration project, young Ruby was cared for by her auntie. Soon, however, Ching could not expect her kin to take care of Ruby full time and quit work when the Luks' situation improved and intensive mothering was needed. She put it in terms of not bothering others, but she had more complex goals for her daughter's future than kin could meet: "We must care for our own children, our parents are too old. We don't want to burden them. Mother-in-Law won't help. In China, she had a servant. She isn't good with kids. She only knows how to criticize them. So one child will be enough for me!" When asked why, in her affluent household, she took on so much family work herself, she raised practical arguments against hiring a full-time maid, justified by negative stereotypes of servants (Constable 1997): "There's no point. She'd cost HKD 4,000 and you have to give her a place to live, meals, and two plane tickets home to the Philippines every year. I'd have to wear proper clothes around the house, and she'll chatter on the phone." Instead, the Luks hired a Cantonese woman to housekeep part-time. Even so, "Then we went around and cleaned anyway! There's no point in spending the money." It was not only money, but the ambivalence of a woman faced with the sharp choice of doing intensive mothering or working as a low-paid clerk.

Ching defended her choice: "Your boss may say you are pretty and smart when he needs you to work late, but doesn't really care about you or your family. When he does not need you he changes, then you have nothing." Hong Kong employers demand that their workers demonstrate commitment by making work the central focus of their lives—but for Ching, family came first (Blair-Loy 2003). To care for the family and to be seen as caring was her role.

Hong Kong society also honors mothering, yet with its focus on the bottom line, public views of doing family work are ambiguous (Wong 2008). Still, women in Ching's situation do not have low self-esteem (Carr 2004). To Ching, as to others in her cohort, family work defined the unique contribution she made, and she did not regret it. Doing family work secured her self-respect. Ching ultimately felt that a contemporary family, especially a migrant family, needed an organic emotional center as well as an economic base (Hochschild 1990). "If everyone went their own way, they would not meet their potential. They would fragment."

Marriage Is My Compromise

As emigrant planners, the Luks justified their leisure activities within the goal of emigration. In his spare time, Cheung-Kwok applied his strong memory and acumen with figures to mahjong and horse racing. Sitting in front of the television watching the horse-racing channel, he used a modem to bet online, keeping separate bank accounts so that gambling and stocks did not eat into family savings. His gambling track record was good, averaging a modest but steady HKD 500 a week. Depositing these winnings in Ruby's study abroad educational fund, he portrayed gambling as supporting their emigration project.

Instead of seeking demanding employment, Ching, a social powerhouse, developed her skills in golf and dance. She took up these activities in Hong Kong's low-cost Fan Ling public driving range, and in community center dance classes. She maintained that the wider value of these diversions fit into the family's ongoing emigration goals because in Canada she could continue these pastimes even more cheaply. She fit lessons around her family tasks.

Although complementary in many areas, their family recreation activities illustrated their differences as a couple. Ching enjoyed leisure time as a family, whereas Cheung-Kwok preferred the solitary pastime of gambling. Long ago, Ching made a pact with herself that she would be the one to compromise so that her marriage would endure. When they traveled together, Cheung-Kwok's preferences dictated their vacation spots and activities. Once, on their return from a trip in 1993, I asked Ching, "Do you know your husband's friends?" She replied, "Some of them. They like to play mahjong and do horse racing, things businessmen like to do. It's boring." When I asked, "Does he know your friends?" she retorted: "No. He says my friends are gossipy. Actually we don't have the same person-alities. We're not at all alike. He's serious and quiet, I'm lively. We'd go somewhere and I'd book lots of things to see. He'd complain, 'Why do you have to make so many arrangements?' On a holiday, he likes to sleep!" To avoid these conflicts, she invited along people whom Cheung-Kwok likes, and managed their time so that holidays went the way he wanted. Still, on these family trips, Ching and Cheung-Kwok often spend their leisure time apart, choosing to dote on Ruby separately while the other was busy doing things they preferred.

Ching feared that in Canada, when a retired Cheung-Kwok would have too much leisure, their separate interests would harm their marriage. She based her fears on the experiences of others, for example her golf coach, who discussed the problems he faced in Canada. A former accountant, waiting for his citizenship and without employment, he developed his golf skills. He and his wife quarreled over their disappointing Canadian life and divorced. After returning to Hong Kong, he turned his golf pastime into a job. This story was emblazoned in Ching's mind as an emigration warning: the displacements of migration might exacerbate marriage problems.

As Ruby matured, the Luks' outings more closely catered to her development and drew them together as a family toward achieving these goals. Ching designed family holidays to advance Ruby's learning, and her husband went along more enthusiastically than before.

The Broader Family Needs Work Too

"In life you only have your family."
— Ching Luk

Another cornerstone to her identity, Ching ventured that she has always done more conscientious kin care than her sisters, and was the one they all counted on. Ching seemed resentful over her sister's minimal oversight: "Elder Sister may live near Mother, but Mother has to shop and do everything by herself." Ching brought her parents to doctors, filled their prescriptions, organized outings, took them shopping, and arranged family ritual celebrations.

In these, she again put her principles into action, each activity meeting two goals. For example, while attending the funeral of her mother's sister in Guangzhou, she warmed up relations with her family members. She bought train tickets for her cousins and visited her father's family, trying to reunite the two feuding brothers. During the same trip, she dropped in on her husband's brother and sister-in-law. Whenever possible, Ching organized her time as efficiently as possible, applying the same strategies to kin care as to the family migration project.

One pleasant sunny afternoon in June 1993, she arranged for a ferry trip to one of Hong Kong's many outlying islands off Saikung, where we could have a seafood lunch and walk around. Three-year-old Ruby easily accommodated the adults, leaving us time to chat about Ching's important role as family caregiver. She pointed out that her kin work avoided costly incidents. Earlier that year, when Cheung-Kwok was betting at the Happy Valley race course, she dropped in on her parents and found her father perspiring heavily: "He had high blood pressure, and no one knew it. It was a hot day. He went out, waited for a bus, and took a one-hour bus ride. He got very sick. Mother is a typical Chinese woman who doesn't know what to do in a pinch. It was fate that I was there to send him to the doctor!" Ching's identity was one of competence. She valued being responsible in her varied activities and family roles. She was proud of being able to fulfill her family roles and other roles and still have time for leisure. Given her linking and cohesion-building role in the Luk and Ngai families, managing her kinship responsibilities from abroad became increasingly problem laden.

Changing Plans

While still waiting in Hong Kong for their immigration interview, emigration began to appear costly. The migration patterns of others in their network shifted: peers who had once encouraged migration discouraged it. Emigrant Hong Kong friends phoned them from Vancouver to tell them of a country rich in minerals and raw materials that was doing poorly. They were also distressed to find that their colleagues appeared to have lost their former Hong Kong work drive. Their approach to business—to look for new opportunities on all fronts—had succumbed to an easygoing Canadian life. A friend they visited had become *too* Canadian. "He was very active in Hong Kong, bought houses and made lots of money. In Vancouver, he changed 100 percent. Doesn't work weekends or buy and sell. He says, 'Why bother?' He doesn't care anymore. The local environment did it!" As Ching put it, "In Hong Kong, you have to struggle, and be commercially minded, keeping up. It is said that Canadians do not like to work." These experiences added to their growing concerns about migration.

When author Janet Salaff was invited to meet Cheung-Kwok's colleagues in 1994, talk centered on the personal costs of migration. The occasion was a Christmas barbecue in a well-to-do mixed Chinese-expatriate gated community in the New Territories. Two Mongolian firepots on gas burners were laid out on long tables in the backyard patio. We dipped sweet shrimp, crab, scallops, chunks of fresh fish, meatballs, and marinated pork. Two maids cared for the tiniest charges while the adults chatted and the teenagers urged food on the guests.

This small get-together mirrored the professional community's migrant status: three of the four families had applied to immigrate. Of the three, one did not intend to leave, one was an astronaut, and one still awaited Canadian landing papers (the Luks).

The nonemigrant host, a construction engineer, had gone to Cheung-Kwok's middle school. "We've thirty years of friendship!" Cheung-Kwok said proudly. The host offered that it was too costly to get immigration papers for Canada: "There's no reason to emigrate. It is a crisis of confidence. If you get a passport to leave and then return, it's a waste of time. You might as well stay here. It's not necessary to have a passport. I can send my children to England to study without one. If things are really bad, you can leave as a refugee!" Another guest, Wong, had already served his three years' residence stint in Canada, become a citizen, and returned to Hong Kong as an astronaut. His wife, whose mother lives in Toronto, remained. They had gone to Canada to join her, but Wong had not tried to find work:

"Hong Kong people build tall buildings, and they are quite complex, but Toronto builds mostly low buildings. All construction is in the hands of Italians, and they are very skillful. I didn't even send out resumes."

Instead, while waiting out what was commonly referred to as the immigrant jail period for landed immigrants to become citizens, Wong developed a computer software package that tracked trends in FOREX money market. He took advantage of Toronto's low-cost community centers to swim every day, and practiced martial arts. He summed up his Canadian experience: "No, there wasn't much I could learn from Canada. In fact, Canadian construction rules are so cumbersome, you take three years to apply for all the paperwork. Within that time, the building here would've been finished." Despite their friends' negative experiences, the Luks still entertained their own emigration project; after all, there was Ruby to think about.

During the 1990s, Hong Kong's economic boom significantly advanced Cheung-Kwok's career. In the early part of the decade, a colleague put him on contract for a start-up building firm, part of a consortium, at HKD 40,000 a month, with considerable professional autonomy. By 1995, Cheung-Kwok was full-time, earning HKD 60,000 a month plus a share in the firm's profits and commissions for their completion. Still committed to building capital for emigration, he also directed his own small interior design business but found that "running your own business isn't worth it. It's better to be an employee and buy stocks. At least I pay lots of taxes, that'll show the Canadian government my worth!" In 1995, soon after their acceptance as immigrants and his promotion to a full-time employment, he sold the side business to a Mainland Chinese firm. He was too busy to handle two jobs.

Though the economic boom made Cheung-Kwok's job of providing funds for their family emigration project a little easier, it was also more difficult to leave established networks. In a skilled profession, he was very much in demand, driving his ambitions further. Exhibiting his self-made Hong Konger approach to business—to look for new opportunities on all fronts— over time it became apparent to Cheung-Kwok that Canada had far fewer opportunities than pre-handover Hong Kong. The failure of yet another Canadian investment shored this belief.

Cheung-Kwok, still in Hong Kong but intending to emigrate, joined five former coworkers and friends in a startup window frame company in Markham, a Toronto suburb. This would enable him to get points to immigrate in the investment category and earn money at the same time. After a slow start, business picked up when new Hong Kong immigrants, used to having steel bars outside their windows, replaced their Canadian wooden frames with sturdier material. The business expanded, but they could not break out of the enclave into the local market, because "houses are far apart, not like Hong Kong, and Canadians don't want heavy windows."

The investors next cooked up a transnational venture: "Canada makes plastic molding machines that mold egg cartons. We're hoping to make them and sell them to China." Part of the problem was the transnationalism of its business partners, as they rotated their time between Canada and Hong Kong to maintain their dual residence. After one partner met his six-month-yearly Canadian residency requirements, he returned to Hong Kong to be replaced by another fulfilling his stint. After becoming citizens, they retired from the firm altogether. Although some researchers find local markets and return visits aid transnational entrepreneurship (Landolt 2001; Wong and Ng 2002), in this case it did not. In fact, the transnational migrant investors' lack of information and contacts with local markets doomed the project from the outset. Their social contacts were not part of social fields with knowledge of suitable businesses in Canada. Troubled by lack of information or commitment, unable to develop markets, and stuck with inventory, the company folded.

As life went on in Hong Kong, the Luks found it hard to break entirely from the economic conditions, family relations, and other ties that held them there. Even after obtaining his Canadian permanent resident's permit in 1995, Cheung-Kwok delayed his withdrawal from the fast-paced Hong Kong business environment. Construction projects related to the handover boomed and skills were in demand, so Cheung-Kwok postponed retirement to save for his family's emigration.

In 1994, still in Hong Kong, they invested in a three-bedroom apartment in North Point, a turning point in their migration plans. This new home would double their living space in an area with status, but substantial mortgage payments were barriers to emigration. Luk proudly entered the site grounds while it was under construction to monitor the progress. Trees lined the walkway leading to their high-rise. Buses, minivans, and street cars drove below them at all hours, but high above bustling Hong Kong, the flat was secluded. After moving in, they quickly filled this apartment with toys, which spilled from bookcases to the couch and the corners of the living room. There were two computers with one for Ruby, who learned to load her computer games before her little hands could clutch the mouse. The walls were adorned with the fruits of her years of drawing classes.

Even here they bought few household goods—they did not repair their audio equipment when it broke, except for maintaining the VCR for Ruby's Disney cartoons. Their flat lacked the trendy decor being promoted to middle-class families in glossy magazines and shops. They remained unwilling to encumber their emigration plans.

Fulfilling their kin responsibilities, they also bought an apartment for Mother Luk. Luk's younger brother and family share the apartment and the care of the older woman as well. The expense of a car was no obstacle. Apart from Cheung-Kwok's travels to work sites, they used the car to drive Ruby the distance to visit her grandparents and to transport grandparents home after family dinners and Ching to play golf. When they changed their car, Ruby chose its blue color.

The Luks had mixed feelings about living in Canada. Their ambivalence meant that Cheung-Kwok did not quit his Hong Kong job, and they hired an immigration lawyer to arrange for them to return to live in Hong Kong without jeopardizing their landed status. Immigrant colleagues helped them navigate the Canadian housing market:

> I was going to buy three apartments in Mississauga. My friend faxed details to me in Hong Kong. They were reasonable, but I knew I could get them cheaper. I looked up the construction costs and figured they should cost CAD 120 per square foot to build, and I thought I could get them close to that price, but someone got there first. Friends suggested, "Rent and live here for a year before you buy, see the market and where you want to live." You need such people who can give you good advice. We may even live for free; a friend who will return to Hong Kong offered to let us live in his place.

They perused the slick advertisements of places with names like Pacific Place that borrow the aura of well-situated Hong Kong locales. Finally, while visiting Canada in 1996, they bought an apartment in North Toronto, but then immediately returned to Hong Kong.

Cheung-Kwok was unable to establish a life in Canada. His firm did not give him a long leave to go abroad. All of his Canadian investments failed, and his extensive experience in construction projects did not translate into Canadian experience. Moreover, networks are key in the construction industry. They are part of the social fields underlying the normative structures that run the industry. In Hong Kong, Cheung-Kwok has built useful networks with those who completed the grueling evening-school stint with him, and with colleagues he has met on projects. They got jobs for each other: "We all have good jobs in government or large firms. We're too busy for reunions, but we know where the others work. We look each other up when we need a job done."

He started his interior design firm with two schoolmates and secured his current job from a former colleague: "Networks are important in this field.

Work has always come to me. People know if I'm dissatisfied with my job and call me up. I don't have to look in the want ads." These networks did not extend into Canada. At the same time, his credentials were not recognized either. His experience as a site manager supervising construction of high rise hotels was not useful in Canada.

He was not alone in his unfulfilled career abroad. Half a dozen of Cheung-Kwok's friends who had quit their jobs and emigrated to Toronto returned to Hong Kong for similar reasons. Since Cheung-Kwok stayed at his post, his networks enabled him not only to change his mind, but to help other returnees as well. Cheung-Kwok's company was under pressure to complete key construction jobs at the new Hong Kong airport and he arranged contracts for several colleagues. Having invested much of their lives in Hong Kong, the older the Luks get, the more returns their personal networks give them. Several years later, few in their circle remain in Toronto. Their collegial social networks who cheered each other on to emigrate created the bandwagon to return.

In the end Cheung-Kwok had little choice. The large-scale regulative differences between the political economies of Hong Kong and Canada, the unexpected opportunities in Hong Kong, and the problems at the normative level of accessing Canadian social fields compelled him to continue his employment in Hong Kong. Though Ching could stay in Toronto with Ruby, benefiting from access to Canada's education system, she worried that lengthy separations would threaten her marriage. The Luks decided on a short-term astronaut arrangement; Ching and Ruby would spend just one year in Toronto, long enough to qualify them for citizenship with their lawyer's help. So in 1997, the same year that Hong Kong was officially handed over to China, Ching and Ruby left for Canada. In 1998, they rejoined Cheung-Kwok in Hong Kong. During their qualifying year Cheung-Kwok only visited his family on holidays.

While in Toronto, Ching continued to oversee family relations at a distance. She planned ahead, grooming her sister-in-law as her successor to do kin work. But even when involving other family members as her support team, Ching had not lost her leadership in the kin group. On her return, she again took up her role as organizer of family gatherings and other important ritual events she'd missed while away (Imber-Black et al. 1988; Stone et al. 2005).

Although they initially planned to become new Canadians in the full sense of the term, the Luk family altered their plans. The failure to rebuild their family economy abroad was the first step undermining their resolve. They could not rebuild their strong social and economic positions in Toronto. Cheung-Kwok's credentials went unrecognized and his business investments did not earn money. Furthermore, his Hong Kong colleagues were not well integrated into Toronto's economic life, and they could not help him connect to the social fields needed to secure a living abroad. One by one, friends who, like Luk, expected to continue their careers abroad reached the end of their savings and returned. From an enthusiastic embrace of the emigration move the Luks, too, drew back.

And so, the Luks reframed their migration plans. With booming Hong Kong business opportunities in Cheung-Kwok's field flowing to him from his networks there, with the passage of time and their changing life course, a permanent family move was unlikely. The Luks' emigration family economy now focused on their daughter's education abroad.

Passing The Baton: 1996–2005

Returning to Hong Kong after their year's residence in Toronto, the Luks shifted their attention to Ruby's future career as an overseas student. Ching planned her family time anew to meet the educational imperatives. Unable to combine intensive mothering with long work hours, Ching quit her position in software sales to devote herself to her daughter's study when Ruby was ten and approaching the crucial school placement tests. "My boss is too demanding! He can't accept it if I don't work overtime or stay late at night. I need to take care of the little girl because for the past two years when I was working, I couldn't spend too much time on her school work or on Chinese culture. Her low results reflect it. Ruby doesn't concentrate. The teacher tells me, 'She is so naughty, always ignores instructions, always chats with classmates.' So I need to teach the little girl this whole year." After this, Ching no longer contributed money to the emigration project, declining to work in favor of Ruby's education.

Ching's work with Ruby paid off. The following year, Ching proudly announced, "Ruby studies more now, likes it, her grades have risen." The teacher expected more of Ruby, appointing her as class monitor. Ruby was accepted into a Band 1 (gifted) school stream.[1] Even so, Ching maintained that the Canadian school system was superior: "The class ratio here is forty-five to one; there's no way the school can teach a child well in that setting. Band 1 school means Band 1 parents!" Ching steeled herself for this level of personal attention to Ruby's schoolwork, all the while keeping her eye on the ultimate goal, sending Ruby to school overseas.

To help prepare Ruby for school abroad, Ching worked hard to expand her daughter's all-around learning, intent on shaping her character. She studied tennis, putonghua (standard modern Chinese language), and saxophone, and attended English-language camp in Australia: "Ruby needs to have good food, rest, sports, arts, and to study. I think they have thirteen days of tests in her first year of secondary school [Form 1]. Ruby can't stop everything because of exams. She's only age thirteen and has many more years of exams ahead. I didn't cancel any of her sports or other activities; only windsurfing, which takes a whole day to set up the sail, surf, and wash the boat." The level of attention that Ching paid to Ruby's development was matched by the teacher's involvement. This was part of the daily pressure on young Ruby, which posed academic achievement as her overriding purpose in that stage of life. This created a stressful atmosphere (Leung 2006). But Ching was determined to do all she could to give Ruby the required family backing for achievement.

In 2003, the year before Ruby sat for her next set of major exams, Ching spent a week in Toronto with her immigrant friends to update her plans for Ruby's overseas schooling by asking questions: How were their children doing in school? When was the optimal time to send her daughter to Canada? How should she pursue the family migration project, without separating from her husband? If Ruby went to boarding school, would they become a divided family?

She figured out that high school was optimal time for Ruby to go abroad: "The high school teacher works on the student's creativity. They go over their essays and vocabulary. My friends' children have to stay up all night at least twice a week to do their high school projects. Then once you get to university, it all changes. Getting in takes good grades. To get into a professional school like architecture, you need a 90 percent average! Also they don't correct you there. It's very difficult. You have to work very hard. So Ruby needs to start high school in Canada to get the training she needs to do well in college." Pondering all sides of her daughter's future, including her identity, Ching openly wondered if they'd lose Ruby to Canada: "I observed what the young generation Chinese immigrant does. If they go to junior secondary school in Canada, they are likely to go on to college, and then get a job and stay there. If they go to university only, they are not likely to have the connections to get the best jobs, and they'll return to Hong Kong." Nevertheless, Ching draws on the world's educational offerings for Ruby's educational trajectory, "Maybe she will go on to college in Toronto, and then maybe to Europe."

To balance the needs of their family members, some mothers establish a home in Toronto or other Western cities where they help their school-age children, leaving the father behind as an astronaut. Ching was against this; her friends warned her about philandering astronaut husbands. She considered sending Ruby to Toronto alone the following year: "She'll only be fourteen, and it's not safe for her to live alone. But if I go with her, it will be three years away from Hong Kong." She realized that if she remained with Ruby in Toronto, "My husband won't be happy and it may be bad for us." Ching began to explore boarding schools for Ruby.

Cheung-Kwok continued to build savings for Ruby's education while gradually becoming more directly involved. Then, like Ching, Cheung-Kwok's focus narrowed. Ruby already considered working in the housing field, perhaps in interior design. That did not match her parents' aspirations. Cheung-Kwok brought Ruby to his office where she manipulated architectural designs on the computer. That summer they took a family trip to six European cities. Cheung-Kwok happily went along, understanding that the function of this holiday was educating Ruby. Gazing at the old tall buildings, daughter Ruby had a revelation. As Cheung-Kwok proudly reported, "My daughter wants to be an architect!"

Ching's systematic long-term plan to help Ruby adapt to living abroad appears tailored to this ambition, but Ruby's goal gives Cheung-Kwok pause. His own experience attuned him to the relations she needs to work as an architect—her social capital. He knew that the building industry in Hong Kong closed itself against a foreign-trained architect who returns to Hong Kong without contacts in the local field. But this was not enough to change Ching's decision to send Ruby to a Canadian school. And so Cheung-Kwok postponed retirement, explaining that the cost of boarding school fees demanded he continue work "for at least another million Hong Kong dollars!"

Without warning, in 2003, retirement was forced on Cheung-Kwok by shifts in the company's leadership and policies. The company director quit and sold his shares to the umbrella group that now controlled Cheung-Kwok's profitable construction firm. Having to lay off his junior staff frustrated him, and he complained that Hong Kong firms were hard-boiled: "Work life has become functional. Neither employers nor employees get too involved in relationships anymore. Hong Kong employers are short-sighted. Whenever there are some problems with the business, the first thing they think of is to lay off staff." However, the new head of the company urged Cheung-Kwok to stay on for a time in order to help the transition of the firm's business and rehired him as general manager to prepare a bid for new high-rise buildings in Macao. The job was an exciting challenge that he could not refuse and other project management jobs followed. By this time, Cheung-Kwok's ambivalence about the costs of migration had overwhelmed him. Although the family emigration project was evolving, it appeared that it would not, at least not in the near future, include Cheung-Kwok or Ching's physical move to Canada.

The likelihood that Ruby would ever be joined by her family diminished further with the transformation of Cheung-Kwok's attitudes toward Hong Kong. His view of Hong Kong's politics evolved from almost overwhelming anxiety to contained criticism, disapproving of the political situation, but no longer fearful. Cheung-Kwok stated, "During the transition, for ten to twenty years, there will not be that much effect, but a child will have less freedom and her intellectual world will be limited."

Over the years another theme emerged: self-reliance. Those who pulled their families from poverty held that people should depend on themselves and even rebuild their family fortunes should the economy take a downturn. Thus in 2005, Cheung-Kwok described Hong Kong society as worn out, unable to recover from the economic recession with no hope to soar again. He disparaged the first Hong Kong Chief Executive, Tung Chee-hwa (who inherited his father's family business that bankrupted and was bailed out with the help of the Mainland government) as unable to rule Hong Kong—"He has not built his kingdom himself." Furthermore, "the government did too little to prevent and deal with the problem of SARS when the outbreak was most serious." He went on to blame people's lack of self-reliance: "Our generation learned to count on ourselves. Today's younger people have become lazy. They blame Tung Chee-hwa for everything. Last night, on the [2004] Asian tsunami fundraising TV show, [media stars] Michael Hui and Jackie Hui joked that 'A person trips and falls, Tung is to blame!' We can't blame Tung for everything!" The Luks' family script has decidedly shifted. By criticizing those who are not as self-reliant and determined as he is and who can't face new crises, Cheung-Kwok accounted for the new turn to his family emigration project from flight abroad to investing abroad. In this case, the human capital of his daughter was the investment.

Investigations of PRC immigrant professionals report on the immense strains placed on marriage (Chan and Chia 2003; Salaff and Greve 2006). Uneven access to employment and loss of support systems take their toll. Ching is aware of this probable development of events. Hearing Cheung-Kwok's insistence on living a comfortable life in Toronto after retiring, she imagined a scenario in which their marital relations worsen.

> A man that works hard his whole life is at a loss if he retires in a strange place. In Hong Kong, we live our separate lives. He's not in my hair; he has his friends, I have mine, and Ruby hers. I go dancing and play golf. He plays mahjong, and on the weekends we all go to our families. If we were in Toronto and couldn't afford two cars, how could I go anywhere by myself and take the car? If it

rained, he'd be mad. If he wanted to drive to the casino in Windsor, he couldn't. We'd fight every day and maybe divorce. So we don't go to Toronto.

Over the years, Ruby has spent more time in Canada than her parents. After the year they lived in Toronto, she often spent summers staying with her friends and going to the University of Toronto summer day camp. So when it came time for boarding school applications in 2005, Ruby went to Canada for the interview and entrance exam on her own. An elite Toronto boarding school accepted her, cementing her move abroad. For her part, Ruby was excited by her prospects. There was no culture shock. She stated, "I always knew that I was going to go to school abroad." In 2006, on the eve of leaving for boarding school, she enthused, "I'm not afraid, just curious with whom I will room. I don't have any brothers or sisters, so I never lived with anyone. I wonder what it will be like."

It seems unlikely that the Luks will ever emigrate as a family. Yet the position of their daughter is pivotal. Whether Ruby returns to Hong Kong to rejoin her family or plays a role in the family's migration is still uncertain (Orellana et al. 2001).

Summary: A Family Emigration Project

The Luks planned their family life around emigration, but over the years their views about its value shifted from an anxiety-driven exit to an investment in their daughter. Initially, the structures in which they were embedded worked together to propel their departure. Cheung-Kwok suspected the institutions that had gained them economic success in Hong Kong would not survive PRC rule, an anxiety that was sharpened by their families' past suffering in China. Sharing these thoughts within their Hong Kong professional circles with similar histories enabled their transnational networks to link them to communities of like-minded people leaving for Canada. These sense-making mechanisms scripted their emigration.

They made their move, yet after landing, the poorly fitting institutions caused settlement hardships. Although they met the immigration requirements in Canada, Cheung-Kwok could not break into a profession without recognition of his engineering credentials. His transnational networks weren't integrated into similar Canadian social fields; thus, his entrepreneurial ventures failed. Keeping active contacts in Hong Kong over time (in fact, Cheung-Kwok never quit his Hong Kong base), he and his colleagues reshaped their interpretation of Hong Kong's institutional structures and opportunities, ultimately revaluing Hong Kong and reaffirming their position there.

Instead of espousing politically motivated emigration, the Luks articulated a desire to take advantage of global opportunities for their daughter.

There is one essential continuity: At all times, the survival of the family underpinned emigration motives. The family script that centered on survival and advancing the family has been transformed. The Luks foresee that they can meet these commitments at home better than abroad. They no longer plan to migrate as a family; only Ruby now has that chance.

CHAPTER FOUR

The Chou and Leung Families

Immigrant Entrepreneurs

As Hong Kong reverted to China, many businessmen considered leaving. They worried about institutional stability and the safety of their enterprises, while investment programs of foreign governments offered further inducements. Although many people think of business people as individualists, in fact, they heed those in their circles (Greve and Salaff 2003). Aware that many others were doing the same, emigration seemed a good bet. By settling their families in a comfortable home at a fraction of the Hong Kong price, they would further improve their lifestyle, while a foreign diploma would boost their children's cultural capital. So, on the eve of the handover, with investment plans on the drawing board and money to back them, many Hong Kong entrepreneurs became business immigrants to Canada and elsewhere (Li 2005; Wang and Lo 2005).[1] However, the outcomes of their ventures were often unsuccessful, prompting large numbers into a transnational way of life, the theme of this chapter.

We meet here the Chous and Leungs, two immigrant entrepreneur families related by marriage. Both families were accepted as investment immigrants; however, they occupied different economic niches. Mr. Chou managed a string of integrated enterprises in the transportation industry with associated investments and many contacts in this trade. The Leungs, laboring entrepreneurs, shouldered a hardware business. Though state institutions favored their entry, neither family could establish successful businesses in Canada. They became astronauts to continue their Hong Kong businesses, the mainstay of the family economy.

Some argue that transnational migration is primarily a flow of capital and that it represents the entrepreneurs' success in seizing investment opportunities. They further interpret transnationalism as a form of integration (Portes 2001). Others, in contrast, find that transnational immigrants are not well incorporated into society (Hiebert and Ley 2003). So, too, their astronaut activities did not signal business success in the lives of these two families and their friends. For them, the deficient reach of their social fields in Toronto gave rise to transnationalism and was a failure in settlement. We see this by contrasting their Hong Kong and Toronto businesses. We begin with Uncle Chou, our main respondent over the years.

Building a Business from Scratch

Clement Chou was a successful businessman in Hong Kong who started out poor at a time when everyone was poor and when Hong Kong was in the early stages of development. He did business in ways that he could never repeat in North America. A rags-to-riches businessman, he is a Hong Kong icon. News of those who break through poverty and go on to build an empire against odds breathes faith into many hopefuls. This was as true in the halcyon days of the rise of entrepreneurs as it is today as small firms are being marginalized and even disappearing under the pressure of economic restructuring (Sun and Wong 2008). Chou presents himself as just such an iconic self-made man. He appeared with a mobile phone in hand and wearing a deep-purple Hawaiian shirt, not the suave suited garb of the company man. He was as well-known for his acting in a popular television series in which he played the role of the genial sailor "Uncle Chou" as he was for his business exploits. Since Hong Kong people familiarly refer to him as "Uncle," we'll dub him that as well. When we met Uncle Chou in 1992, he had already become a Canadian citizen. He was an astronaut, while his wife and three children lived in Toronto.

Uncle Chou was Hong Kong-born; the city gave him his start and the supportive contacts that built his small empire. His father arrived in the colony from Chaozhou in 1913, ran a small store, and raised a large family. Uncle Chou, born in Hong Kong in 1933, was the eldest son. Though during the Pacific War his family had sought refuge in their Chaozhou village, they later lost that contact with China. The war cost Uncle Chou a chance at formal education. Returning to Hong Kong in 1945 when he was just thirteen, he went straight to work.

In this transitional early industrial period, many poorly educated men went into factory or hawking jobs, saved funds, and started marginal businesses, hoping for a breakthrough (Wong 1999). A circular career from worker to petty entrepreneur back to worker was common for the hardworking poor. Chou also started his business career modestly and advanced through his ability at seizing opportunities and making contacts. He began in this turbulent period by hawking goods in Hong Kong's Kwun Tong factory district, turned to a small garment factory, and was promoted to supervisor. He saved and bought the firm, but like many of the day, it floundered. Marrying Olivia (also Hong Kong born) in 1963, he badly needed to earn a family wage. He tried a convenience store and a restaurant in Taiwan, among other ventures, none of which would prove to be the break he was looking for.

Fortunes turned in 1970 when Chou drove an unlicensed taxi, a common way for unemployed Hong Kong workers to earn a living. One of his regular customers, Dr. Shik, rode with him when pregnant with her first child, Angela. A general practitioner in Kwuntong, she recognized Chou's extraordinary sense of personal responsibility. The physician soon relied on him to ferry her ill patients to her clinic doors and back home again safely. She also recommended Chou as a driver to her friend, the director of a newly established television station, who happened to be of Chaozhou background.

From the driver's seat Chou made programming suggestions for this new popular station. He drew on his large network to help the director locate extras from different walks of life for the show 72 *Kinds of Jobs*. Although not an actor by trade, he landed his own job playing Uncle Chou. His role was the "nice father" in a typical Hong Kong Chinese working family. Olivia, who worked alongside Chou in many of his enterprises, played his wife. Poking fun at government scandals of the day, the program became popular among working class people who were just then buying their first TVs.

But Chou was first and foremost a businessman, and he soon took on the transportation business for the entire station. Starting with driving television crews for movie shoots, he branched into the trucking business and his fleet expanded. In 1977 a newspaper editor, looking for a chance to serve the growing mass media market, saw Uncle Chou's large transportation fleet parked along the streets and approached him. Teaming up with major newspaper chains and financially backed by a large investor (Hutcheson group), they founded a logistics group. This firm contracted to handle deliveries of newspapers and other Hong Kong consumer goods to convenience stores, later to MTR stations, and to other chain outlets. The company's business swelled as new food-chain stores offered free delivery of purchases. Hong Kong's major property cartels that owned the chains soon started to drive down the prices paid the truckers, which ultimately brought down Uncle Chou's delivery franchise (but that was after he left) (Chung 2005).

It was this string of events that marked Chou's accomplishments as the emergent industrial society of the 1970s was transformed to the service society of the 1990s. As he moved forward from one venture to another in

Hong Kong, it was not something he would be able to repeat in another setting, although he tried.

Emigration as a Family Project: 1981–86

"It was not because of '97 that we emigrated," Uncle Chou stated. He had not planned his family emigration project much before making his move. Uncle Chou was not a refugee from Communism. The notion of immigration to Canada arose because his family was enmeshed in global institutions.

Chou's Views Toward Reversion

Uncle Chou had not actually lived under Communist Chinese rule, had no ties to his hometown in China, and thought traveling there was troublesome. His business did not involve trade with China, and he did not expect to either profit or lose by reversion. Given his lack of firsthand experience there, Uncle Chou's negative opinions reflected what many businessmen around him thought. He accused the Mainland government of incompetence and felt sure they could not raise China's standard of living. For example, he repeatedly insisted that "under the people's government, people are really miserable! Under the Chinese Communist Party rule, nobody can speak the truth."

On the other hand, neither was he attracted by the idea of popular rule in Hong Kong. Unwilling to put his fate in the hands of ordinary people, Chou doubted that Hong Kong's low-paid politicians would dedicate themselves to their political work. In all, retrocession did not play a role in his family's emigration.

Suzanne Makes her Move

Daughter Suzanne became the family's first migrant several years before retrocession became an issue, initiating her family's move overseas. In 1981, Suzanne and her classmates were in Form 3, attending a church-run secondary school. Pondering the approaching advanced level (A level) tests, the girls predicted they would not do well. Some children facing the competitive, exam-based Hong Kong school system may submit to the intense reviewing routine while others rebel and drop out (Lin 2000). The well-off chose another path: studying abroad to build cultural capital (Waters 2005). One day, her classmates turned to each other and agreed, "Now's the time!" For Suzanne, plans were easily made.

In Suzanne's search for a place in school abroad she was following the reach of global institutions. Educational institutions were becoming similar, making it possible to transfer to faraway places. As headmasters met and did the groundwork for international students to move about as fee-payers, education was becoming a commodity. Her secondary school had arrangements in place with Canadian schools, churches, and home-stay families that made it easy for their charges to become visa students. A school in Toronto would receive them; church host families would board them.

Since the program was considered reliable, Suzanne's parents agreed and paid the fees. But her sudden departure without much forethought and living apart from her family for the first time caused Suzanne to become desperately lonely. While visiting his daughter in 1982, Uncle Chou came up with the idea of emigrating to Canada. "I thought that if we emigrated, our daughter could then live together with us, and the whole family could have a better environment too. It would also be good for our sons' education. The issue of 1997 had not yet arisen." At that time, elder son Elic was nineteen and younger son Kin-yam was fourteen; both were lackadaisical students. Uncle Chou was certain that this was the family direction to take; still, he wanted their assent: "The most important thing was whether my two sons would want to go." Taking the whole family on a tour of Toronto, the sons agreed to emigrate as a family. Olivia, by then responsible for the home life of their growing family and without ties to China, was eager to try a Western life. Only then did emigration become a family project. Uncle Chou easily amassed the funds to apply under the investment category. In 1984 the family moved to Toronto's growing immigrant suburbs in Scarborough.

The Chous were not strangers to emigration. Three of their eleven siblings also exited, but unlike the dependent networks of poorer families, they were not a tightly linked migration chain. They did not lend money or find jobs and places to stay for each other abroad. Countries accepted them mainly on their human or financial capital, not kin ties.

The Chous had the ability to compare local institutions with those abroad and to seize emergent opportunities for themselves and the next generation. More concretely, the transnational connections of their daughter's school system generated knowledge of and contacts in a new country. Finally, the promise of the desirable Western lifestyle meshed with their identity and prompted the move. With their economic capital accepted, emigration became an available option, something to be tried.

Transnationalism: 1986–96

Business Troubles in Toronto

As an investment immigrant, Uncle Chou established several small companies in Toronto, which he was required to do. Having built successful businesses in Hong Kong, Chou expected that his knowledge of how to do business and of the world outside Hong Kong would allow him to succeed. He also hoped that he could wind down his Hong Kong ventures and work in Toronto full time. He further assumed that, compared with much of Asia, Canada's stable institutional environment for entrepreneurs would ease his investment. As much as he could, he followed his Hong Kong pattern. But doing business also requires bridges to people and organizations in his field. Lacking the institutional and network supports he had known in Hong Kong, Uncle Chou struggled to set up a profitable business in Canada.

Chou entered his initial investment in 1984 virtually sight unseen with two Hong Kong Chinese business friends who had settled earlier and led the way. But his friends did not know much more about investing in Canada than he did. Thinking property would be as safe a bet as it was in Hong Kong, the three partners bought a hotel on Sherbourne Street, unaware that it was in a declining area of town. Within two years they sold it at a loss. Successful in their own countries, abroad they were outsiders who could not break in.

By default, Chou next turned to the emerging middle-class ethnic enclave in the expanding Hong Kong Chinese suburbs north of Toronto. Doing business in the enclave resembled the business culture and networking that he was used to in Hong Kong, where lunch accompanied most business dealings. He and his colleagues recognized each other as culturally familiar and trustworthy. Social fields and their business practices fit together into a social system, an interwoven set of practices and approaches. Most crucial was their familiarity with doing business *the Chinese way.*

Others have argued that since businesses can cross-fertilize each other, merchants' experiences on one side of the sea can turn into new opportunities on the other shore. In Uncle Chou's case, the decade of transnational migration did not benefit his Toronto investments. His string of business ventures (including an audio-visual shop, a restaurant, and residential properties) in the Chinese suburbs did not perform well. "It is a wrong concept that investing in Canadian properties is profitable now. I can see no area in Canada which is worth investing in either," he grumbled. Despite having brought resources with them, many Hong Kong investors also had disappointing results and had to cut back (Ley 2006; Wong and Ng 2002).

Chou held onto his enterprises as part of his identity and also his obligation under the immigration strictures, but in the end, doing business in Canada could not truly hold him. Instead, he spent his time in Canada (as required to build his residency) responding to the opportunities afforded by streams of Hong Kong immigrants. He advised newcomers and dabbled in the booming field of Hong Kong language-television programming in Toronto, perhaps his real love.

Business in Hong Kong Continues to Build

It was Chou's Hong Kong business that thrived, despite or because of his transnationalism. For three years, Uncle Chou lived in Toronto, making short trips back to Hong Kong for his business. While in Toronto, Chou got ideas from the Canadian postal system about computerized delivery methods; he applied these to his logistics business in Hong Kong. Inputting the addresses of Hong Kong factories, schools, clinics, and fast-food chains on networked computers enabled his vans to deliver papers quickly. He stressed the service he could now give: "We are actually earning from what we have saved. Our customers can also benefit!" The firm's motto of success was "People flow, goods flow, and then money flows." And so, transnationalism proved productive in Chou's Hong Kong delivery company.

Chou's East-West approach combined the latest Western organizational tools and centuries-old Asian paternalism. We saw this in 1993 when we were escorted around his 1,500–square-foot office in a To Kwa Wan industrial building. Maps of Hong Kong covered the walls. Computer printouts listing Hong Kong street names and industrial buildings were piled precariously high on all available surfaces. At their peak, Uncle Chou's integrated transportation companies included two car parks and a repair site. There were over 150 vehicles, 40 staff and 5 managers, 2,000 delivery orders per day, and an annual turnover of millions of Hong Kong dollars (Chung 2005).

The five managers' offices were divided by glass walls so Chou could see them from his desk. This panopticon vision enforced control, but he stressed his traditional paternal ties with his employees. "I treat my employees like my sons and daughters. I teach them many things. Our relations are very good."

Elic Chou, Uncle's eldest son, held another view: "Being from the 'old generation,' Father would never be able to manage in the same style in Canada. If Father wants to work, he has to work in Hong Kong. There's no point in his trying to work in Canada—he won't understand the Canadian way. He expects people to do his bidding if he pays them. They won't do that in Canada. They don't even do so in Hong Kong anymore."

However, Uncle Chou's business troubles in Canada were due to more fundamental issues than to cultural style. His networks did not reach into the social fields that would enable him to do the kind of business that he knew about. As a result, once he had obtained Canadian citizenship, he returned to his Hong Kong business.

A Divided Family: Home away From Home: 1986–96

Chou's transnational moves resulted primarily from his poor integration into North American business networks, a deficiency at the level of work relations. Others might blame the immigrants' commitment to their Asian identity for their transnationalism. Many well-off Hong Kongers, used to frequenting restaurants, clubs, and shops, seek a lively street-scene-based lifestyle like that they left behind. They find the Canadian lifestyle—based on private cars, dispersed communities, and maintenance of the family home and a summer cottage retreat—alienating and lonely, deliberately isolating themselves (Lam 1994).

This was not the case for the Chous, whose family migration owed its success to their appreciation of Canadian ways. After the demanding business-cum-social whirl in Hong Kong, Uncle Chou and Olivia enjoyed the privatized familism of North American urban life. Nonetheless, their goal of integration was unevenly attained. More than cultural values held back their integration.

Uncle Chou's stay in Canada was short-lived because his Canadian investments did poorly. For a decade, he lived the life of an astronaut, residing first in a Hong Kong service hotel, then buying a modest studio flat in the miniature city-like apartment complex of Whampoa Gardens (managed by Francis Kwong, chapter 5), and commuting to visit his family. Retaining his Hong Kong businesses served several functions. They were what he did, what gave meaning to his life, but most important, the Hong Kong operations fed capital that sustained family life and businesses in Toronto. Like others, he timed his final move to Canada to mesh with his retirement (Ley and Kobayashi 2005).

Meanwhile, Olivia and their three children began to build their lives in Toronto. Elic entered a trade college, Suzanne started at a university, but youngest son Kin-yam struggled to adapt to the school system. Eventually, his inability to master college-level English drove him back to Hong Kong where he apprenticed as a mechanic in a car repair firm jointly owned by his father and his father's sister.

Integration was also hard for Olivia. Her role as a wife and mother often pulled her back to Asia, and lack of a work role also hampered intermixing. Without professional training, she tried a number of part-time jobs in Toronto—entered data for a bank, sold video discs and audio tapes in her husband's store, and sold tickets in a movie box office. These might have led her into the community, but eventually Uncle Chou persuaded her that she was working hard without material need. "If your requirements are not high, it's usually not hard to find a job in Canada. But if there's no necessity to work, why not let someone who needs the job more do it?" He surely felt labor jobs were beneath her status, although they are common among the new immigrant middle-class who cannot reclaim their fields (Salaff and Greve 2006; Man 2004). His counsel prevailed, but he overruled her desire to be part of the world outside her home sphere.

Olivia mainly adapted to a leisured life in Canada. She addressed her spotty education, studied Japanese and French, and earned a vocational training certificate. She did not bother too much about building social networks and had only a small number of friends in both places. "I'm not a complex person." She enjoyed watching the Cantonese TV channel and practiced singing along with karaoke music videos at home. She liked to play mahjong and recounted with a sparkle her interest in social dance. She learned the dance steps with friends, but without her husband to partner her, danced less often than she wanted to. She studied flower arranging and played golf. "These lessons are very cheap in Toronto! Only rich people can golf in Hong Kong," she pointed out.

Choice of neighborhood was another hurdle in their intention to meld with Canadian society. The Chous opposed living in a Chinese enclave, but it was hard to find another kind of neighborhood. Hong Kong affluent immigrants arrived all at one time, overwhelming local neighborhoods. Newcomers had to buy houses when there were vacancies, usually in areas in transition or new developments (Myles and Hou 2004). The Chous bought their first house in a mixed ethnic neighborhood in transition near Elic's college campus. But soon afterwards, more Hong Kong Chinese residents entered their area. Wishing to integrate, the Chous moved to upscale Richmond Hill in 1992, then a newly developed suburb with as many families of Italian origin as Chinese. Another surge of Hong Kong immigrants found the area, with its large lots and reasonable prices, attractive. This community, too, quickly became identified with well-off Hong Kong Chinese.[2]

The Chous' home mirrored their transnational situation, spectacularly mixing Chinese and Canadian decor. With an apparent bow to integration, they decorated their house in an East-West manner. Familiar symbols identified the exterior of the residence as Chinese. Two large cement lions guarded the front door; inside were white and pink Italian marble floors, popular among Hong Kong designers. The Chous had brought dining room furniture with them—carved wood chairs and a table, framed calligraphy that hung on the walls, a painted Chinese screen, and a thick rug with the characters for "long life" woven in the center.

A long white sofa and easy chairs and a low glass coffee table gave the living room a Western look. The fax machine in Uncle Chou's first-floor study helped him keep in touch with his Hong Kong office while he was away. A long winding staircase led to four bedrooms upstairs. The finished basement was the heart of the family space. Uncle Chou liked to putter in one basement corner; his tools and fix-it equipment hanging from the ceiling gave the clue. In another corner was an entertainment center with a karaoke system where they entertained friends. Friends shared up-to-date Hong Kong laser discs in their basement.

Such Eastern influences increased over the period we knew them as Uncle Chou retired and the family used the house more. A few years later, Chou added a Guanyin statue for family safety and well-being in the living room, three "Happiness, Prosperity, Longevity" statues, and an old Dehua porcelain Guangong statue representing the martial spirit symbolized trust and valor. It was like all gods and goddesses were living in his house. Uncle Chou was hedging his bets and put them there for peace of mind. He quipped, "Actually, I don't believe in any religion because no one had ever visited heaven to come back and tell me how it was."

Uncle Chou's choice of leisure also reproduced a Hong Kong way of life in Toronto. He spent his free time in Toronto giving advice on settlement to Hong Kong newcomers and working with the Cantonese TV station. As one example, he joined the organizing committee of the 1993 lunar New Year cultural event, held at a motion picture studio.[3] The entrance to the festive site was through a reconstructed Wang Tai Sin MTR station. To the immediate right was a room with a replica of the shrine to the Wong Tai Sin goddess of immigrant and refugee health (Lang and Ragvald 1993). In Hong Kong, people visited fortune tellers at the foot of the goddess's temple to forecast their fate after emigration. Many people were worshipping before it, burning incense, and praying for a better future in Canada. Chinese cultural troupes, kung fu boxing, and a lion dance were filmed for TV viewing and judged. Afterwards, everybody ate small dim sum snacks on rough benches. The mud paths that led to the site of the Lunar New Year events and the quickly thrown-up card tables attested to the recent expansion of the Hong Kong community. Uncle Chou disappeared often to talk with the many people he knew. The master of ceremonies, a television actor who had immigrated to Canada, was Chou's close friend.

Uncle Chou repeatedly stated that he liked to do what Canadian people did: "Although it's quite hard to switch from working more than ten hours a day in Hong Kong, I like this lifestyle in Toronto. It's less tense, and people are not chasing after materialistic things." During the summer he enthusiastically mowed the grass and decorated the outside of his house; in the winter he cleared the snow outside and decorated the inside. Chou and Olivia happily recounted their Canadian activities: "Mostly, we go to garage sales and flea markets."

Uncle Chou thought he was an integrationist. Hoping to participate in the wider Canadian society, he refused to depend on other Chinese just because they were country cousins. "We have little in common. We only meet during major festivals." Instead, Chou thought it was important to be open-minded and sociable and to make friends with a wide number of people. Nevertheless, his best friends were Hong Kong business contacts who spanned the seas. "We know more than a hundred families in Canada. Whenever I return, I'm busy visiting friends. No time to feel bored." He summed up, "Actually, my sense of kinship is very weak. Friends are much more important to me."

How immigrants settle is hotly contested. Immigrants' "acculturation space" refers to their involvement with the larger society combined with the degree to which they maintain their heritage culture (Berry et al. 2006). American ideology and institutions stress blending in. In this melting-pot mode, immigrants should interact with the larger society, letting their own culture go (Bloemraad 2006). Canadian multiculturalism supports separate forms of cultural expression, while encouraging immigrants to participate in mainstream institutions as well. Such an acculturation space most fits Canadian immigrants in this book, Uncle Chou included. He was still attached to his culture, did not speak English, and preferred to enjoy leisure with his Hong Kong friends. But he also sought bridges to the Canadian mainstream, was intent on investing in mainstream property, and chose to live in what he saw as an integrated setting.

Events brought about a retreat from cultural tolerance in Canada (Brown and Bean 2006). Immigrant groups encounter racism and are pressured to act like locals. Chou's efforts at integration were hampered not by his will, but by the structures around him. He lacked the social contacts to truly cross the sociocultural divide. His investments failed, his residential area filled with other affluent Asians. Finding it hard to overcome his difficulties with integration, he coped by means of his astronaut way of life.

Uncle Chou hoped to become as much part of North American society as he could, given his Chinese upbringing, and drew the line at living in ethnic enclaves. He had moved to Richmond Hill because it appeared to be a mixed ethnic upper-middle-class location. But the large numbers who immigrated shortly after he did changed this. Chou perceived that Hong Kong immigrants were becoming a critical mass, to the point of tipping the community in which he lived toward becoming a wholly Chinese enclave. The issue of integration was fought in his backyard.

By the mid-1990s, racism was coming to the fore, incited by locals' animosity to the many well-off Hong Kong arrivals. Their immigration, a product of Canadian immigration policies, coincided with a recession (Preston and Lo 2000). Heightened ethnic competition played itself out in disputes over the representation of culture in housing and commercial outlets. The Caucasian Scarborough mayor accused the Chinese community of being insular because their storefront signs sported mainly Chinese characters. The press played up the issue of what they called "monster" homes, and from Vancouver to Montreal, charged Chinese with "overbuilding" homes to the edge of their lots, tearing down old trees, and in other ways not abiding by "real Canadian" values (Anderson 1991; Li 1994).

Closer to home, a legal battle raged over the planned construction of Bayview Landmark, a Richmond Hill Hong Kong Chinese theme mall. A theme mall has a myriad of small, owner-operated shops selling diverse products, with a chaotic look novel to Toronto's suburbs. The Hong Kong developer, eager to profit from one of the few growing consumer markets in the 1990s, had already sold most of the shops of the unbuilt mall to investment immigrants. The opposition was Canadian large-business interests, promoting the dominant Canadian standard shopping complex with a large anchor store, usually a supermarket, and premises leased to international chain-store outlets. They feared that the Chinese-style mall would attract even more Chinese residents and shoppers, and that the nonwhite ethnic minority would grow and might even dominate the district, resulting in racial tipping. Numerous commissioned traffic studies projected, while others denied, the crowding that would follow commercial development of the area. The odd combination of interests pitted Chinese business developers and the Canadian Civil Liberties Union—alerted by the racial overtones—against the Canadian developers. Author Janet Salaff testified as an expert witness on the importance of respecting diversity. Eventually, Canadian businesses fought successfully to avoid another "Chinatown" mall in this affluent suburban neighborhood.

The Chous opposed such a theme mall around their corner, arguing it would make the area too Chinese. "You can see how many Chinese plazas there are already!" To bring home his point, Uncle Chou drove us around his neighborhood on a mini tour, first visiting a coffee shop for Hong Kong milk tea, where the decor had reproduced the Wanchai skyline, giving it a "mini-Hong Kong" look. We continued to a Chaozhou restaurant with murals of the tall mountains of Southeast China. A waitress immediately came to greet Uncle Chou. Apparently he often dined there. Other Chinese theme malls followed.

On the surface, the theme mall was an issue of Chinese versus Western concepts of city planning. On the popular level, it was an instance of competing views of what immigrants expect they need to do to join their new community versus what locals think. That the new immigrants of color have more money to spend than the locals they settled among fired up the situation. Not genuine refugees, the Hong Kong business and professional immigrants had little claim to local sympathies.

Such controversy reflects deeper contradictions in the institutional environment. The Canadian immigration policy draws in wealthy Chinese investors, but their lack of bridging networks forces the newcomers into their own business enclaves where they depend on their traditional ethnic resources. Without means to do business in the mainstream Canadian economy, many become astronauts. Their frequent departure and returns further exacerbate local animosity, leading to accusations of holding passports of convenience, or *flexible* citizenship (Ong 1999). Further, they are numerous enough to create an institutionally complete community. This is tolerated as long as it does not go too far and shift the balance of the local economy. Then it is held against them. At the level of identity, the newcomers, Chou and his friends, feel both Canadian and Chinese, although others may not view them so.

After Uncle Chou had been an astronaut for a decade, he finally retired and returned to Canada in 1996 for good to live the family-centered life that he long imagined.

The Next Generation: Life Continuing in Toronto

Imparting his desire for an easier life to the next generation, Uncle Chou moved the family to Canada. His goal was explicit: to give the children a good education and environment. North America held out the best promise for his children's future. But would they feel the same? Exploring the pulls of their two homes on the next generation, researchers with a transnational perspective expect that youths having continued contact with their place of origin will be more open to identifying with those back home (Levitt 2002). Continual interaction will reveal attractions of their former patria and they will hold back from commitment to the new land. In contrast, the segmented assimilation view expects those immigrant youth who maintain contact with their ethnic culture to cope better and eventually to identify with the local way of life (Zhou 1997). As parents, the Chous were committed to living like Canadians; nevertheless, the whole family engaged in transnationalism to various degrees. We found that the degree of their contact with Hong Kong made a difference as to where the younger Chous felt their allegiances.

After she led the migration foray to Toronto, Suzanne finished a college accounting course and married a computer programmer whom she met in a Hong Kong Chinese Christian organization. They settled down and both work for large Canadian firms. Although Suzanne's husband was also originally from Hong Kong, they rarely return. As parents, they live a diluted version of Chinese life. Suzanne prods their two children to learn Chinese, teasing them when they couldn't understand as our Cantonese conversation flowed around them.

As sons of a prosperous businessman, would Uncle Chou's boys become heirs to their father's legacy? Business people commonly try to pass on entrepreneurship to their children by giving them assets—whether capital and social networks—or by being role models (Aldrich et al. 1998; Delmar and Gunnarsson 2004). Uncle Chou's companies were partnerships built on his networks and he could not automatically bequeath them to his offspring. Nor did he involve his sons in the family business from an early age (unlike the Leungs whom we meet later).

Migration cut off Elic Chou from the social networks needed for such entrepreneurship. Elic was finishing secondary school when the family began its move. After taking an English course for two years he studied computer programming at Seneca College in Toronto. Upon graduation in 1990 he held a series of technical jobs in telecommunications.

Although his father's entrepreneurial goals rubbed off on him, having been brought to Canada meant that Elic could not easily craft the social networks necessary to run his father's service-oriented transportation business located in Hong Kong. He set up a computer repair service with classmates and Hong Kong friends using a unit in his father's commercial property, but the service was unprofitable. "Mother asked me to manage my father's properties, so I do, and I took an empty unit for myself. I don't pay rent. My cotenants are my schoolmates. In the beginning when they were setting up business, they asked me for advice, and I suggested they buy monitors in bulk and repair them. I let them share my unit; after all I'm not using it fully. At first, I didn't charge rent, or they'd be bankrupt already. Now they pay CAD 250, not enough even to cover utilities!"

Aiming for business success in Canada, Elic made business decisions that were not always good for the bottom line. He called it "taking the standpoint of my customers."

> I recently fixed a computer for a company introduced by another of my good customers. The woman called me in a panic, "It's the hard drive! Another company estimated the repair bill at CAD 1,000." I said, "Maybe it's not. If it's the battery I could fix it for CAD 85." In fact I thought to myself, I might drop the price for goodwill; after all, the battery only cost me CAD 45. It turned out it was the battery, but the computers were networked; the repair took four hours. But I had told them the price, and I didn't raise it. My wife was mad: "You worked there for four hours for only CAD 85!" And then it turned out that they will move to California and won't call me again! Never mind, other customers will hear about it.

So, while he analyzed it from a positive point of view, Elic could not make ends meet.

Uncle Chou did not wish this son to return to Hong Kong. "Hong Kong is too 'complicated' [competitive and with lots of speculation]. Canada is simple, I want my children to live here." Looking back, Uncle Chou reflected, "I started business at a time when anybody could make a good living in Hong Kong so long as they work hard. Times are different now. In order to be successful in Hong Kong, one not only needs to work hard—a good education is also a must! Those business opportunities are harder to come by today."

Elic, more transnational than his sister, returned often for visits. He had, however, little attachment to life in Hong Kong. Elic agreed that he was not suited to Hong Kong's work life. "I've been away eight years. I don't know my way around. Father's contacts there won't treat me as an equal. And he's in authority, what he says goes. I'd be spending my time socializing with Father. There's no point, all I'd get is a free lunch. I won't be able to learn anything. It's better to stay here. Maybe later on, I may return to Hong Kong as a computer advisor."

In 1992, Elic Chou had traveled to Hong Kong, where he attended a class reunion at the house of one of his former teachers. There he caught up with his high school classmate Ong Wong. Their friendship quickly progressed, and after a brief courtship, they were married and Ong immigrated to Canada. Olivia and Uncle Chou never approved of Elic's marriage to Ong, who was not well educated nor from a business family. Instead, they wanted Elic to marry the daughter of one of Uncle Chou's business friends. Elic justified his refusal on avoiding generational conflict: "If things didn't work out right with that woman, I'd be in trouble with my family!" As it turned out, he was right.

Ong's Hong Kong training as a nursery school teacher was not recognized in Ontario. After arriving in Toronto, she didn't have enough to do. Her husband and in-laws tried to shelter her, discouraging Ong from driving, preferring to take her where she wanted to go. She looked forward to taking ESL classes, and eventually going back to teaching. But at the beginning she didn't have any friends and was isolated in Elic's family. She began working in Elic's small office in his father's mall. She organized the files and desiring to win her mother-in-law's approval, cleaned the office toilet so well that Olivia was invited to inspect it. Luckily, the Leungs, related to Ong through her brother Po-Shek's marriage into their family, had also arrived. They provided a social outlet for her. (Our story turns to the Leungs below.)

The arrival of Elic and Ong's only child, a daughter named Olive, eased family tensions somewhat. Both mother and grandmother gained respected social roles. Ong threw herself into Olive's care. Olivia babysat and amused her granddaughter. Nevertheless, Ong was unhappy. As was customary, the two family units lived in the Chous' large suburban home, where Ong felt under scrutiny. She had also been plucked from the Hong Kong setting she knew for its Toronto replica, which had new rules and where she had fewer contacts. Surely underneath her moodiness was her inability to find work in her field and her husband's subordination to his family, who watched and guarded her moves and on whose largess Elic depended. After several years, Elic and Ong's union ended in divorce.

After their separation, Ong had custody of Olive, but since Olive had been enrolled in the Chous' well-appointed neighborhood school, the child remained in the Chous' home from Monday through Friday, returning to her mother's on weekends. Olivia bought learning books for Olive and by devoting herself to Olive's education finally found an engrossing Canadian role.

Angela Shik (Janet Salaff's student), whose mother, Dr. Shik, was Uncle Chou's early taxi customer in Hong Kong, had attended the same Toronto Cantonese church as Suzanne. Angela arranged a large reunion for the authors in Toronto in 2006 to catch up with family news. It was then that we learned the fate of youngest child, Kin-yam. The most transnational of the three children, Kin-yam took up his father's business challenge. Uneasy about the demand to matriculate in English in Toronto, he had finished school in Hong Kong. After apprenticing in his aunt's car repair firm, he moved to Toronto and began a small repair shop. He sold it at a profit and bought a share of his father's Hong Kong transportation firm. Cantonese-speaking and familiar with the mechanics of the business, he built on the family's social networks in Hong Kong. Referring to his son, Uncle Chou emphasized that he needed to develop his social relations himself: "I'm not helping him with his business because he needs to learn to run his business on his own."

Nevertheless, the low price that Kin-yam paid for the shares was a sort of fatherly bequest. In the Chou family, the only member of the second generation to continue the Hong Kong business values is the one who was never physically disconnected from his family's kin and business networks in Hong Kong. Kin-yam's integration into local social networks underlay this business success.

Entrepreneurial Kin, the Leung Family

Ong introduced us to the Leungs, also investment immigrants. Ong's brother Po-Shek had married into the Leung family, who incorporated him into their business in Hong Kong. Here is another example of a transnational entrepreneurial family who were unsuccessful in the Canadian market and ended up with the Hong Kong firm carrying the costs.

Around 1970, Father Leung had begun Five Metals, an industrial hardware store in the Tai Kok Tsui district, home to small machine-tool industries and car repair shops. Over the years, three of Father Leung's four children worked there. After Father Leung retired, his eldest son, Kit-Wai, became the main operator. Two sisters did the store's accounts part time. Five Metals underwrote the Leungs' migration project to Toronto. During a long foray, family members gradually disengaged from the store while keeping it running. The funds from Five Metals and the family members flowed into their Toronto business and living venture.

Five Metals was known throughout the old industrial district for stocking the most complete collection of machine tools and metal supplies in the area. At the time the Leungs emigrated, Five Metals was prospering, as a result of Hong Kong's integration with South China. Originally serving neighboring firms needing their equipment, as these firms moved to South China, they continued their orders. Mainland Chinese firms from Dongguan, a rapidly developing city in Guangdong Province, also placed orders with them.

We visited Five Metals with Elic Chou. Po-Shek proudly showed us around. He had been a security guard at the Vietnamese relocation centers, which were closing. His wife, Cindy, had brought her husband in to work at Five Metals when the company was short on manpower because her brothers were emigrating to Canada. Now Po-Shek was an established member of the sales team.

Five Metals had two stores and a warehouse. Like nearby shops, the cramped main storefront opened to the street. On our visit there in December 1994, we stepped over pipes and brushed by measures. Rubber tubing hung from the ceiling. A counter was on one side of the store, a metal-cutting machine on the other. Shelves lined the back room with a myriad of supplies. The second store had higher ceilings for storing large metal pipes and the adjacent warehouse kept more stock. There was no computer-based scanning equipment to update stock, since Kit-Wai knew where everything was.

Po-Shek explained this small firm's niche: "Factories will fax an order, we send back prices or photos. Luckily for us, China is making money, we are okay." He commented on the incompetence of Mainland workers at the time, a view shared by local businesses. "A Chinese company will buy four of the same items, though they can't use them all. One they use, one they lose, one is stolen. The workers grind down and break the fourth. So we sell four of them! They are so young now. They need to learn slowly. Sometimes salespeople get angry. I say, 'Don't yell at them, thank them. Because if they didn't break things, how could we sell so much!'"

Po-Shek went on about the idiosyncratic PRC managers who, unaccustomed to the Hong Kong business world, did not follow what he considered common sense:

> They like to bargain. This spanner, made in Sweden, costs us over USD 2,000. They try to get it for several hundred. I tell them, "I'm not cheating you, you tell me where to buy it cheaper and I'll buy it too." They can buy one made in China for less, 'cause labor is cheap, but the quality isn't good. Nothing they have is good. Doing business is easy, there's lots of opportunities, but there are other sides, too. I just say [to his shopkeeper neighbors], "Don't worry. Don't be frightened. But when you do business on the mainland, don't talk politics!"

Having learned much from his brother-in-law's sales skills, Po-Shek emphasized,

> Brother-in-Law Kit-Wai is really good with people. People believe in him. He goes out in the street and chats with people, then brings them back in to buy things. Not every customer knows how much to buy. Sometimes someone comes in and rather naively asks, "Do you have this, or that?" This little thing he asks for may be worth USD 30; Kit-Wai chats a bit, and then the customer might buy the whole box! The customer might end up buying hundreds, even thousands of dollars worth of things and leave. It has happened! We provide a one-stop industrial hardware store. Customers always come back, because they can find whatever they want. They say, "Five Metals has what we need, no point in going elsewhere."

Pointing to a small spearhead for drilling, Po-Shek says, "This little round thing costs HKD 600. Some things are worth so much that they are just investments. Some things no one wants, yet if they want it, here it is."

Five Metals was the Leungs' bridge to the new Toronto economy. The Leungs had systematically brought their family members from their family firm to their new family economic base in Toronto. Then they recruited Po Shek to help in their family store in Hong Kong. In Toronto, they re-created a family setting which would work together and ease the settlement transition. Their family division of labor drew on each member's strengths. To do so, they lived under one roof, and all contributed their earnings and other resources. This modernized version of the traditional Chinese household, which reproduced an old family institution in a new setting, struck us as a powerful means for new immigrants to establish themselves.

The first members of the Leung family arrived in Toronto in 1992. Intent on reuniting there, the elder Leungs bought a five-bedroom, 2,000–square-foot house in Toronto's Greek town, which borders Chinatown East, a working-class district dominated by Chinese from Vietnam. It was a newly built house whose Greek owner was selling cheaply to pay for the construction costs because of a sudden downturn in property prices. Like many other immigrants, the Leungs did not have a credit rating, and had to buy the house in cash. Mother Leung exclaimed over the nearby community, where she could "shop without knowing English."

The Leungs gave an impression of a confident family, full of plans for the future. The first immigrants were Father Leung, his wife, and their youngest son, Chi-Cheung. An unmarried chemist in his twenties, Chi-Cheung was legally a dependent and eligible to immigrate with his parents. He had just applied to bring his fiancée, who was heavily pregnant. She wanted to have her child in Canada.

In Hong Kong, eldest son Kit-Wai and his family had lived with his parents. He worked in Five Metals, and Mother Leung had looked after his three children. Naturally, Mother Leung wanted Kit-Wai's family to come to Toronto and join them. Kit-Wai was visiting when we arrived and was busy drawing up immigrant investment plans for the Ontario government to approve. Kit-Wai couldn't open a shop like Five Metals in Toronto, where large chain stores like Canadian Tire and later on, Wal-Mart, fully occupied that industrial field. He was looking for a business that could be a bridge to local Canadians.

On our visit to the Leung family's Toronto home on Lunar New Year's Eve in early 1993, we counted eleven people living in the family home. Older Brother Kit-Wai and his family had two rooms on the second floor.

The younger son lived with his wife and infant in a basement room where they had just installed their matching bedroom furniture from Hong Kong. He was recredentialing, earning another chemistry degree at Ryerson Polytechnic (although the course reading repeated what he already knew) and he hoped to teach secondary school. Joy, an unmarried daughter and former accountant for Five Metals, was immigrating and had just arrived.

The sisters-in-law now worked in a factory making mobile phones and beepers, where almost all the other workers were new Chinese immigrants. They were happy they could speak Chinese there. They proudly learned to drive and came to work together. Mother Leung cared for the newborn, in addition to the three school-aged children.

The Leungs' dynamic force also drew in others. People only distantly related became part of their family network. Visitors enlarged the festive gathering as the Leung clan began to rebuild their social network with whoever was at hand. Pang, an engineer and distant cousin, his wife, her mother, and two children arrived, bringing extra dishes of food, which the two dowager mothers set about serving. Pang recalled, "I've known the Leung family for so long! As a kid, I even appeared in their photos so that they could get a larger Resettlement Estate flat!" Elic sketched Pang's kinship relation to the Leungs on a napkin. Father Leung showed a video of his trip home to his Chinese village, an hour from Shantou. Mother Leung beamed, surrounded by her new enlarged household.

In summer 1994, Janet Salaff visited the family and enjoyed a backyard barbecue featuring small hot dogs and chicken wings, a great treat for the children. They had come back from fishing and gleefully described the large salmon they had seen struggling against the currents in the Humber River the previous fall. It was said that the Chinese, who arrived in groups and cooperated to snare their active catch, were better at this sport than were single Canadian fishermen. The children were so keen on such Canadian activities that when they visited Hong Kong at New Year's they broke out in tears in the airport, distressed that they might be returning for good.

We learned that Older Brother Kit-Wai's immigrant investment plans had been approved by the Ontario government. "I'm going into the bakery business. Why? It's because people in Canada always have to eat. Even Canadians will eat our bread. They have coffee in the morning and a piece of bread, like the kind we eat in Hong Kong." He had brought in a distant relative as a partner, a chef in charge of pastry in a West Chinatown restaurant. "I'm learning to cook from him. I'm an apprentice. It's quicker than going to school." Kit-Wai voiced the family's long-term plans: "After it's profitable, the shop'll give work to my wife and sister-in-law. Then, we'll shut down the shop in Hong Kong. We immigrants must stick together, especially in the beginning."

Back in Hong Kong, to maintain local confidence, Five Metals kept up the appearance of business as usual. We revisited the Hong Kong family branch in December 1994. Only Cindy remained in Hong Kong with her husband. Ong's brother Po-Shek was now the main family worker at Five Metals. He explained, "Older Brother-In-Law Kit-Wai stays in Canada most of the time. He has to return to Hong Kong for the coming Lunar New Year. Otherwise people will believe we're quitting the business to emigrate. We aren't. In Hong Kong you must depend on trust to do business. We depend on people, to get things from them. If people think you are leaving, they will not give you good credit. They will hold the reins more tightly. We're not leaving!" he reassured us loudly, as if to dispel the neighborhood doubts.

The turn of events proved otherwise. On a 2005 return visit, we learned that in the past few years Five Metals was no longer doing well. PRC joint ventures and Mainland firms could now make their own quality metal parts themselves. They did not need to buy from Hong Kong. Their customer base having narrowed, the Leungs had closed the warehouse and sold the remaining Five Metals store to a distant cousin in 1999. The entire family completed the migration journey.

The Leungs' family firm in Hong Kong was the basis of their family emigrant economy. It had given all the members work in Hong Kong and then transformed its function as it became part of their border-spanning economic practices (Landolt 2001). In this role, it was not a transnational firm. The family's businesses in Hong Kong were not related to those in Toronto, which eventually failed. However, the Hong Kong firm provided capital, the basis of the family's social organization, and a moral purpose. Five Metals served as a coherent center—the spirit of the family—in both Hong Kong and Toronto, while its profits launched the family immigration project. Five Metals supported their efforts to keep the family together during the settlement period in many ways.

This transition took seven years, from the arrival of the first family members in Toronto in 1992 to the sale of Five Metals in 1999. It featured their efforts to locate as ordinary people, living in an ethnic enclave—but not doing business there—and using the range of services offered new immigrants. They collaborated with the Ontario government investment counselors, used the school system to recertify, and found small-business opportunities to reestablish themselves. They carried forward to Toronto their family division of labor that had been developed over the years in Five Metals. All family members lived under one roof, contributing their earnings and other resources. They also drew in distant kin for ceremonial gatherings and work projects. The dynamic household was a magnet.

Summary: Entrepreneurs' Settlement Problems

Uncle Chou and the Leungs are immigrant entrepreneurs who succeeded in business in Hong Kong but not in Canada. Their stories illustrate what happens when institutional frameworks do not mesh. Their inability to build crucial business-related networks in the new locale is their undoing.

In Hong Kong, Uncle Chou was integrated into larger networks on which he founded his profitable transportation firm. Likewise, the Leung family's hardware firm was networked into the small-business communities of Hong Kong and China. When the Chou and Leung families confidently tried to establish companies in Toronto (as demanded by Canadian immigration policies), without similar connections they failed. They aimed to do business in the North American mainstream and wanted locals to see them as legitimate. They needed sources of information, ideas about what works and what fails. They needed access to local supply chains and markets. They needed links to local trade and professional associations and networks (Greve and Salaff 2003; Kim and Aldrich 2005). As recent arrivals, the Chous and Leungs were not connected to such circles. Although they desired to be part of Canadian life, in both cases, their loss-making ventures forced them into astronaut activity to support their families.

The importance of keeping the family economy going led to years of transnational moves as they used their Hong Kong capital to motor their families' settlement. For the Leungs, the family business provided the concrete arena, a place where the family economic division of labor was organized socially; they transferred their family-based economic division of labor to Toronto. For both families, closing their Hong Kong businesses completed their migration projects.

The next generation reestablished their households as full members of the Hong Kong Chinese-Canadian communities, going to school, marrying members of their ethnic group, attending the community church, and raising their children to be part of merged cultural worlds. They also belonged to the native Canadian scene as well. Unable to reestablish a business in Canada, two of Chou's children entered the local Canadian firms their parents might have wished to link up with. These entrepreneurs and their families adapted to the migration process and took on new identities. After ten years of astronaut transnational migration, they settled into the kind of quiet, family-centered life in Canada that they had longed for.

CHAPTER FIVE

FRANCIS KWONG
The Professional's Dilemma

"No one wants to leave Hong Kong, but . . ."
—Francis Kwong

Institutional forces linking global structures, professional roles, and identities drove Francis Kwong's emigration plans. The field of property development is a cornerstone of the contemporary Hong Kong economy and Francis had been professionally trained to manage large estates, adhering to an outlook of standards and procedures that rewarded performance. His upbringing and career committed him ideologically to British values and way of life. Expecting progress toward democracy, he then perceived that this Anglicized world would collapse around him. His colleagues and professional kin had left, pulling him into their aura of shared views. Adding to the pressure to emigrate was his desire to protect his family, wife Siu-Foon and their only child Ka-Tit. Francis wanted Ka-Tit to grow up in an environment where he could speak his mind—something Francis did not believe would be possible under Chinese rule. With his own professional identity at stake and concerned for his family's future, Francis started his family on a migration journey that would span almost a decade.

Entering Canada in 1995, Francis Kwong was treated as an outsider and with no recognition of his professional experiences. Unable to reestablish his career, Francis lost scaffolding for his identity and sacrificed an income for his family as well. This created the professional's dilemma: remaining in the new country where his professional accomplishments are unrecognized threatens his identity, the protection of which, ironically, had led to his exit. Returning to Hong Kong as an astronaut would distort his family's life, undermining the goal of protecting them. To resolve the dilemma, Francis ultimately settled for a lower-status job in Canada.

Early Days in Hong Kong: An Anglicized Life

Francis's and Siu-Foon's early days in Hong Kong bred them for a British-identified life. Born into comfortable Hong Kong families, they were schooled in English-speaking, elite secondary schools—a minority option. These institutions prepared privileged students for jobs in the civil service, British trading firms, and professions such as law and medicine. In 1967, twenty-year-old Francis began his career in the civil service. His older brother also worked in the civil service and his sister was in property management—like Francis would soon be.

By this time, the property development industry was key to riches in Hong Kong. As Hong Kong's economy boomed, mountains were leveled and the landscape filled with private luxury high-rises, hotels, and government housing blocks—the construction of which engineer Luk (chapter 3) oversaw. Entrepreneurs invested in hotels and as tourism grew, so too did their wealth. As China liberalized its markets, these rich Hong Kong property investors joined Mainland entrepreneurs and moved into China's property market. Francis Kwong's career emerged from these activities.

Initially, Siu-Foon was also professionally ambitious, hoping to become a doctor or a lawyer, as did many in her elite secondary school. However, failing to earn one of the few university places available at the time, she taught kindergarten for two years, then trained to become a midwife. She met Francis, one year her senior, during a stint of community volunteer work in Hong Kong and they married several years later. Their son Ka-Tit was born in 1973.

Both enthusiastically recalled how much they enjoyed that carefree period of their lives. They were good at talking with each other, and saw the other as their main confidant. They were comfortable holding hands in others' presence, not often seen among Chinese of their generation. Yet beginning with Siu-Foon's pregnancy, life became more constrained.

In the year that Siu-Foon became pregnant, Francis took on more challenging government service work, which meant he could not help her much. After Ka-Tit's birth, Siu-Foon's life became centered on her small family and her deteriorating health. Beginning late in her pregnancy and worsening with her newborn, Siu-Foon suffered from symptoms of depression. In pain after an unexpected Cesarean section, she was unable to take care of her baby and was troubled by her inability to soothe his cries. The family had moved in with Francis's mother so that Siu-Foon could get the help she needed, but rather than easing her isolation, things took a turn for the worse. The unsympathetic views of her mother-in-law, who did not believe Siu-Foon was doing everything she could to care for her new baby, added to Siu-Foon's woes.

Siu-Foon's mother tentatively tried to step into the helper role. Unfortunately, Siu-Foon had never been close to her own mother. Ashamed that her mother-in-law—by rights the person in authority—was not helping her enough, Siu-Foon rebuffed her own mother's offerings of nourishing food and support. This painful period put its stamp on their family in unfortunate ways: Siu-Foon's health remained poor, and her ties with her mother and mother-in-law were forever strained. For Francis, these outcomes generated a desire to create a better life for his wife, contributing to his motivation to emigrate.

Building A Modern Career: 1979–88

Francis advanced steadily in his career, adding to his education and training in his chosen field. Over the years, he obtained a master's degree and completed diploma courses in Hong Kong and London, credentials highly valued under British rule.

As he advanced, his family was drawn into the British way of life as well. In 1979, Francis took up his first demanding private-sector job managing a housing estate. As a perk, the Kwongs were given a luxurious apartment within the expatriate compound in entirely non-Chinese surroundings. Such integrated family and work roles were part of his job, and allowed Francis to become fluent in English. "No Chinese spoken there at all," he recalled. Siu-Foon, however, did not work after Ka-Tit's birth, and felt this socially isolated living environment as an added strain.

Francis became a leader in his profession, helping inaugurate a local association of property market professionals. As a member of governing and auditing boards, he aimed to raise professional standards in Hong Kong and China. He traveled to Britain and participated in conferences. In Francis's view, he deserved the high income, status, and privileges that he had achieved. He was, after all, highly qualified, as distinct from untrained amateurs.

Francis took his professional identity as his personal goals. The quality of his work, on-the-job obligations to colleagues, career structures, and a range of other collaborations in which he participated strengthened his sense of purpose. Francis admired the Hong Kong way of life. He respected Britain's orderly laws that underlay his professional career. From the beginning, their early childhood education and background had taught Francis and his two siblings to appreciate a British perspective. His British education gave him greater appreciation of freedom and the British way of life, and his management job in the modern housing sector placed him in a global setting where he became committed to what he thought of as an international way of management. In his opinion, Britain had brought predictable, legal methods of handling commerce and property to Hong Kong (Faure 2008). These everyday arrangements made sense.

The conclusion of talks about retrocession in 1984 planted the first seeds of doubt about his future in Hong Kong. Francis worried that Britain's reliable economic organizations would not be maintained through retrocession, but would become watered down or overlaid by the unpredictable, even arbitrary methods known in China. Worse, he worried that the Chinese government would not appreciate his qualifications or his professional status. Ultimately Francis came to view the retrocession agreement as a threat to both his profession and his identity.

Deciding to Emigrate: 1985–94

As Hong Kong merged with the People's Republic of China (PRC), the world of property development started to change. The profession now included the PRC in their social fields, and industry leaders felt responsible for bringing their Mainland colleagues up to standard (Mathews et al. 2008). Representing his employer and the professional associations, Francis traveled to the Mainland and into the classroom. He lectured in Hong Kong and China, organized study tours, and taught estate management in universities. Just as he feared, during these visits, Francis encountered illogical bureaucratic decrees. "I once went to China for a lecture. I brought books and pamphlets on housing to distribute these scarce materials to my audience. But they were confiscated at the border! Even if you wish to help China modernize, it is hard. It will take forty years for China to allow us to help them!"

This firsthand experience showed Francis the face of a closed society, raising concerns about how China's entrance into Hong Kong would affect the flow of information on which professional development depends. Francis's sister, who traveled to China on behalf of her firm, bemoaned that the Hong Kong's investments there were beset by corruption. All around were portents that Chinese rule would interfere with Francis's profession and the life that he and his family enjoyed.

Francis had spent his lifetime in self-improvement and hoped to pass on his knowledge, saying, "I have Chinese blood. I wish to help China modernize." However, the confiscation of his books showed that the Mainland government paid education little attention. "We want to help, but several hundreds of us to educate a billion is like a drop of water in the ocean!" Francis noted that "the future of Hong Kong and China is just like mixing lemon tea and water. Hong Kong will be worse because she shares her benefits with China. China will be better because she gets Hong Kong's benefits."

Francis believed that his education and qualifications gave him the right, even the obligation, to express his opinions. But his professional activities and especially his leadership in the housing field were already bringing him into political conflict with Mainland Chinese representatives in Hong Kong as he searched in vain for democratic practices. As a spokesperson for his profession, he took part in committees that met to smooth the transition. During the drafting of the Basic Law between 1988 and 1989, Mainland representatives in Hong Kong courted professional associations to get them on board. The PRC representative addressed the members of Francis's professional association about their opinions on the Basic Law. Francis raised a question about the qualifications of a person who could be the first chief executive of Hong Kong SAR, but he was brushed aside. This revealed that the Chinese government did not respect their opinions; his confidence in the new order fell to its lowest point.

His concern that freedom of speech would become limited under Chinese rule extended to his son Ka-Tit, now a teenager. Whether or not Francis was projecting his own fears on Ka-Tit, not an outspoken lad, as a father he was building his son's moral environment. Francis wanted to do his best to provide an alternative world where his son could express his ideas. Also, since performing well in the competitive Hong Kong school system was not Ka-Tit's strong point, Francis hoped to give him a more flexible educational environment. A Hong Kong school kid who did poorly was stigmatized (Lin 2000). Francis began to think seriously about emigration. His commitment to emigrate increased further in the early 1990s as the conflict between the Chinese and British governments intensified over Beijing's mistrust of the British introduction of a somewhat widened democratization in the 1991 and 1995 elections. This turned the transition into a tug-of-war (Chan 2003).

We asked Francis whether the political deadlock affected his trust in the Chinese government. He replied, "It only further confirmed to me that the 'one country, two systems' proposal was insincere!" Standing on the side of the British leadership, he was astounded at the rhetoric, which he thought unprofessional. "Did you know that the Chinese officials denounced Patten as 'sinner of a millennium'!"

Francis was exasperated by the increased opportunism in Hong Kong politics. He noted that the Chinese and Hong Kong deadlock over forming the new SAR government compelled civil servants to choose sides. Civil servants sided with the incoming power holders, and Hong Kong's last British governor, Chris Patten, lost support. Francis believed that because of their interest in their pocketbooks, local Hong Kong leaders would not risk taking significant action against the Chinese government. In 1993, he said, "All Governor Patten's advisors quit the Executive Council, and after waiting for a few months, are now on China's side—even those who were pro-government before. Power corrupts! How can you be pro-government and then change? People don't favor Patten now. The Hang Seng index is up."[1]

Even closer to home, with the Mainland housing market promising immense profits, Francis watched as his Hong Kong Chinese employer bypassed channels to invest in China. He foresaw that it would get worse: "We have a double standard. If you build in Hong Kong, it's simple. You can get gas, water, light. In China, it's hard. You have to visit the units—gas, water, light—one by one. You have to go to the higher-ups, and only then can you get service. When we go there, we pay, give people gifts. There's lots of corruption. It'll come to Hong Kong."

Identified with the Western model, Francis felt marginalized as the British gradually moved off stage. He complained that those around him lacked ability and scruples, and anticipated that his new master's degree wouldn't get him promoted in his Chinese firm. "Only Western companies emphasize training. In a Chinese system, training is nothing. They have no work system." Without hope of passing on his experience, finding his profession co-opted by the advantages of investing in China, and concerned for his family's future, Francis reluctantly decided that emigration was his best choice. Yet he hesitated to leave Hong Kong.

Lukewarm Emigrants

The term "reluctant emigrant" fits Francis Kwong well (Skeldon 1994). The term refers to an avoidance strategy by Hong Kong professionals who applied in droves for papers to leave a situation expected to turn bad. They hedged their bets, not quitting their jobs or selling their apartments. For Francis, applying for passports did not mean that the family move was imminent; instead, it was "like buying an insurance policy. When you have bought the insurance policy, you put it aside. You renew it when it's ready to expire. When you need it, you can use it." People with the education and funds to make them acceptable to foreign governments seized the opportunity to apply for multiple sets of papers. The Kwongs weighed their options.

Francis's employer encouraged the managerial staff to secure the Right of Abode in Singapore, because the brain drain associated with emigration was affecting the company's internal operations. The Right of Abode in Singapore or England allowed the holder to keep this status for several years without exercising it; that is, without actually having to move there to establish their residency. For Singapore, they only needed a job offer, which Francis's transnational company arranged through their Singapore contacts. Many Hong Kong companies during the time used this tactic, believing that if employees who were anxious about the future could get the precious Right of Abode documents, they would remain longer on the job in Hong Kong. Consequently, Francis first got Singapore papers. He also successfully applied to England, the United States, and Canada, countries that courted skilled immigrants.

Yet Francis postponed the hard decision, saying, "I will leave whenever the situation gets worse." His inaction stemmed from his inability to give up his Hong Kong career and from concern over his prospects abroad. In 1992, Francis acknowledged his likely problems in getting a good job abroad: "I am now forty-five years old. By 1997, I'd be an old man." But he also knew colleagues who were working in Canada, giving him hope. "My friends there in housing got jobs. I have a friend in Vancouver, even older than me, with a job in estate management. I have a friend in Toronto in the same field as well. Of course you have to take a cut in wages, but still you survive." His career was only part of the story, though, and contributing to his ambivalence, neither Siu-Foon nor Ka-Tit wished to emigrate.

Siu-Foon and Ka-Tit: Unwilling Emigrants

The daily round of activities for Siu-Foon and Ka-Tit was circumscribed to more narrow spheres. Siu-Foon did not have an active social life. She was not part of wider family networks. She concerned herself with cleaning their apartment, which she decorated in purple and lavender colors, and took charge of homemaking tasks. She shopped daily for nourishing food, traveling some distance, avoiding costly shops in their housing complex. Apart from maintaining the home, she had a penchant for playing the stock market, an exciting hobby that she could engage in by herself or with friends. Francis acquiesced to Siu-Foon's passion and gave her some spending money, although he did not actively endorse gambling. When she was low on funds, as a kind of window-shopping experience she thrilled in watching the Hang Seng index's rise and fall against her mental purchases. Since she thought that these special gambling activities were best conducted in Hong Kong, she leaned toward staying there, remaining untroubled by Hong Kong's future and fearing the disruption that emigration would bring to her life.

For his part, Ka-Tit was placed in the international secondary school in Hong Kong, which prepares youth to study abroad. However, he could not keep up at the level his white-collar career his parents wished for him, and fellow students bullied him because he didn't fit their "smart guy" image. He was happier when in diploma courses, first studying food and beverages in hotel management. Unfortunately, during the practical placement, he could not survive the hotel politics. He also took courses in criminology and social work, and at Francis's urgings, property management.

Ka-Tit resisted Francis's urgings to study abroad. He wished to take on the role of a protector by joining the security services as a police officer or a firefighter—an interest that may have stemmed from his own experiences of being bullied. He followed news reports of real-life rescues, watched videos of heroes fighting villains, and recounted the problems caused by serious accidents on Hong Kong roads. He wanted to maintain law and order, and shoot "bad guys."

When we met him in 1992, Ka-Tit's room in the Kwongs' modern Hong Kong apartment was filled with the latest genre of powerful toy guns. With a keen interest in marksmanship, Ka-Tit also hoped to join a gun club. Francis mounted a realistic cardboard human figure and Ka-Tit practiced shooting rubber-tipped bullets at villains from his plastic pistol. His shelf contained books on Chinese dynastic history, rebels, and conquerors. A well-read copy of *Shui Hu Chuan*,[2] the Sung Dynasty epic tale of a band of Robin Hood-like bandit patriots protecting the emperor against a despotic prime minister, jostled with videos about heroes and fighting, the powerful triad societies, and branches of armed Hong Kong Chinese underground gangs. He studied them to learn how to beat them. His fantasies sheltered him from reality, further confining his world.

In the end, Ka-Tit came closer to his ideal in Hong Kong's booming security industry where positions as guards in malls and gated apartment houses of the affluent middle class were readily available. It was a world in which he felt comfortable; one that he, too, was reluctant to give up through migration.

The lack of enthusiasm from his immediate family delayed him, but as retrocession grew near, Francis determined to go. He was not leaving for a better material life. Migration meant protecting Francis's integrity as a cosmopolitan and trained professional, devoted to achieving competence in his work and searching for freedom of expression. He aimed to preserve his family's right to be themselves and not have to follow illegitimate orders. Even so, predicting his family's future life in a foreign country, Francis admitted, "the house will be bigger, the air fresher, the environment prettier.

That's all. No one wants to leave Hong Kong, but the environment forces us to. Emigration is a last resort. There are too many uncertainties in Hong Kong's future."

Emigration: But Where?

For the Kwongs, the decision as to where to immigrate proved more complicated than getting their papers. With family in the United States and Canada, firsthand experiences as tourists to numerous destinations, and papers in hand, one might have thought there were many potential destinations. But few fit all their criteria. Between the two of them, Francis and Siu-Foon had eleven fairly prosperous siblings, most of whom had papers to live abroad. Nonetheless, when deciding where to go, they did not follow a working class-style migration chain by relying on kin for concrete support (Salaff et al. 1999). Like most affluent families in our study, Francis felt that it was wiser not to be too dependent on immigrant kin. He explained, "My brother and sister have their own family. They can handle their business in their own ways. The issue of emigration is just like that of religion—we talk little about it. After the decision has been made, we will inform each other, but we scarcely discuss it beforehand."

Not surprisingly, Britain appealed to Francis, since he admired Britain's legal system, its degree of liberty, and living environment. He could also get help in settling from friends. "Our relationships are very good. A surveyor I know can help me find a place to live, but I don't anticipate their help in getting work. They wouldn't let me compete with their rice bowl!" He thought that he might gain employment on his own merits. But the more people he spoke to, the less optimistic he became. He complained that few antidiscrimination policies were enforced, saying, "It's difficult for Chinese people to get a job there. Even if they get one, it is usually as laborers in restaurants and the wages will be very low. They won't choose me for a high position, and will reject me for lower ones saying I'm too old." Realizing that the employment situation for Chinese was not favorable, he excluded Britain.

Siu-Foon felt comfortable going to Singapore, a Chinese society, but Francis worried that it would not provide him with enough professional opportunities either. Further, with his liberal perspective, Singapore would not be a step forward. "Singapore is too small and likes to compete with Hong Kong. Employers will offer a lower position to Hong Kong people than they deserve, to show that Singaporeans are superior. Besides, there are too many constraints in Singaporean life, which is too parental, such as the prohibition against chewing gum. Even if Singapore can achieve that aim, it is not a real success. Its people follow the rules but they do not really obey them in their hearts."

Siu-Foon's sister in the United States immigrated there years before, but despite this family link, lack of colleagues and the prospect of unemployment for Francis ruled it out. By contrast, he expected more from Canada, and even though he downplayed the connections, kin surely planted the idea of migrating to Canada in his mind, where seven relatives had or were in the process of immigrating. These included Siu-Foon's mother, two sisters, and a brother, all of whom landed in the 1980s. Francis's brother, sister, and their families had gone to Canada around 1988. His younger brother Kong-Jin was contemplating the move. Francis simply expected kin to ease the move for his wife, who liked to be near her sister. So they decided to go to Canada.

Settlement Woes: 1994–99

Francis resigned from his Hong Kong job at the peak of his management career. It had to be like this—if he waited until he retired, he wouldn't qualify as a skilled worker. The economic balance between the two cities (Hong Kong and Toronto) was in the Hong Kongers' favor. Francis put his retirement fund and the substantial sums earned from selling their modern apartment into a less costly townhouse in Toronto. They also earned enough to buy a modest flat in Mei Foo, Hong Kong's first middle-class housing development (Rosen 1976). Because the flat was fairly run down, they got it at a savings. Lacking the elegance of their previous family home, it looked temporary in appearance.

Their new Mei Foo abode symbolized the Kwongs' reluctance to leave. Francis boxed his papers and books and left them in the corner of a room, knowing from those around him that he might return. He was loath to let go his collection of professional materials completely. In their absence, they let a nephew live there—he needed the Mei Foo address to be eligible for a good neighborhood school. This was a graphic example of the underlying ambivalence of Hong Kong migrants: even as they were boarding the plane, they were preparing a place to return to. They were unable to make a total break with their Hong Kong base.

Soon after landing in Canada in 1995, the Kwongs moved into their compact three-bedroom townhouse in multicultural Scarborough, North Toronto. Cantonese-speaking facilities, Chinese churches, and Chinese restaurants were nearby. Large grocery stores sold the particular Asian products they needed, from lap cheung sausages to rice cookers. In mall promenades, bins of dried fungi competed for space with a Shanghainese vendor displaying samples of flooring made from special woods he imported from China.

This sort of community has been referred to as an "institutionally complete" environment for immigrants, since it contains professional and social services and places for leisure and worship in the language of the dominant immigrant group, in this case the Cantonese (Breton 1964). The inhabitants need not travel far for work, shopping, and other daily needs. However, institutionally complete communities are especially suited to working-class immigrants, and while the types of occupations are diverse, aspiring professionals often find such an ethnic environment less attractive, since most jobs there serve the immigrant community (Li 2001). In particular, there were none for people with Francis's professional background. He knew he couldn't live long on his savings; he still had to work.

As for Siu-Foon and Ka-Tit, such familiar surroundings were perfect, since neither felt at home mixing with non-Cantonese speakers. Though initially concerned about the impact of migration on her health, Siu-Foon's sisters had reassured her that she could live her daily life without change or strain. What they said proved to be true, at least partly.

Francis's older brother and sister-in-law landed in Toronto, and despite Francis's dim view of kin ties, shared the townhouse Francis bought. Eventually, neither family occupied the townhouse full-time anyway, since both became astronauts. But living together, even off and on, was not congenial. Francis was dissatisfied, feeling that his brother and sister-in-law were not contributing their share. Siu-Foon complained that when Francis was away, they criticized her and Ka-Tit's behavior, remarking that, "I just always stay at home, watch TV, and sleep. When I go to play mahjong, or shop for food I ask them to drive me, since I don't drive. That gives them more chances to comment."

At age twenty-two, Ka-Tit met with his own difficulties in adapting to Canadian life. Whereas in Hong Kong he found a niche independent of his parents, in Canada both Francis and Siu-Foon ran the risk of stifling Ka-Tit as he tried to find a place for himself in his new home. Worried that his son's poor education would limit his future, Francis was reluctant to let Ka-Tit go his own way and enrolled him in courses at a nearby community college. Francis was torn between a view that he should let his son choose his own activities and his concern that his son was not practiced enough to choose wisely.

Siu-Foon also urged Ka-Tit to persist at his studies, seizing every opportunity (such as when the authors visited) to urge Ka-Tit to speak English. She felt that if he could be exposed to more subjects and possibilities, he might discover something that really fit him. At the same time she feared that he could not take care of himself and would follow whatever was before him; Siu-Foon was uneasy if he was out of her sight. In her protectiveness, she anticipated all his needs to the point where her sister urged her to let her son become more independent. "If I ask Ka-Tit does he want an orange, and he says no, I drop the subject. If it's his mother, she'll ask him again, tell him about vitamin C, and that he has to eat it, peels it for him, urges upon him one section, and then another!" In this example, however, Siu-Foon could not be distinguished from most Chinese mothers, who incorporated their children's needs into their own until they could not tell them apart (Lam 2007; Ho et al. 2006).

Siu-Foon acknowledged that she probably contributed to Ka-Tit's over-dependence by making him a central concern of her life and planning everything for him. She felt guilty that she hadn't given him a chance to take initiative and do things himself. As things were, she expected that she and Francis would have to take care of him for life.

Ka-Tit seemed resigned to this parental oversight. With conflicting messages about independence coming from his parents, he sought the comfort of a familiar environment in Toronto's Cantonese-Canadian communities. He joined a neighborhood bible study group; Francis hired a church member to fetch Ka-Tit and bring him home when he was away. Ka-Tit also watched the Chinese news channel that beamed news from Hong Kong, and used a cheap calling card to place bets on Hong Kong horse races by long-distance. Ka-Tit, whose name Francis had invoked in justifying emigration, found it hard to live a Canadian life. He was happier back in Hong Kong in the setting he understood back.

Francis sought a job in his field but was frustrated that this Western city, with its narrow institutional scope, did not recognize his training and experience (Kee and Skeldon 1994; Mak 2006; Salaff and Greve 2006). Though Francis was never completely optimistic, reality seemed much worse than anticipated. Malls in Toronto do not resemble the gigantic integrated living and office complexes—a total environment—in Hong Kong and China (Lui 2001). Francis could not adjust to the drop from being in charge of a Hong Kong super mall to being a superintendent in an apartment house—more a working-class handyman's job than a professional position. "In Canada condos are not so complex; it's hard to find an equivalent job." Nor was his master's degree recognized. There were interviews, but no offers. Employers cited his lack of Canadian experience, to which he protested, "I've no Canadian experience but I can do the job. There're lots of local regulations, and I know them. But they don't believe it. It's always, 'You need Canadian experience,' so the problem is getting the first job." Francis's age was also a factor. "Why should they hire someone like me who costs 1.5 times as much as young people? They want to hire cheaply, and don't think they need experienced people."

Realizing that he would not land a job that suited him, he got papers that enabled him to return to Hong Kong for one year without giving up his Canadian status. Francis made the return journey to Hong Kong in 1995 and immediately was sent to work on the Mainland with its expanding market in construction. Over the next five years, Francis built on his previous reputation and was in great demand as Hong Kong firms invested in China's property market. In stark contrast to his degrading experience in Canada, he even had the luxury of turning down questionable work. Nevertheless, serving the Mainland Chinese companies and property market was problematic. Francis sensed he was even more directly working with firms that engaged in the fraudulent practices that had worried him in the past. And psychologically he was farther from his family than before.

But on the Hong Kong front, things had changed for this transnational migrant. Years as an astronaut lost him his local networks, there was a recession in building, and he could no longer land Hong Kong jobs. At the same time, job offers in China were declining as well because Mainland professionals were able to do the work themselves. Frances explained, "I anticipated that they would soon no longer need consultants to manage buildings in China and I was right. They have their own people now who are capable and less costly." He also said, "People don't call me for work in Hong Kong. I am advised by another friend that I stand little chance of getting a property management job in Hong Kong now that I have been away for too long. He said that most employers will think that I do not have an intimate knowledge of the property management industry, which is not true of course. I better make a go of it in Toronto."

Over the five years of her husband's astronaut period, Siu-Foon traveled to Hong Kong to share time with Francis when he was there, always returning to Toronto to build her residency period. But China was foreign turf to her. Ka-Tit often traveled with Siu-Foon as well, logging over a half dozen cross-Pacific trips in the period. The whole family had become frequent flyers.

Having bounced back and forth for a period, Ka-Tit eventually decided to remain in Hong Kong. He returned to his former niche as a security guard, watching on a TV monitor as people came and went. Although the pay was not high, living rent free in the family's apartment enabled the move (Salaff et al. 2008). His aunt was on the lookout for Ka-Tit's needs while Francis was working in China. There was easy public transportation and small cafes and fast-food outlets where he could grab a bite to eat. In this protective society he could live more independently. But his parents saw things differently. Ka-Tit's lack of career prospects and the rough culture of the security business concerned them.

Ultimately, Francis's moves had broken his career chain. The institutional regulative environment and nonrecognition of credentials created problems finding jobs in Canada. This was compounded by his lack of bridging social fields in Toronto; his access to job circles in Hong Kong had been disrupted as well. All in all, by 2000, Francis decided to try to make things work in Toronto. He returned to Toronto for work experience and to qualify for citizenship.

Accepting Migration: 2000–2006

Back in Toronto in 2000, Francis renewed his job search, still vexed by the Canadian profession's nonrecognition of his experience. Studying had long been Francis's solution to career advancement—yet, as a proud professional, he refused to redo an undergraduate diploma in the field where he already had a master's degree. He did not take a downgraded practical degree like many skilled immigrants did in response to the noncertification of their professional credentials from their home country institutions (Salaff and Greve 2006). Miffed at the denial of acknowledgment of his degree, he protested that he would not continue in property management. "It's too late to start, and things aren't organized the same. They want a superintendent, not an estate manager."

He tried to change his field instead. But he seemed to lack focus, taking courses whose main attraction was their low cost and their apparent relevance to the needs of other family members. He studied Web design and related computer courses in community college, thinking he could open a business repairing personal computers and that his son could work with him. He took a driving instructor class, and considered opening a driving school or a garage, hoping to involve King-jin, his mechanic brother.

As it turned out, King-jin, with his hands-on skills, had less trouble recouping his preimmigration job level. Practical skills are easily recognized and not controlled by professional bodies. Further, King-jin met a need in the Cantonese immigrant community that had little experience of second-hand car ownership. Though his earlier credentials in car repair were not recognized, he had quickly recertified and found work in a car dealership. Francis stated ironically, "He doesn't earn all that much but he earns more than me! He's well known in the Cantonese community. Newspaper and

radio programs interview him on how people like us should go about buying vehicles. We don't buy them in Hong Kong."

Francis did know people in Toronto—his elite secondary-school classmates regularly held reunions. Former colleagues, some of whom managed
modest apartment complexes or sold real estate or insurance policies, com-
miserated. But none were able to help him find work. Thus, his social fields
did not reach into the realms he needed for professional or managerial-level
positions in property development.

Volunteer work is a common path for new immigrants to get Canadian
work experience and find contacts in their fields (Carrasco et al. 1999).
Under a government program (which also gave him training), Francis offered service to senior citizens in two community centers, helping them use
computers to do their taxes. Later, as a citizen, he joined the New Democratic
Party to help with election campaigning. In this way, Francis furthered his
dream of democratic participation. He worked so hard that they invited
him to become office manager, but the pay was too low to live on. None of
these stints were in fields remotely close to his.

The family had survived on their savings, but the downturn in the stock
market after "9/11" wreaked havoc with his mutual funds, and Francis worried about supporting his family. After two years without a job, in 2002, he
finally settled for his first overseas paid position in Toronto's Chinese enclave.
Francis managed apartments and condominiums for a firm owned by a
wealthy Hong Kong-originating family. The company owned four hundred
apartments in Toronto and shopping malls in Calgary and Vancouver. It did
not rent solely to Chinese, but was nonetheless an enclave job by virtue of
its Chinese family ownership, management practices, and hiring preferences
(Greve and Salaff 2005). "I saw an ad in the Chinese language press every
day for two weeks, something about property development. Why not give it
a try? They don't develop; they rent out property to client firms. First thing
they said to me was, 'We don't give benefits; we are a Chinese company!'
They are very tight. They want me to go to meetings in Calgary on Friday
afternoons and stay until Wednesday without overtime pay so I can take a
cheaper weekend flight!"

As a jack-of-all-trades in this position, Francis worked on leases and
other management issues including searching records and going to small
claims court to garnish clients who had not paid rent. At first, Francis offered suggestions from his experience on how to reduce customer turnover
and manage efficiently. "The company is poorly managed. The boss's two
children come in and don't work much. My supervisor sits in his office all

day and reads e-mail. Even though he is around the corner from me, he won't drop by to talk. Yet he's unable to solve the simplest problems." The company could benefit from his experience, but he got no hearing.

> They waste too much time and money. For one example, I try to convince them not to have conference calls to Calgary when they could use e-mail instead. Also, we have many empty locations but they don't solicit the real estate people to find out why. They need to find out. Is it too expensive? What do we need to do to fill them? Once, when I found a company to rent the last set of flats on a floor, the boss found many reasons to change or deny the lease! Can you imagine? You'd think a boss would want to show how good he was, renting everything out! The company probably doesn't earn. I don't know how they keep on going. I tread lightly. I want to tell them what is wrong, but they don't want to hear.

Though Francis's fellow colleagues, some of whom held jobs managing housing units, congratulated him on landing this job, he feared for his reputation. "I'm losing their respect because my boss keeps on changing the terms of the leases, and I have to ask colleagues for favors. For instance, I had to find a place for the tenant that I took on, but that later the boss didn't want!"

Francis endured and got a long stint of Canadian experience. But his employer wanted a yes-man and was not interested in Francis's suggestions on good management practices. In 2006, without warning, Francis was laid off. He e-mailed: "It's the first time in my life that I got sacked, for being overtly more competent than my incompetent boss. So, unfortunately, I won't have a Happy Chinese New Year this time."

The firm gave him only two months' severance pay after four years' employment. A decade after landing in Canada, Francis accepted that his only possible path was upgrading his credentials in the housing management field. He began a certificate program supported by unemployment insurance. As he e-mailed at the start of the course, "I will be taking a 6–months' course at a community college in order to get a housing management certificate. What a shame that I had to go back to basics in Canada and start it all over again, at the age of 59!"

Francis finally got back on the track, hired as a property manager of three groups of townhouses. "I'm doing the sort of work that I did in my first private sector job in Hong Kong [1979]. None of my previous experience seems to count. And it seems that my master's degree in housing management, achieved over three years of hard work, is totally disregarded. It isn't as good as a certificate that I got here in seven months! What a shame." The position would have been good for a new graduate, but for Francis, it fell short of full recognition. And while he got back on a career of sorts linked to his former field, Francis Kwong could recoup only to a small degree his past status, not to mention earnings.

Having settled his work status and gotten citizenship, Francis turned to the issue of his divided family. He recalled Ka-Tit from Hong Kong and took up the problem of his education. Francis thought he could help Ka-Tit more in a career that followed his own footsteps, and urged him to take the same courses that he had taken in his field so he could help him study better. He regretted that he had not been around earlier to supervise his son.

Selling their Hong Kong flat closed the question of settlement in Canada for the whole family. Francis had a newly minted degree, Siu-Foon was familiar with and settled in Canada by now, and their son was living with them. Yet whether Ka-Tit, who was out of step with Canadian life, would stay or find a way to return to Hong Kong, is an open question.

Summary: Migration Dilemmas of a Professional Manager

A professional manager with British and Hong Kong credentials, Francis perceived that the impending regime change was distorting Hong Kong's systems of professional governance. As Hong Kong reverted to Mainland rule, he saw all around him portents of loss of professional autonomy. He feared that the heavy hand of PRC control over professional jurisdictions would be applied in Hong Kong. He also saw how Hong Kong's monied interests, intent on developing property in China, were changing the configuration of his field in Hong Kong itself. His concern that the popular voice was being muzzled further spurred his intent. We also saw that social fields create, maintain, and anchor identities. When a field changes, it threatens an identity, and the new identity may not be acceptable. Francis's struggles highlight this process. With his identity coming under attack, migration appealed to this middle-class professional.

Equally important, Francis was protective of his family. He perceived Canada—with its better social services—would be a more supportive society than Hong Kong for his wife, who needed medical attention, and his son, who needed career help. He felt that emigration would be best for them all.

As this chapter shows, regulative structures can ease immigration for those who are sought after, but at the same time are not universal and may impede settlement. Francis was attractive to immigration officials but barred from working. The professions withheld recognition of his credentials, and potential employers followed their lead.

Social networks added to these job-related problems; Francis's contacts—his brother and other kin, schoolmates, and even former colleagues—were not in social fields that could access his profession. Further, social networks change when people move, and their reach into specific fields also changes. Having made his move, Francis broke with his occupational networks in Hong Kong and truncated his career. Without the same well-connected networks in the Canadian economy, getting good jobs was difficult there, and when he sought to return to Hong Kong, Francis could not regain where he had left off before emigrating.

Francis's derailed career led to his transnational migration. With neither formal nor informal recognition, human capital immigrants like Francis face sharp choices: Remain in Canada without having their credentials recognized? Or return to the uncertain fray in Hong Kong and China, which had led to their exit to begin with? Francis found neither of these choices fully satisfactory. Further, because his family did not completely go along with the decision to emigrate, they, too, could not settle completely. Thus, the Kwongs' move to Toronto was not a once-and-for-all act. The complications of migration preoccupied their family for years as Francis went back and forth between Asia and Canada, searching for meaningful and well-paid work while his family tried to settle. In this case, as in that of the professionals and businessmen we met earlier, transnational forays became the means to resolve the inconsistencies of institutions.

After a period as an astronaut, Francis finally made Toronto his permanent home and began to rebuild his career while caring for his family. Francis's final decision to stay in Toronto was rooted in his concern for his family's well-being and the ultimate recognition that he needed to work where he lived. Emigration and the mismatched institutions on the two sides of the ocean had unsettled his family enough.

PART TWO

THE ROOTED:
TIES TO HONG KONG
DETER MIGRATION

Our theme—that their institutional position sets families' migration hopes as well as their success—can be seen in three families who are rooted in place. They either have not entertained or have given up migration projects. Applications from the Gungs (chapter 6) and Wans (chapter 8) were rejected; the Ongs (chapter 7) did not apply. Surprisingly, these families have a lot in common. Given their middling incomes and human resources, they could not gain acceptance at the larger regulatory level. At the level of social relations, all of the Gungs' and Ongs' kin are local, and hence they have only local social fields. In contrast, Brian Wan's emigrant kin extended the promise of work abroad, sparking his interest in emigration, while his wife is the rooted one. Since the Wans' resources cannot get them past the regulatory gatekeepers, they, too, remain in Hong Kong.

Three of the five wage earners have local careers and lack connections to global institutions. Without the bandwagon effect of migrant peers, two of the three families have little interest in emigration. Consequently, all three families, whether rejected or nonapplicants, are de facto rooted in Hong Kong. They build their family ethos around securing modest prosperity through local opportunities. Even the rejected emigrants redefine their way of life in Hong Kong as "good enough."

CHAPTER SIX

The Gung Family
Hong Kong Locals

"We're not going anywhere!"
—Kai Gung

Staving off the emigration fever, Kai and Aloe Gung remain in Hong Kong. For one thing, this ordinary family had less opportunity to migrate than did the better-off families we met. When, as a young clerk, Aloe applied for the Right of Abode in Britain, she did not meet the basic requirements and was rejected by the immigration authorities. After marrying Kai, both gradually improved their social positions enough that they might have been accepted had they reapplied. Yet they never again tried to emigrate. Their daily lives are embedded in a Hong Kong-based kinship network that they do not want to compromise, and their careers are also rooted in local structures. Further, at the cognitive level of identity, the Gungs prize security and familiarity. Aloe's civil service work engenders trust in—not anxiety about—local institutions, while the Gungs' two young daughters give their Hong Kong life meaning. Their story reveals their assurance that by emigrating they'd risk what they worked so hard to achieve: family and careers.

In recounting their approach to life, the Gungs emphasize their considered approach to family improvement. Inheriting a past of family poverty and division, they determined to exert control in their own lives. In fact, survival became part of their family script. Their view of their past creates a reference point that they revisit in their imagination and update for present needs. This is the stuff that family culture is made of, and the Gungs are ongoing participants in this cultural construction. Their family members understand this family script, which is based on their previously shared past and validates their "meaning frames" (Ho and Ng 2008; Benton and Snow 2000). The Gungs marshal this family account, infused with meanings, to support their goals of upgrading their family life in Hong Kong. Emigration does not fit the picture.

Their parents, like the majority of ordinary people in Hong Kong, fled China not because their wealth was confiscated but to escape village poverty. This gave them a different perspective on reversion from those whose property was confiscated under Communism, for the Gungs did not anticipate another sudden loss of family position.

In the early 1950s, Kai's father left Bao'an County's unreliable soil seeking work at the Hong Kong dockyard in order to send money to his family back home.[1] The unexpected closure of the border divided his family, but Father traveled back and forth to visit. Kai was born in China in 1960, and in 1963, Kai's mother joined thousands of other poor peasants and brought her eight children, Kai among them, to Hong Kong. The family reunited in a small hut in Shau Kei Wan's squatter area and struggled to boost the large household out of poverty. The times demanded sacrifices.

Kai says, "In those days, most new immigrants from China suffered. Father had a trade and worked hard, but it wasn't easy when only one person worked. Sometimes Mother took temporary jobs to help support the family. After being apart for so long, we were happy enough to be able to live and eat under one roof, however small. We didn't think it was crowded. People solved that with three levels of beds! We even slept head to toe next to one another. It was very lively and noisy when we ate and studied together."

Memories of this period evoked a sense of resourcefulness at having overcome difficulties. Kai remembered, "I went out to work at a very early age. I found a part-time job, and Elder Brother also helped me with my secondary school fees." Looking back, Kai saw the fruits of their labor: "Only when we all went out to work could we move from the squatter area," he proudly recounted. The family resettled in government housing, which they viewed as an achievement (Lee and Yip 2006). "Now we've all married and live on our own," he reflected on their ultimate accomplishment.

Aloe, whose parents were Hakka from Wai Yeung County, Guangdong Province, recalled a similar past of poverty. Aloe, their second child, was born in Hong Kong in 1963. Her mother, an uneducated woman, was not well and could barely do the odd manual jobs that fell to her. When Aloe was a teenager, she and her younger sister Yan-Yi went to work part time while going to school. Their mother died and in 1985; their father remarried another Wai Yeung villager who could not pass through China's closed borders until Hong Kong rejoined China in 1997. By then, they had three children.

Commenting about her childhood, Aloe stressed, "We just worked and worked." Laboring at a young age did not stand in the way of getting an education, however. Poor families succeeded through mutual cooperation;

older siblings got jobs so they could pay for their younger siblings' school and help their parents make ends meet. Aloe recounted, "Before marriage, I brought home half of what I earned. It wasn't calculated. Just a lump sum so my parents could have spending money and pass their days well. It was enough, but if there was a crisis we gave more. For instance when my father was injured, we chipped in nearly HKD 30,000 for medicine."

As time passed, her siblings got part-time jobs to pay for their own schooling and soon could contribute to their parents' support. Yet as part of their leadership role, older siblings gave more. Aloe revealed, "Now, my younger brothers and sisters are working, but it's no longer necessary for them to give much to our parents. So what happens is that I and my elder sister give more and my younger brothers and sisters give less." Such family cooperation, which would continue in smaller ways even after marriage, contributed to lasting family ties (Salaff 1981).

Mutual support was also the norm in Kai's family. He proudly recalled, "I've given my parents money since I started to work. Before I married, I contributed half my salary. Now, it's around HKD 2,000. It's the same for my other brothers and sisters who are working." This family responsibility also motivated Kai's brothers and sisters to rebuild their family home in China although they had long moved out. They saw it as a family house: "Our old village house wasn't sturdy anymore. It cost around HKD 100,000 to rebuild it totally. At first, I didn't really like the idea of building a house there, because we won't let Father live alone in China. We can look after him better here. But he wanted a place to stay when he visits for a vacation. So we decided to renovate. We can all go there for weekends and enjoy it."

Themes of family cooperation, frugality, and planning were noticeable in their narratives. Brothers and sisters who worked together for the family's sake felt that all gained by pooling some of their earnings and improving the family economy. Gradually as their careers developed, they continued this system of cooperation not for survival, but for the meaningful goal of family reciprocity itself. These experiences shaped their identities as a people forged by hardships who can endure an uncertain future.

Now past extreme poverty, this first generation of Hong Kongers became curious about their Chinese heritage. This curiosity figures in the Gungs' own story of becoming a couple. They met each other during their first tourist visit to Guangzhou, an underdeveloped place at the time. The visit was jarring and they were desperate to find something familiar. Aloe recalled,

It was around Christmas, and really cold. Yan-Yi and I took the cheapest night train. We were only in our early twenties and a bit lonely. We thought that a train going to Guangzhou must have someone from Hong Kong on it! My sister, who's pretty brave, walked around and saw Gung's group of friends and we felt some kind of kindred spirit. We introduced ourselves, and later went sightseeing together. Then they returned to Hong Kong because they had finished their trip, while we kept on going. We exchanged phone numbers, and when we got back in Hong Kong we got together to look at our photos.

Kai thought it was fate: "Luckily we went on that particular train!"

Deciding to Stay: The Early 1990s

Putting their past of family division and poverty behind them, Aloe and Kai wanted a modern marriage in which they made their decisions together. They planned carefully to make the most of their resources. As part of this plan, they both spent years in part-time evening study and waited until graduation to marry.

In 1991 when emigration fever hit Hong Kong, Aloe, still single, was working in sales in the high-pressure garment industry in Hong Kong—a job she had taken to support her family after finishing secondary school and taking her exams. Her sister Yan-Yi was studying garment merchandizing in Britain and encouraged Aloe to join her. Proximate in age and having similar experiences as they grew up, and working in the same industry, they were particularly close. Yan-Yi urged Aloe to file for the Right of Abode to join her in Britain.

When we met the Gungs in 1993, Aloe had not yet heard about the status of her application. She explained that she was not keen on leaving Hong Kong. "I applied because there was an opportunity. Actually, I was not so anxious to go. But it didn't take a lot of time. I don't care much, not like others who approach consultants and lawyers. It was two years ago. I'd almost forgotten, until I was asked to go for an interview earlier today. If I get it, I'll accept it, if not, I won't worry about it." She planned to take the Right of Abode in Britain, if offered, as sanctuary from an ambiguous political situation (and to join her sister). "Actually, I never thought of living there, because it's not easy to find a job. But there's no harm in applying. The advantage of the Right of Abode is that you are not required to go right away. It's for the worst-case situation—if something happens, then at least you have a way out."

Aloe and Kai share the theme of overcoming hardships, a cornerstone of their family identity. Their past difficulties forged them into the kind of people who could confront adversity and survive, confidently facing Hong Kong's uncertain future. "We came from a poor family; we went through a lot before we reached what we are now," Kai stated repeatedly. They viewed themselves as competent and responsible in their work and family roles (Bird and Schnurman-Crook 2005). As they focused on their careers and planned for family life together in Hong Kong, they revised the meaning of emigration as escapism.

Knowing that she wanted her own family, Aloe planned to move out of the private sector where the hectic activity and competition did not mesh with her family-oriented goals. She wanted a stable career with regular hours and saw the civil service as her ideal job (a view that she would come to question following reversion). For six years, while still holding down her private-sector job, Aloe worked toward a degree in business studies. She said, "I thought I ought to be more comfortable. The private sector was tiring. If you're not very aggressive and don't like to compete for power, a government post is best. You have to be industrious and there are things you may have to worry about, but you don't have to struggle. The chances are there, but you have to wait to climb up. Some people think job satisfaction is greater in private work, but in the civil service, you can enjoy life more. So, I sacrificed interesting but frantic work for quality of life."

Upon graduation in 1991 she joined the Colonial civil service as an executive officer. She married Kai a few months later. As they began to work out their family strategy together, marriage soon turned Aloe's attention from looking for a way out to building their life in Hong Kong. By the time she heard that her right of abode application had been rejected, their careers and family events had progressed. Whatever Aloe had decided on her own before marriage now became a joint decision (Berger and Kellner 1977). The couple chose not to reapply.

In her civil service position, Aloe did general "office administration, internal work, personnel, finance, accounting." An executive officer, when transferred to different departments, Aloe applied the procedures she had already learned and found the noncompetitive nature of the work a relief. "Everything's according to policy, everyone's treated the same. You just stick to the rules." She distinguished herself from administrative officers, who were keen on politics. She herself was not concerned, and felt her bureaucratic position suited her cautious personality.

Kai had worked his way bit by bit into the engineering world. Starting as an accounting clerk in a construction company, he, too, took night courses for six years to earn his higher certificate in engineering. Cathay Pacific Airlines bought his firm and assigned it maintenance projects at the airport, construction of government housing authority buildings, and the design of the Disneyland project. Kai planned construction, prepared drawings, and coordinated departments. "The department gives out a contract, and our company is contractor. I work in the office and track the progress of the projects." The firm's large size and prospects appealed to him, as he said, "The field of engineering is quite tough—at least I don't need to do the practical work myself. We usually discuss how to coordinate the progress of the project and other administrative tasks in indoor meetings. And our company has lots of benefits, like cheaper plane tickets!"

Hong Kong was a conduit for financing the construction industry in South China, drawing engineers like Kai (and site engineer Luk, chapter 3) into diverse projects. Radical changes after reversion could only be guessed at: How would Hong Kong's political merger with China affect Kai's position? Would his company lose their projects in Hong Kong and China to cheaper Mainland workers? Although both Kai and Luk saw drawbacks to Chinese presence, Kai envisioned fewer downsides. To his view, the booming economy proved that reversion to China would benefit them. In 1993, Kai interpreted the unfamiliar future optimistically, saying that his company would land the projects because of their better work. "I'm not afraid of competition. We already hire Mainland Chinese, it doesn't influence us much. People in China work differently. They don't check their work carefully. They don't belong to engineering associations. They can't meet our standards. They build a building however they please. There's no planning and preparation, that's why it always ends up in a mess. So we don't worry. Our work can't be compared." The great demand for employees with technical and administrative skills gave Kai confidence, bolstering his decision to stay in Hong Kong.

Trusting Hong Kong's Institutional Order

Their faith in Hong Kong, the strength of the economy, and the importance of social stability contributed to the Gungs' decision to remain. They felt sure that Hong Kong was strong enough to survive anything. As Kai put it, "I think the most important thing is to make the society a safe place. If we keep our laws and maintain political order, then I don't think the society will be in trouble." Kai's views reflected his experiences as an engineer in the airport, where contracts favored those from the home country. He opted to end the Colonial status: "Hong Kong can stand on its own, with or without China, and even without the UK. The UK discriminates against us in many ways. Without those two countries, Hong Kong will still do very well. So, if you are asking me who should 'own' the place, I don't think it matters. As long as they can give what Hong Kong requires, then whoever they are doesn't matter. Just don't create so many problems because it will do Hong Kong more bad than good."

"Reversion doesn't matter" became a key theme in the Gungs' narratives leading up to 1997 and they raised the issue of reversion in ways that emphasized ordinariness. As Kai told us, "Nothing much will change with reversion. We will still be the same." Still, the Gungs did express some concerns over the unknown. Kai emphasized the importance of ordinary folk enjoying everyday activities, saying, "We don't really know what is going to happen economically to Hong Kong in 1997. If the environment is very chaotic, it would make us worry. As to what I see now, the chance is minimal. If you can still do your daily activities like watching movies, or seeing friends, then I don't think it will be very bad."

The Gungs dealt with their concerns by drawing on their family histories and their family script of survival, affirming that their experiences steeled them for hardship. "Since we came from a tough family and had some hard times, we don't really worry a lot. For me, the worst is not so bad. The worst we can do is to go through hard times, just like before. But those who haven't been through hard times at all will find this a difficult time." To clinch the argument they referred to wisdom of the elders, saying, "You notice that the older generation doesn't seem to take the threat of '97 seriously? They have been through a lot, so they know better than to panic. And you can see that they're not worried at all."

In addition to their trust in the ability of Hong Kong's institutions to withstand change following reversion, part of the reason the Gungs remained nonchalant about 1997 may have been due to their ambivalence about the political process. Although they had joined the huge number of Hong Kongers who protested the June 4, 1989, Tiananmen crackdown, by 1993 they had reevaluated its significance. They no longer saw this as an event that might recur under Chinese rule, and they did not join subsequent memorials.

Aloe's trust in the viability of Hong Kong's basic institutions resonated with her civil service employment. From her standpoint as a government official, she now had a different view of Tiananmen: "At that time I felt the Chinese government made a mistake. But looking back at it, I believe they have their own reasons for doing what they did. Overall, I can't say who was right and who wrong. Only those on top will know what was going on behind the scenes. So, we don't really know what the causes are."

They downplayed the significance of the democratic process altogether and with it the significance of the transition. After the historic first election of the Legislative Council in 1991, they did not bother to vote. Aloe said,

I voted in 1991, I forget for whom, because I'm not really keen about the person. When I voted for him, I couldn't actually say that this was the right person. I did consider whether he is really capable of doing the things he promises. Still, there are so many candidates that it makes things difficult. We don't know much about them and find it hard to choose. What people get out of the elections all depends on what they put into it. The election doesn't mean anything to me. As long as it doesn't affect me adversely, then it is okay. But I won't waste my time on it. I won't feel bad if my candidate lost. For me, it doesn't make any difference.

The Gungs argued that the right to vote would not greatly improve governance in the short run. Further, they mistrusted the efforts of others and believed that few people took politics seriously. In Aloe's words, "A lot of Hong Kong people, including me, don't know how to see what is right and what is wrong. We don't really know who is right. And not all our decisions are right all the time." Kai made a comparison that he meant as serious: "It's just like horse racing. Some just bet for fun, while some really study the horses' achievements before placing their bet. Elections are also like that; it depends on the seriousness of the person making the vote. If I am going to spend a lot of time knowing the candidate, I might as well play the horses!"

Their expressed concerns about reversion were also mediated by an increasing sense of Chinese heritage. For example, in 1996, Kai thought that social issues were not explosive. He foretold that

> there might be a period of unrest during the transition. Hong Kong people will mix with Chinese people. And I think there will be small arguments over opposing ideas, but I don't think it would be a big problem, and I don't think it will last long. Either the Hong Kong people accept the fact of change or the Chinese will adapt to the system. Nothing much will change. We will still be the same. In Canada, people may think that we'll have changes because their culture is different, and they rely so much on news reports about us. But we Hong Kong people know the style of Mainlanders—we know they are also Chinese like us, so it's not a threat anymore.

The Colonial withdrawal gave the Gungs pride in their Chinese identity. But they were not single-minded over the effects of reversion. When we first met in 1993, Aloe retorted, "How do I feel about reversion to China? I am Chinese, and so I feel a sense of closeness. But I also feel a struggle within me." She struggled between her Chinese identity and background and her training that made her a staunch supporter of the Hong Kong system of governance in which she was involved. Integration with China did present some trouble to Hong Kong. Overall, however, in the personal and family sphere, the Gungs downplayed potential political and economic problems when Hong Kong reverted to China. They were Chinese after all. They had overcome poverty and turmoil and could do so again. In this way, they assuaged their concerns over Hong Kong's future.

Reactions of Others in the Gungs' Social Circles

The downside of migration itself was also a deterrent. The Gungs had numerous opportunities through emigrant colleagues to view life in other countries and felt up to date on how Westernized Chinese lived. Aloe realized her civil service experience was unlikely to be transferable to other countries (Wong and Salaff 1998).

"It's difficult to compare the UK and Hong Kong. The lifestyle's totally different. If you have an average job, then any place is the same. But when it comes to a professional job, I think Hong Kong's better. We know from the papers that the economy in the UK isn't so good. If you just hang around without work, it's not so good; it's not really like a vacation!" Moreover, with poor prospects elsewhere, their overseas kin and colleagues were re-grouping in Hong Kong. As Kai told us, "Getting a job is a problem. A lot of friends who lived in Canada and Australia still prefer to come back and work here, even after years of staying there."

For example, in 1996 when Aloe's sister and fiancé were returning to Hong Kong for their wedding, they stayed in Hong Kong. With her newly minted foreign degree in garment merchandizing, Yan-Yi was a hot commodity and quickly found work. Her husband, trained as a research chemist, took a job testing beer-brewing facilities in China—somewhat under his skill level but paying well enough. Yan-Yi had been the sole family relationship Aloe had abroad; her return further released Aloe from an interest in emigration.

Kai was also aware that his engineering skills could not be transferred abroad. The Gungs now were certain that remaining in Hong Kong was the best use of their talents. Familiarity with the larger world helped them evaluate what life might be like elsewhere for people like themselves and they realized how much they had to lose. As Kai reflected on emigration, he increasingly drew the line around who was staying and who left. "Those who stand to lose the most are those like us, the middle classes. Neither of us like to gamble, so we don't think of those things. Those that emigrate are risk takers, businessmen who invest in life abroad. Emigration is strategic planning. It's a kind of gamble. If you are wealthy, you won't suffer a big loss."

The Gungs believed that those who most wanted to emigrate were the wealthy or who had a different family background.

Some people are really afraid of '97, they fear the Communist Party will come, so they leave in a rush, then have trouble living there. Businessmen and politicians are frightened by the ploys of Britain, Hong Kong leadership, and China. But we're not so fearful, so why should we go abroad and have to suffer? We're not afraid because we've no particular bad experience with them. We can't think of what to be afraid of. In my family we don't think '97 is a big thing. We don't plan for it. Come to think of it, comparing the impact of '97 on us here with it on those who are moving somewhere else, I think the pressure is less on us than them. That's why we prefer to stay here.

Over the years, both spouses built careers within their fields as the first in their families to enter the middle class. Ultimately, they decided that the success and security available in Hong Kong were much more desirable than the risks of emigration. They were satisfied with the lives they were achieving in Hong Kong.

The Transition Years: Their First Child

The Gungs planned their family life carefully. They spent years in part-time evening study, waited until graduation to marry, banked much of their income, and paid off their first flat quickly. They were already in their thirties when they had children. Aloe proudly distinguished her generation of Hong Kongers who delayed marriage and childbearing from that of traditional Chinese who had many children without preparing themselves financially. In 1996, they welcomed their first child, daughter Yuk-Ping.

Aloe found her woman's roles growing heavy. With no mother to aid her, she was responsible for most of the household chores as well as her government job. Her routine was hectic. She woke up at six-thirty every morning, fed the baby and then took her on the MTR to Tai Koo, where Kai's younger sister, their babysitter, met them. Aloe proceeded to her job in Wanchai and returned to fetch Yuk-Ping in the evening. When she arrived home, she played with the baby for an hour before preparing a simple dinner of steamed pork or fish and soup and rice. When Kai was not in China, he played with Yuk-Ping after work and they all ate dinner together. But he admitted that he had little time to spend with the baby.

Similar to their counterparts elsewhere and like many Hong Kong professionals at the time, Aloe and Kai lacked time, not money (Hochschild 1990). Working hard in Hong Kong's booming economy, Kai could barely carve out time to see his daughter or be with his extended family. Neither Kai nor Aloe ever predicted this side issue of retrocession—the area's hot economy—which gradually took its toll on Aloe.

By 1996, the Gungs saw reunion with China as economically profitable, creating a stable economy. Kai said, "I believe the future belongs to China. And now, China is starting to improve its economy. That's why reversion doesn't matter." But as the skill gap between the labor force in China and Hong Kong closed, Kai realized that his working conditions were not static. Still, unlike manufacturing workers, instead of fearing for job security, his firm profited from investment on both sides of the border. In 1996, Kai reflected positively on the changes he saw while working for his company in China:

> Chinese workers are now more cooperative and are willing to work hard to earn more, whereas in the past they just killed time. I'm quite pleased, because it means more jobs for us. Mostly we're stationed in Hong Kong. But because manpower's cheap there, and people now are willing to work, we're building a factory in Zhu Hai to do construction and repair machinery and equipment for the airport. I go three or so days a month to supervise. So we don't worry about having nothing to do after '97! In economic terms, I think China's getting better. A lot of people are investing there, and it makes a big difference. I have a stable job now, so I don't think I'll be changing in the near future. I've just been promoted to senior engineer, and I now have to do overtime because we've lost some manpower.

Kai's working hours lengthened. He monitored construction at the new Shenzhen airport and his company provided him with a car so that he could return home late at night. He also upgraded his qualifications through a part-time distance-learning master's program organized by the Hong Kong Polytechnic University and University of Warwick. All of this meant that despite his success—or perhaps because of it—Kai was not available for his family.

Aloe, too, found her workload increasing since the many new immigrants from China burdened the system. In contrast to Kai, she felt that her job situation was worse. As she put it, "The two ways of life in Hong Kong and China have formed two peoples; those from China have different living environments, different interpretations. They are not used to trusting government rules. They bargain. You have to explain more. It gives us a lot of administrative work. Being a civil servant isn't easy."

Political changes added to her stress. She believed in the civil service ethos of ruling by policy, not politics. But as Britain and China jockeyed over the terms of the post-handover government, her working environment became increasingly politicized. Despite working for the Colonial civil service, Aloe was not committed to the British Empire. She suspected the motives of politicians who advocated democratic elections; they were stirring up an uninformed public. As she said, "I feel Governor Patten is hurrying things a bit. And I doubt what he does is for the benefit of the Hong Kong people. He just thinks for himself and for the British who asked him to come here.

Sometimes I feel that he doesn't work for us." In her view, the belated discussion of the expansion of franchise was part of the British exit scenario; they were creating a social movement that left behind favorable views of their rule and were not genuinely interested in reforms. "Reforms that are too fast are unsafe," she said.

In the district office, she was involved with local organizations and residents, writing weekly reports on government reforms about which she was not enthusiastic. Aloe was finding herself unable to opt out of politics:

> One of our duties is to "reflect" public opinion. The political reform is one of those hot topics we have to write about. I wish I could choose another, more interesting topic. It's hard to know whether the voting reforms are right or not. I feel there are hidden government motives that we have no information about that involve us in the political games between China and England. The administrative office should be concerned with politics because they often have to make policy. But we belong to the executive, so actually we don't really need to know much about politics. It just happens that I'm in the district office, so I have to write about these things—very painfully!

In the waning years of Colonial rule and the early transitional years of the new SAR regime, political complexities destabilized the civil service-based political system. The transition leadership changed the structure to widen their political base. Governor Patten directed the civil service to make its policies more user friendly, adding to Aloe's work.

Aloe saw morale plummet. "Governor Patten proclaimed a 'performance patch.'[2] That means we have to be more responsible, work faster, be more careful." Aloe believed that the civil service did its job by following policy guidelines, not by embracing public opinion. She stated, "Having to explain what we do takes time. People should let us get on with our work." Although she could not object to the underlying rationale, she resented the increased work pace and humbling of the once-proud service.

> After Governor Patten passed an "access to information" law, the public can ask "What do you have about me?" and get their dossier. This department needs a strong reason, such as high security, to refuse. People don't fully trust our decisions about them, and they appeal. It's very time-consuming. For instance, someone asks, "Why didn't you allocate public housing to me?" And we have to tell them about the rules, and then they ask, "Why do you have such rules?"—especially those from China. In Hong Kong, people follow the rules of the game; they know policy and are only concerned about applicability. Maybe the reform is necessary, but not every request is reasonable and they misinterpret; there're lots of appeal cases on procedures. We have to justify all the decisions we make. In the past we just made a balanced decision, and it was

accepted. But now we see the decision appealed many times. When things are politicized it takes more time. Now that Hong Kong belongs "to the people," people want more from the government; they want more openness, more accountability, just more!

As she grew more dissatisfied with her job, instead of dreaming about emigration, Aloe became more and more focused on her family life, which included a second child.

Post-reversion: 1997–2005

Soon after reversion, Hong Kong was hit by the Asian economic crisis and suffered government mismanagement. The engineering trade took a nosedive, and the new SAR administration severely cut back the civil service. The Gungs took this as a sign that their cautious approach to their family economy had paid off. Emigration became even more remote. With a second child on the way, paradoxically, the Gungs' narrowed opportunities convinced them to remain with what they knew rather than venturing to the unknown.

Their second daughter, Yuk-Yan, was born in 1999. With the reduction in the civil service workforce, Aloe's workload became even heavier and she was forced to parcel out her family jobs. They hired a low-waged live-in immigrant domestic helper. They sold their first flat at a low price to Aloe's younger sister Yan-Yi and bought a larger apartment in Junk Bay for HKD 1.5 million, paid in full. To solve the space problem, Kai planned "to buy a triple-decker bed for the children's room. Then the two kids and the domestic can have their own sleeping space." Whether their servant—or children—needed their own private space didn't enter his plans. Without irony, they had come full circle to Kai's youth, with a difference: the children and servant now crowd together on bunk beds in a high-rise apartment, not a shantytown.

Aloe's job continued to worsen with the growing pains of the new SAR regime. She had been a strong supporter of the civil service, which she thought symbolized efficiency, stability, and prosperity through its guidelines of impartiality and rules. To Aloe, the restructuring of the civil service that Patten began and the SAR continued was a way to blame civil servants for the executive's political blunders. The executive was building a political system it could control. Aloe did not worry about losing her job, although she no longer counted on promotion. Nevertheless, given the mounting problems, she increasingly drew into her family.

Reversion to China also changed their broader family life in an unscheduled manner. Aloe's father sponsored his second wife and their three children for the Right of Abode in Hong Kong. Their arrival gave Aloe another role in the family, that of a substitute mother. She was torn, because as a daughter, she was not expected to advise the older generation, but she did not agree with her father's actions and could not stand aside. "He's traditional. He raises them like he raised us, uses the stick; it doesn't really work now. He never helps them or takes them out. He only thinks of expenses. Every once in a while I try to tell him how to raise them in a more modern way. Their grades are mediocre. I tell him to get a tutor. He says, 'It costs too much, it's because they are lazy!' I say, 'It's because they came from a different educational background.' Let's just hope the kids don't rebel and create problems for Hong Kong society." Although she believed she knew how children should be raised, eventually Aloe, as a working mother, enmeshed with her own husband and children, had no time to care for two families. She gave up her mission of turning her half-siblings into exemplary Hong Kong citizens.

Focusing on the Future: Yuk-Ping and Yuk-Yan

Middle-class parents—wanting their children to develop their full potential, to retain their family status, and to have good careers—tend to be quite hands-on in raising them. They absorb educational philosophies of the time and do not stint on their lessons and training (Clausen 1968). Those Chinese parents the authors met go further, shaping their children's hopes, habits, occupational goals, and even their personalities (Ho et al. 2006). Each family does this in their own way, partly dictated by their economic strength and social fields. Improving their children's chances in the competitive world begins with their education. Those like the Luks (chapter 3) and Uncle Chou (chapter 4) who can manage the costs emigrate for their children's sake or send them abroad on their own (Waters 2005). Those with fewer resources cannot make this sacrifice. With their solid local family ties and concern for their parents and other siblings, the Gungs did not value giving up Hong Kong life for the sake of a foreign education. Instead, they developed strategies to get top-quality schooling for their daughters in Hong Kong.

Selectively combining their traditional upbringing with new ways, they chose a private Chinese Christian language school with a strong academic tradition. Hearing that a world-famous mathematician had graduated from that school, they stood in line from dawn to get application papers and prepared Yuk-Ping for the oral interview for school entrance. Aloe's civil service allowance would pay half the HKD 2,000 monthly tuition for each child attending school. They knew they could not duplicate these perks outside of Hong Kong. As was the school's tradition, they expected their second child would be able to follow.

When it came to shaping the children's personalities, the Gungs trained their daughters to fit into the family circle, important to them as parents in their own right. No longer needing to pool their resources to survive, the Gungs looked for occasions to teach their daughters to cooperate. As the elder sister, Yuk-Ping was expected to take the lead. During a Sunday afternoon outing on the beach at Lamma Island, Kai turned to Yuk-Ping and asked, "What color candy do you think your younger sister wants?" Yuk-Ping guessed purple. Kai went to a kiosk, bought a box of purple candies, and encouraged Yuk-Ping to give it to Yuk-Yan as a gift. Catching on, Yuk-Yan offered some back to her older sister. If they wanted candy, they had to share.

The younger sister was eager to follow the lead of her older sister in swimming, piano, and drawing. To her this was a sign of growing up. Aloe used this inclination to draw Yuk-Yan into activities through imitation. Aloe sat with Yuk-Ping while she practiced the piano, because she felt that "lessons are work for a child." When Yuk-Yan saw Aloe going off with her older sister to piano lessons, she thought "It's a special time," and became eager to take lessons herself.

Lunching in a restaurant, Kai murmured encouragement for her youngest to finish her noodle dish, telling her that if she ate more, she could do more things she liked. "Posted signs at Ocean Park [a popular amusement park] give the height measurements before a child is allowed on the rides. My younger daughter is eager to qualify. I tell her 'Eat more then you will grow higher and can go on more rides,' so she does." This ploy to get their daughters to willingly do what they wanted seemed to work.

When they visited the authors' Lamma apartment in 2003, drawing pencils and papers emerged from big backpacks (prepared by the parents) as soon as they arrived. They came up to the rooftop terrace, and the children were eager to begin drawing. "When the younger sees Yuk-Ping draw, she copies it."

On this visit, Aloe revealed how discouraged she was with her paid job. "Morale is very bad now. They may have a goal in cutting pay, but they should approach it by explaining the bad environment; instead they talk about the civil service being overpaid and a deficit. How could you say that, until 1997, the civil service is an asset and all of a sudden the same people become a liability? So of course there is bad morale! Those that are left have more work to do. So there is a kind of internal resentment."

Luckily, she did not fear losing her own job, since she needed to continue working to invest in their children's future. The Gungs considered getting a larger apartment, but as Aloe told us, "We want more space but I'm very cautious. This apartment is all paid off. I don't want to get in debt to the bank, so we're waiting." The acceptance of the status quo was essential to tolerating life in Hong Kong after reversion to China. Aloe said, "There are some people who are crazy to earn a lot of money, always preoccupied with work. Some of them expect to earn a lot, but they risk losing it. I'm happy with this life. Maybe I don't expect much of myself. I think my background also matters. They say if you're used to sad experiences, small happiness means a lot. My lifestyle is ordinary. If I want to do something, I can do it. But my expectations are not very high. This is already good enough."

Referring to their family concerns, she stated, "Apart from having a good job and a good lifestyle, a stable family life is what makes you secure; you have a definite place to go. I think this is very important." It is this set of concerns, their family script, which the Gungs referred to when times got tough. Having achieved balance, stability had taken the place of survival.

Aloe and Kai felt they were achieving a "balanced family life" of which they could be proud. Their commitment to Hong Kong is evidence of this balance and of their need to seek certainty in their lives. Stability in Hong Kong became the core of their family script—their identity. Their script is rooted in their careers, their related political views, and beyond these, the family; structures that bound them to the local place.

Summary: Adapting to a Changing Hong Kong

In their making sense of and adapting to the changing Hong Kong scene, the Gungs interwove the rules, norms, and their family culture, developed from the institutional structures of their daily lives. Aloe had not succeeded in her early migration effort, partly due to mistiming. A few years younger than the Luks (chapter 3) or Kwongs (chapter 5), Aloe experienced the Tiananmen uprising—a major political issue that spurred those others to emigrate—before settling in her career. Hence, Aloe did not satisfy the British admission requirements.

By the time the Gungs' careers in bureaucratic organizations developed, emigration was no longer desirable. They were aware that emigration would cut them off from their institutional fields. A civil servant could hardly hope to find a similar bureaucratic position abroad, and an engineer with a career in only one firm and whose credentials were not recognized abroad would also have trouble.

In terms of social relations, finding that many of their emigrant colleagues and kin were returning reinforced the Gungs' decision to stay put. Beyond these experiences with return migration, their local family networks—all located in Hong Kong—played a major role in their lives.

Cognitively, they perceive and make sense of the transition period through narratives about their family, whose imageries are associated with caution, planning for the future, and pride in survival. In the Gungs' view, migration does not accord with these themes. Migrants take chances; emigration is riskier to their family than is staying in Hong Kong. The Gungs see themselves as cautious planners, content to enjoy their modest achievements, which are rooted in local structures.

CHAPTER SEVEN

The Ongs

A Nonemigrant Trading Family

> "The difference is roots. . . . I just continue."
> —Ong

Like most of others who just earned enough to get by, Mr. and Mrs. Ong did not really consider emigrating, and the way they lived contrasts starkly with the well-to-do people we met. Economics was not the only issue in their being nonmigrants. With his traditional education in Chinese village schools, Ong would not appeal to today's immigration authorities. At the height of emigration fervor surrounding 1997, he was nearing retirement age and typified the many who had come to Hong Kong from China with traditional skills. Tied to a time-honored, cross-border trade and without Western education or a modern career, it was hard to consider emigration.

Nor did the Ongs' social fields reach to the West. The key institutions to which they were connected were regional, reaching China, Japan, and Southeast Asia. As for kin ties, when the border firmly closed, their family became divided, most remaining permanently on the Mainland side. After that, with their rich, overlapping personal ties linking them to China, feelings of duty and strong kinship ties dictated remaining. These participants in a life firmly attached to the region had no thought of exiting.

Finally, the Ongs were cultural patriots, taking pride in both their Hong Kong identity and their Chinese roots. In their meaning frame, retrocession was historically right because China's long cultural heritage preceded British occupation of Hong Kong. But like all such frames, ideology and emotions figured in this account, not only cognition. For the Ongs always saw Hong Kong existing within China. Put simply, dedicated to the region, remaining in Hong Kong embodied structural forces as well as rich personal dynamics.

This was reflected in the authors' visits to the Ongs in Hong Kong's traditional Sheung Wan district, where place and person resonate with tradition. We arranged to meet Ong in 1993 at his apartment in Sheung Wan, followed by a walk to his store. Still one of the most traditional Chinese districts in Hong Kong, Sheung Wan was the earliest place settled by the British forces in 1842 (Leeming 1977). The foot of Possession Street, then on the shoreline, has now retreated inland with reclamation. The location of dockyards, food imports, and warehouses through the 1930s, Sheung Wan is adjacent to the Edwardian-style Western Market, which was built in 1858. Once a "wet market" selling meat, fish, and vegetables, it has been refurbished for tourism. The four-star restaurant (which replaced the food stalls on the top floor) turns into a practice spot for ballroom dance aficionados at tea time, while clerks and transport workers slurp noodle soup in alleys behind it.

Here, in the Sheung Wan community, winding streets house the old China trades—gold, tea, Chinese medicine, and dried seafood. The heart of Sheung Wan is the North-South import-export trade ("nam pak hong"), with congregations of Fujian, Chaozhou, and other trading groups. Their clientele and contacts are densely connected through subethnic links that are constantly fed from the rural hinterland of South China (Lin 2002). The store where Ong has worked for forty years, North-South Dispensary, conducts a triangular trade in bird's nests, sharks fins, abalone, fungi and other luxury dried food from China and Japan. Several companies on the street are in the same business as Ong.

Ong's street has had facelifts. Banks of narrow granite-and-marble buildings replaced stucco, and cement street-level, open-faced markets display bushels of dried salted fish and vacuum-packed macadamia nuts jostling with rattan baskets of dried scallops. Middle-aged customers pick the good from the bad. In the interior of his building, electronically controlled freezers store abalone for up to three years to meet demand on the world market. The time-honored dried foodstuffs industry, a foundation of Hong Kong crossborder trade, has seen changes in sources and storage, but not in methods of sales. The city still concentrates employees from the same Guangdong places like Nan Hai or San Shui. Salesmen play cards, sitting on overturned bushel baskets in front of the building, their abacus at the ready, giving the impression that the trade continues exactly as it has for the past century. And that is how the Ongs fit into our study—as a living representative of earlier times.

The Early Years: From China to Hong Kong

Traditional Roots: 1930–51

The Ongs' attachments to China shaped them as unlikely migrants. Their local roots extend from their childhood in once-prosperous Guangdong villages in the early 1930s through to their family's residence there today. At a time when there were no public education in the villages, Ong benefited from the school that his prosperous clan association set up (Freedman 1958). It taught sons Chinese literature and history, which remained his hobby. He recalled, "The Ong surname is famous. Our family is big and owned lots of land, which we later donated to our province. My parents didn't need to pay my school fees. We always had a share of roast pork at the New Year's Feast, so much that we could eat pork for about four months."

Like many traditional sons, Ong was channeled into the kin group's trade, import-export of luxury foods. As a teenager in the mid-1940s, he began working alongside his brother in their kin-run Guangzhou store selling bird's nests. Then the rapacious post-World War II period in China forced Ong to escape China or face army service. "At that time, China had lousy military defense. There was so much corruption and political complications—the Communists, Sun Yat Sen's people, so chaotic. Every year, the Guomindang recruited kids from each area for the army. Our village usually raised enough money to give to the officials to pay for substitutes so that we didn't get recruited ourselves. But in those years, we couldn't afford to do that, so my brother and I escaped. He left China at the end of the Japanese occupation; I followed in 1947."

Life in Hong Kong was also hard. Merging knowledge of history with his personal experience, Ong told us, "Right after the war, it was tough to find a job in Hong Kong, and there was no place to stay. Seven or eight families lived in a flat of 1,500 square feet. More than twenty people in the house! Seven people slept on a double bed! Hong Kong started to flourish only after 1948 when crises forced those with money to escape Shanghai."

With formal institutions disrupted, personal networks helped get around military conscription, borders, sanctions, and other regulatory barriers. In those lawless times, there was little distinction between legal and illegal trade. Ong paid Chinese border guards to allow him to pass with large bags of bird's nests for his elder brother to sell in Guangzhou until "Brother Ong was imprisoned by the Guomindang for 'spying.' Our clan connections got Brother out."

Ong was introduced to Hau-Nung (his future wife). Shortly after their marriage in 1949, he returned to Hong Kong for work, leaving his bride in the village of ShaoXing. In 1950, their first daughter was born. In 1952, the border between Hong Kong and China closed, with Ong on one side, his family on the other.

From Sky to Sea: 1952–78

Ong's way of life became permanently centered on cross-boundary relations. His family relied on his material support, but the bird's-nest trade was not good. He recalled, "You need to do a lot of things to clean bird's nests, so it's expensive. Hong Kong people couldn't afford bird's nests. After the rich left China and Hong Kong for New York, Philippines, and Thailand, we sold mostly to those countries. Still, there were some buyers left in China."

Desperate, he turned to his personal networks and followed them, often into survival jobs. "Still, in the early '50s, there wasn't much trade in bird's nests and nobody was hiring. We tried almost everything that friends could get for us. In 1955, a cousin opened a bakery, and I helped in the business for about five years. The van delivered bread at six A.M., so I had to start work at seven, stayed until closing at eleven P.M. For that I earned HKD 80 per day. Room and food were free, but I sent only small amounts home."

Seeking more lucrative work, he turned to the trades of the seas. Bordering on the illegal, these, too, depended on trust between those with personal ties. Everyone relied on each other, relations helping them get around institutional barriers. "For about five years I worked with a former schoolmate in a market stall selling shrimp. Shrimp from China are larger than from Hong Kong and sell well. I got HKD 120 a day, and for the first time also a day off. We didn't have importing licenses or permits to sell the shrimp, so we used another wholesaler's name. We moved them around to avoid sanctions, transferred cargo to another person, and sold under his name."

Pearl cultivation promised even greater profits. The Chinese refer to these precious objects that are born in the sea as "conceived in the brains of dragons," the most powerful mythical beasts. To enter this field, Ong and his friends turned to more distant networks connecting the locales that plied the North-South trade.

In the early twentieth century, the Japanese discovered a technique for inducing the creation of a round pearl in the gonad of an oyster. Until then, pearls grew in the wild and were so scarce that it took several tons of oysters to find a handful of good pearls. This discovery revolutionized the industry, allowing pearl farmers reliably to cultivate large numbers of high-quality pearls at low cost (Dubin 2004). Ong stated, "When pearls became the rage, that schoolmate joined an investor from Taiwan and set up a Hong Kong company to culture pearls. The Taiwanese had learned his skills from the Japanese who started pearl cultivation in Taiwan. Taiwanese bought boats from local fishermen and taught them how to find a pearl and know when it matures. They had to employ someone from Japan with connections to find customers. That's how we here learned to culture pearls."

Suggested through Ong's social contacts, this activity that took so much toil had many production problems. He recalled that

the water in Hong Kong was too hot for pearls to grow properly. If it's hot, usually the oysters move to a cooler spot. In Japan, you have different elevations.

So whenever there's a current, the oysters move to the deeper level. But Hong Kong riverbeds are flat. With all the summer's flooding and typhoons, you're not even sure what you'll end up with. You waited for about four months before oysters started to grow and it took about three summers and lot of oysters to produce one good one. Out of the thousand pearls you collected, only about forty were good enough to use. So many factors affected the culture beds, the outcome wasn't so good. In Japan, they used more equipment and ended up with more production in less time. In Hong Kong, it was manual production, with more time and less output. In the end, Japanese pearls were better. So not enough profit.

I managed around fifteen women in this company, and we did the production together. The company gave us room and board. It was hard work, like "suffering wind and rain." I put the equipment together early in the morning, went to the sea to look after the culture beds. I opened the shells and pried out the pearls. My salary was HKD 100 a day.

In many other poverty-stricken areas, such as Mexico, Fujian, or the Hong Kong New Territories, people left in droves to find better work abroad, creating migrant networks. Among Ong's kin, however, none entertained emigration, so this was not an option for him either. When despite his efforts Ong could barely support his family, he again looked to his confreres for guidance. "That's when we switched to this luxury market. I take care of the accounts," he said. Staying at the sea front, they tried this new avenue, which reinstated their line to their hometown heritage and remained Ong's trade until retirement.

Although involving international trade, it was not a modern global industry. Rather, his centuries-old trade was interwoven with long-established personal relations. In the North-South trade, as in his earlier positions, he was connected to networks of friends, family, and business relations. Products and ways of conducting business are between people who know each other, and trust is important in trading luxury products. Ong's clan-school education suited his place as a staff member in a trade-honoring custom, in a historic part of town; hence his work was prized in this traditional enclave.

Building a Hong Kong Base: 1979–97

Ong's deep commitment to the region flowed through his family and was elaborated through wider ties to kin and quasi-kin workmates. A divided family was not his ideal, but with his wife and children in China, Ong was separated from them not through choice. He regularly sent money home and visited, all the while applying through official channels for his wife to join him. Although he bypassed legal channels in his trade, he rejected bringing his family into Hong Kong illegally (like unskilled workers did; see chapter 11). Doing so "would have been expensive and dangerous." He also realized that this middle-aged country woman was doing better in China than she would in Hong Kong: "My wife visited once in the late '50s and looked for a job. Being illiterate, she didn't get one. She went back to farm in China." Finally, in 1979, Hau-Nung was able to enter Hong Kong, ending decades of family separation. The ultimate admission of his wife under family re-unification policies reinforced Ong's loyalty to his motherland.

Once in Hong Kong, Hau-Nung's surroundings and daily routine maintained the strong kin-based feel that they had in China. The Ongs kept in regular contact with their many kin in Hong Kong and China, linking their worlds of work, kin, friends, and leisure. Their daughters, being both in China, tightened their local cross-border ties. Eldest Daughter remained on the Chinese side, while their youngest, Pui-Pun, would join her parents only in the 1990s.

Ong treasured family life, and he did not care that both children were girls. He believed that Hong Kong residents were liberal-minded with regard to family matters compared with the Mainland. "No, I don't mind not having sons. I don't have a conventional concept to have an heir. I came to Hong Kong so early, I'm open-minded."

Ong's company intertwined family and employment. Initially, Ong lived in company quarters and dined with other employees. Then in 1986, his firm gave out bonuses, which helped him buy a two-bedroom flat in the store's neighborhood for his reunited family. By the time we met the Ongs in 1993, he proudly reckoned that this 300–square-foot apartment, for which he paid HKD 260,000, had appreciated to HKD 1.2 million. However, the meltdown in property values during the 1998 Asian economic crisis reversed most of the gain. The diminutive flat was the Ongs' only asset, leaving them lacking in resources to emigrate, even if they had the notion. So even as panic began to grip better-off Hong Kongers, Ong remained steadfastly tied to his home base.

With only 300 square feet, the flat was tidily arranged. It had two small bedrooms; a wood-paneled sitting room, a set of shelves and drawers, and a folding card table with three stools, on which Ong served us strong Chao-zhou tea in tiny cups. To save electricity, they cooled themselves with electric fans in the sitting room, limiting the use of air conditioners to the bedroom. From the vinyl sofa Ong regularly watched the regional and world news on a small TV that was perched on a ledge no more than four feet in front of the sofa. Ong traversed the globe through the media, interpreting the news through his pan-Chinese meaning frame.

The Ongs' small living room also served as a workplace where, until their eyesight weakened, they cleaned bird's nests. When we visited in 1994, Ong showed us several nests they were working on and described the cleaning process. "High-quality bird's nests fetch high prices, over HKD 10,000 per pound. We remove the feathers, mud, moss and other dirty parts. That's why our place is so dusty. You need about sixteen bird's nests for a pound, and it takes roughly seven hours to clean one pound. It's not hard, but you need to see the impurities."

Loyalty and seniority were a premium in Ong's firm of valuable produce, and only the most trusted workers were allowed to handle bird's nests.

> Usually, we work with those who we knew. People can be negligent. A staff might carelessly give a customer more than they're supposed to. For instance, if they give customers more than one pound, you're already losing about HKD 100 to 200 in that sale. What if they did it one hundred times? That's already a lot of money. Although they don't steal it themselves, it's almost like that.
>
> This is an old occupation. Our business used to rely on verbal promises among buyers and sellers, seldom signing contracts to confirm. However, society's changing, and verbal promises mean nothing now. The business has become more modernized. Fewer and fewer enter this field nowadays, and the company's shrunk. Most of us are quite old, so prefer not to use computers, whereas the second generation is not yet familiar with the market. Even they use the abacus!

As a stalwart member of his kin-linked company, Ong had no desire or ability to try another trade, not to mention living in another country. As he explained in 1993, "I've worked for my schoolmate more than thirty-seven years now; it's become a habit. Raising pearls was the roughest time! What else can I do? I don't have the skills to do other things."

The emigration of Hong Kong's middle class and large numbers of returnees did not change this firm, which remained tied to older routines and customers. "Our customers are mostly older Chinese," Ong said. "We sell more than HKD 300,000 worth a month, but it's seasonal, during festivals like Christmas and Lunar New Year. Lobster and pigeons are highly valued, but you can't compare bird's nests to any other food. Old people buy shark fins and other products that are considered good for the digestive system. It's expensive, but it has its value. The market in bird's nests is also a traditional market. Youngsters may want to eat these products, but they don't know how to prepare them. They eat them only in restaurants."

Proud of their Chinese heritage, Ong and his family also took satisfaction in being Hong Kongers. Even when both daughters were still living on the Chinese side of the border, they did not consider moving back, instead building close ties with those who had chosen life in Hong Kong. For example, Hau-Nung's brother lived in Hong Kong and her nephew, who sold Chinese herbal medicine in Sheung Wan, lived in the Ongs' apartment building. Ong emphasized, "As Chinese, we have a strong family feeling. We keep in touch, help each other, and sometimes my cousin visits after work. In fact we have many relatives in Hong Kong. While not close blood relations, we treasure the bond." Soon, their family began to rebuild itself further.

Family Reunification: The Younger Generation

After years of efforts, in the early 1990s, younger daughter Pui-Pun arrived from China, squeezing into the second bedroom of the Ongs' tiny Sheung Wan flat. After her arrival, Pui-Pun, too, became totally encapsulated within her family's networks to settle and to find work. A victim of Cultural Revolution school disruption, she knew no English or any other technical skills that were in demand. Her cousin found her work in the medicinal shop where he clerked, for HKD 5,000 monthly salary, ten hours a day. Ong defended these conditions in terms of Chinese tradition, saying, "Such a low level of pay is common in traditional Chinese stores, and they give her lunch."

The Ongs primary worry concerned Pui-Pun's marital prospects in this complex city—a matter that overshadowed any worry about retrocession. As Hau-Nung reflected, "Parents' worries about children are without end! Several years ago we worried if our daughter was eligible to be a Hong Kong resident. We missed her so much that we visited three or four times a year. Now we worry about whether she can find a trustworthy husband."

Ong admitted that "we hope Pui-Pun can find a husband. He doesn't need to be rich, but must be hard-working and with no bad habits. However, such kind of 'ideal husband' is hard to find. Even if an ideal match approaches her, we cannot rule out other motives or problems in his background. It doesn't matter whether a child gets married or not, but we parents still hope she can have a family of her own which can give her long-term support and protection. That's one of our traditional concepts."

In 1994, they proudly informed the authors that their younger daughter had found her partner through friends' introductions. They planned months in advance for the divided family to attend the wedding. Always a patriot, Ong was patient, expecting that the Mainland bureaucracy that was still strictly limiting tourist visas would grant them entrance. He happily reported that Mainland kin did attend the wedding: "And when Older Daughter came, she stayed half a year! It was not difficult, only the processing takes a little while."

As was customary for cross-border marriages, they had a bigger celebration in Guangzhou for sixty people, which demonstrated their status. The work entailed and their need for celebrations on both sides of the border illustrates the pent-up demand for easier to-and-fro cross-border movement in everyday lives. Those like the Ongs who worked at maintaining kin ties in the divided country could not easily emigrate farther away.

Following tradition, Pui-Pun lived with her husband's mother in Sheung Wan. Her husband, a cook, held jobs in one fast-food restaurant after another, customary in his trade. Later, when Pui-Pun had her first child, Hau-Nung devotedly cared for him in the Ongs' tiny flat. With Eldest Daughter remaining in China, their family had not truly reunified, but its personal costs were reduced. Ong could look forward to a more complete family life so long as he remained where he was. Hong Kong's reunification with China promised an even more unified life, easing border-crossing for work and family reunion.

Thoughts on Reversion

Ong's traditional education and his readings gave him the frame he used to make sense of Hong Kong's reversion. In the years leading up to reversion, Ong impressed us with his strong awareness of how politics interconnects with history. Beyond improved cross-border personal ties, reversion to China made sense in the long-term flow of Chinese history. He regularly watched the news on TV and read both Hong Kong and Mainland-controlled newspapers because "they contain different views. *Ming Pao* is more comprehensive. It reports both the good news and the bad."

With his strongly analytic personality and knowledge of historic events, he followed through several major themes of retrocession in his discussions. He was concerned with Hong Kong's roots of success and whether they would be lost after reversion. Despite strong ties to China, he appreciated that Hong Kong had developed differently. He attributed Hong Kong's success to its openness, its mixture of cosmopolitanism, and cross-border trade, which he traced to a period before Colonial rule. He noted that "since the Qing dynasty, Guangdong has had no say in politics. But as a coastal region, it can keep open to the rest of the world. The mind of the Guangdong people is more open than that of the Northerners. Northerners are jealous of the comfortable life of Guangdong people and antagonistic to them."

Ong recognized that the British had contributed to Hong Kong; they "have brought us prosperity in the past century," he said. "How important are the British to the Hong Kong people? Very important. In Hong Kong, you have a mixture of nationalities. And it is this mixture that helps Hong Kong. Mainland Chinese have a different culture. The way they deal with people is different. They are not experienced, and sometimes they don't conform to the rules. Mainlanders are so surprised when they see us queuing up for a bus or giving seats to the elderly or pregnant women. You won't have this in China. So I don't think the Chinese can do it by themselves."

At the same time, he argued that before retrocession the British profited more than they gave. "Do I think the Hong Kong government led by Chris Patten and Anson Chan is really good for the Hong Kong people? We should not talk about Hong Kong Government. The so-called Hong Kong government is actually serving the interests of Britain. Don't you see how they take money out of Hong Kong? Like the airport project, many contracts are given to British consultation firms. Like the light railway—the British company that designed it transplanted to Hong Kong regardless of the fact that it is not suitable to the geographical conditions here."

Would China force Hong Kong into the shadows? Despite his emphasis on rational analysis, like others facing their uncertain future, Ong understandably had mixed views about Mainland politics. He put forth one position, and then immediately modified it. While he accepted the direction of change, he lacked complete confidence in China's future, foreseeing that China, facing many paths, might not take the right one.

The Ongs began leisurely explorations of China's outer regions to satisfy Mr. Ong's interest in history. These trips allowed them to reiterate the distinctiveness of the Hong Kong culture. "We've never thought of going north by train, although it will save money. We're different from northern people, who can adapt themselves to the dirty environment. Many of them smoke and shout, sleep, and spit all over. They're rude and less educated than Hong Kong people. You won't enjoy the trip if you go by train."

They toured places with Chinese populations—Shanghai, Beijing, Nanjing, Thailand, and Malaysia—never Western locations. Their trips made them aware of their identity as Chinese and Hong Kongers. Ong learned to distinguish the origins of Chinese in Hong Kong, discriminating between those from the island of Amoy (Xiamen) and the city of Fuzhou. Over the years he tracked the shifting origins of the Chinese in the neighborhoods he knew. In the contradictory mixture that was Hong Kong, he viewed foreign culture as Hong Kong's particular enrichment to the Chinese way of life.

Ong did not judge Hong Kong's future as a Special Administrative Region (SAR) with borrowed political standards. He accepted that China would never resemble Hong Kong or the West. He reflected that policies of democratization were "too theoretical" for Hong Kong, as were attempts to compare China and the West. Referring to Janet Salaff's homeland, he said,

> What is good in Canada are the social benefits. The Communists cannot make it in that area. Their government is poor; they cannot give citizens the benefits that they should have. Many countries have this problem. That's why when someone asks if communism or democracy is better, no one really knows. It's very hard to differentiate between the system and poverty. But again, the Communist countries have their own good points as well. In Canada, control or security might not be so good, whereas in a Communist country, it's the main point of concern. So we can't divide the types with a simple straight line. But communism has already failed.

Thoughts on Emigration

The Ongs were unlikely to become emigrants. While their social life pointed north over the border, at the same time, they felt themselves to be a solid part of Hong Kong life. Their life joined South China and Hong Kong.

The experiences of others further convinced Ong that he could never adjust to life in North America. The Ongs could not easily recall many emigrant kin. When pressed, they came up with a migration chain: Hau-Nung's second cousins had emigrated to Canada with disastrous consequences for their parents, who failed to establish themselves abroad and returned to Hong Kong; Mr. Ong recounted,

> The first to move abroad was Ah Sui's son who went to secondary school in Toronto twenty years ago. It was very easy to go then. After he graduated, he got married and didn't come back. They run a supermarket now. After their second son went to study, they invited Ah Sui to live there. But the older generation finds it hard to adjust. Their father tunes pianos. But he doesn't know English. He can't answer the phone. He has clients, but he has to bring all his tools to tune a piano and he doesn't drive. He doesn't know how to take a bus either. When his son is there, he drives him. But then, his son might not be there all the time.
>
> Then Ah Sui's mother joined the family in 1989. It was winter. One day she went out wearing the same shoes that she wears here in Hong Kong. She nearly got frostbite. They had to bring her to the hospital, where there are mostly foreigners. She only knew how to say bread and tea. So when she needed something or even wanted to phone her son, she could not. Eventually, both parents returned to Hong Kong.

The Ongs did not communicate often with these cousins and did not take them as models. Yet their experiences underlined what Ong learned about through his readings. The macroinstitutional setting abroad was unsuited to people like him. Already marginalized by Hong Kong's restructured economy, he realized that he would live worse abroad. His long tenure in his firm gave him higher status than he could get elsewhere. He told us, "I know a few people who come back, usually after a year, to buy products that they can't buy there. They always tell me how things are. They don't exaggerate nor minimize conditions." His chats and his reading further assured him that because of serious racial discrimination in North America, immigrants would not stand a chance. He pondered transnational migrants who came and went and astutely perceived that the successful overseas Chinese migrants were people with specific skills in demand. People like him were not among them. "Many people who have migrated to Canada have also come back to Hong Kong simply because they are jobless there. There are many specialists and clever people in Hong Kong, however, Canada cannot absorb them and make use of them. On the other hand, the Chinese government has noticed this and recently has invited many Hong Kong Chinese professionals from Canada who are in fact the emigrants from Hong Kong!"

The Ongs have adapted to the living environment in Hong Kong and prefer to make few changes. "Even after I retire I'd choose Hong Kong. Although the living standard in China is improving I would never retire there. I believe that Hong Kong is among the best places in the world," Ong said.

The Handover

It stormed on the evening of the British handover of power. As clouds threatened, people nervously quipped that the gods were protesting the event. For many, this day started in the late afternoon when, despite the steady rain, large crowds lined Upper Albert Road to see ex-governor Patten's limousine pull away from his official residence, a folded British flag on his lap. The throngs included the curious, out for the excitement of witnessing history, well-wishers, and protesters. Ong did not make that climb to the governor's mansion. To Ong, "'97" brought no anxiety. He remained on Queen's Road, waving a small SAR flag to emphasize that "Hong Kong has to exist within China."

He did not have high hopes for Hong Kong's future and in fact predicted that "the peak of the economic development of Hong Kong has already passed. Now it's going to slide. It will be worse in the future. Even if there wasn't the issue of 1997, the economic condition of Hong Kong is going to deteriorate. 1997 only exacerbates the condition. I read about such things."

"Will China catch up?" we asked him.

Ong acknowledged China's successes, saying, "From my frequent visits I realized China's dramatic economic improvement. People are better off and the living standard has risen, especially in the coastal areas, which will move faster than Hong Kong." He saw Shanghai, the most open to the outside, as the place most likely to catch up to and surpass Hong Kong. Then he immediately expressed doubts: "The biggest threat to Hong Kong is if China fails to develop the economy. If China is not successful this time, there will be no other chance; China will turn into a lawless state. Then it will divide into many separate provinces, like the scramble for concessions one hundred years ago, or like the classic *Romance of Three Kingdoms*."[1]

His severest criticism of China flowed from his own commitment to learning, underscored by the experiences of Pui-Pun, whose education was interrupted by political chaos. He worried that the population's low cultural level would affect its future. He predicted,

> Those people who are now ruling China are diligent and they do the best for China. Politics in China are under control now, but not in the long run. Civil society is chaotic. Many people in China know nothing but getting rich. On the one hand, those that have money, power, and social connections are obsessed with making money. On the other hand, those that have nothing tend to be risk takers. They ignore public order, which is the most important thing. When the youth don't have an opportunity to go to school or find work, what else can they do but make trouble? While the Hong Kong people are also obsessed with making money, it's not the same. They don't kill people over it like they do on the Mainland. If the people are one-dimensional like this, the country has no hope.

Despite these qualms, Ong believes in "one country, two systems" because Hong Kong could not survive by itself. His part in North-South trade showed him that "Hong Kong must depend on the Chinese Government socially and economically because Hong Kong cannot produce anything on its own. Most of the products come from other places, like China or overseas. The most the Chinese can do is make this place a special zone, which is what they are trying to do. This doesn't mean that Hong Kong will return back to the old times. They will still remain the same in terms of prosperity and system; the only difference probably [will be] the people handling the system."

Ong also predicted that the character of Hong Kong would be changed by reversion: "I'm sure there will be more corruption. In fact, I feel that Hong Kong might go back to the old Hong Kong [from] the '60s. Still, it won't be disorderly. I believe that Hong Kong will remain prosperous and stable. But there might be troubled times."

Paternalism

Yet even these concerns were overshadowed again by more pressing family worries. Over the years, Ong helped support his daughters and their families. As part of that support, he strongly believed he should guide their activities as much as possible. Giving money and continuously communicating advice were the strongest controls he had.

Ong had counseled Pui-Pun to have only one child so that she could return to work sooner: "Right now, you really need two people to work outside so that they can support the family. If at least both of them are working, then it is safer. If something goes wrong with one, the other one can still support the family." Later, on one of our visits in 1997, Ong informed us in an agitated voice that Pui-Pun had given birth to a second child.

He made an unusual request: Would Janet bring up this grandson in Canada? He said, "If you don't have time to care for him, maybe your friends are interested." Sending a child overseas for education was common enough, but this one was so young. We were also taken by surprise at his assumption that he had so much authority over his daughter that he could make this request on her behalf. This idea he put forward for consideration never took off, but it reflected the ease with which this concerned grandfather forged an East-West bridge, an extension between Hong Kong's traditional Sheung Wan and Toronto.

At one time, the Ongs had commuted often to Mr. Ong's hometown to visit Elder Daughter's family of four grown children and her grandchildren. But after reversion, he kept close contact by phone. Ong paid for the phone when installing a line was costly, sent money, and gave sizable gifts during festivals. He bought a house for the family, justifying the purchase by his hope to spend more time there after retirement. He also bought a van for his son-in-law, a driver, and helped out in emergencies. He was very involved in their lives, even at a distance, to the point where he controlled the details. For instance, when his grandson became sick with "something wrong with his kidney," he contacted his brother's daughter-in-law who worked in the local hospital to ensure that the lad got good treatment. "If you know somebody, the patient is well taken care of." He was proud that he could make that helpful connection. He could continue this cross-border oversight only by residing in Hong Kong and did not expect his eldest daughter's family to move to Hong Kong themselves.

They are better off in China. They know that it is getting harder to find a job in Hong Kong. There're so many people unemployed. Actually, those who came to Hong Kong ten years ago are better off than those who are arriving now [(Chiu et al. 2005)]. Before, even if you didn't speak English, you'd still find a job and have a good way of life. But right now, you must speak at least basic English to compete with others. That's why it's tough for them to find a job. Only the younger generation with good educational background can make it. But in China, the educational level is very bad. My nieces and nephews went to school just after the Cultural Revolution, and the education system was still a mess. Even those who graduated from universities in China can't make it in Hong Kong.

Ong always took his breadwinner role seriously, extending his duties past his wife to include his children's families. His responsibilities and continuous advice, he foresaw, would carry on.

Retirement and Their Older Years: 1998–2003

Family obligations kept Ong working long into his senior years. His earnings supported a modest living, on which he should have been able to retire. But the amount might not have covered his care for other family members whom he saw as his dependents. In 1998, as he approached seventy, we asked about his retirement plans. As his comments made clear, not only getting a job and working, but also retirement depended on personal relationships:

> Some stay on if the company thinks they can handle their jobs. My health's quite good, I can stay as long as I want, but I don't want to work too long. The pressure's too high; I don't want to make mistakes. But since my employer doesn't raise the topic, I just continue.
>
> The company buys us insurance and also sets aside a sum of money for our pensions from the profits earned. The amount depends on the annual gross income of the company. And now the system has improved to giving a pension with the amount ten times one's salary. A person that earns HKD 12,000 per month will get HKD 144,000 pension when he retires.

With economic relationships interwoven with personal ties, Ong's employer did not fire his staff outright, instead urging on them lighter and lighter work until they voluntarily left. But with a change in management that mutual commitment unraveled. So Ong finally retired in his midseventies, proud to have served the company, a desirable employee to the end.

Ong's retirement payment was barely two years' salary. It was supplemented by a monthly social assistance amount of HKD 700, an amount so low it was jokingly referred to as "fruit money," because it was barely enough to buy fresh produce. The Ongs would henceforth live closely dependent on their daughter and son-in-law.

After his retirement, Ong expected to keep a foot in both countries and be close to both daughters' families, so he did not consider moving to China.

"I guess I'll just have to go back and forth, because I also have a daughter here. I also need to help her look after her children." The meaningful life that he envisioned was one immersed in family ties, and this life could not be conducted outside the region.

Then their health worsened. Ong worried over Hau-Nung's cataracts, and his shortness of breath began to concern Hau-Nung. It would soon be time for their daughters to return the care that the parents had devoted to them.

In 2003, the sixth year of Hong Kong as SAR, on our last visit to the Ongs, we learned that they accepted the current government but remained pessimistic over Hong Kong's future. Ong told us,

> In my opinion, some of the people are competent. But if you depend on them to revitalize Hong Kong, the odds are slim that it will happen. It is not that this civil service is incompetent. It is that Tung Chee-hwa is incompetent. He doesn't have the talent. He is kind of patriarchal-minded. In the past when employers hired people, they did it with a patronizing mentality. It's the same now. Tung Chee-hwa still rules Hong Kong with this kind of mentality. That's not going to work. Because things change so fast, the people, and the technologies change really fast. He cannot keep up with them. He says everything's okay. But you must provide some results for people to see.

Hau-Nung commented on a more personal note: "When Tung Chee-hwa talks, he is so sluggish and never talks in a resolute manner." Ong added analytically, "His only merit is his integrity. But being a politician takes more than that. His business empire is not his achievement. It's his old man's. So he doesn't have a decisive character. He is good at execution but is not a charismatic leader. And his team doesn't have one single talented person."

Ong continued his theme that Hong Kong had passed its high point, saying, "Jobs—nobody can create them. This is a task beyond anyone's ability. It's because the economy has changed. I think that it is very difficult for Hong Kong to stay afloat. I have no confidence in Hong Kong's future." Despite this professed lack of belief that they could rely on Hong Kong's future, the request to send their grandchild abroad would prove to be the extent of the Ongs' consideration of emigration.

To make sense of the changes he witnessed, Ong articulated the formation and the dissolution of state boundaries as a long historical process. As he narrated his understanding of these developmental changes, the discourse seemed to empower him to accept and find meaning in reversion. Migration was never part of this meaning. Apart from having no close kin ties linking them to family abroad, their life was rooted in Hong Kong and China. "In each place, there will always be a time of adjustment. But you will get used to it. The difference is roots. Even if you have a good life abroad, your roots will always come back to China."

Summary: A Traditional Hong Kong Identity

Emigration was far from the Ongs' plans, as explained by reference to all three sets of institutions in our analytic framework. For one thing, the Ongs did not meet the strictures of foreign states. Their traditional occupations in the import-export of dried seafood did not correspond to job needs abroad. Although no one in Hong Kong remains untouched by the world economy, the Ongs felt the forces of globalism only indirectly. The wealth of local consumers and their ability to buy his company's luxury food products had the greatest effect on Ong's trade.

The Ongs were most directly affected by their social fields. Ong's supply channels, products, and ways of conducting business changed little over the decades. The networks of friends, family, and business relations are stable and rooted in the neighborhood and region. Tradition seems to rule economic life in this little pocket of Hong Kong. In addition, no one in their immediate circle of family and friends aimed to emigrate.

Finally, Ong's knowledge and understanding, his interest in history, and his rootedness in the area led him to see himself as a local person. The political changeover caused he and his wife no immediate concern. He concluded that the coming together of the two societies was a natural process. It was not just a return of Hong Kong to China, but a new stage for both.

Having lived in both southern China and Hong Kong, the Ongs have seen dramatic economic and institutional changes. They have witnessed poverty, war, migration, revolution, Colonial rule, reforms, and Hong Kong's development into a modern world city and reunification with China. The process affirmed Ong's participation in the local scene; he had few thoughts of moving away. The Ongs are the patriots of Hong Kong.

CHAPTER EIGHT

Brian Wan

The Extended Family Emigrates

Kinship figures in migration in many ways, and in the case of the Wans, whose family economy is organized around property, it takes an obligatory cast (Das Gupta 1999). The Wans' story highlights a Chinese business family who motored its members' migration projects on its behalf. Brian Wan's migration story was tightly linked to his extended family, who emigrated in phases to Toronto. The family firm and family migration were interwoven, since their Hong Kong store funded the migration project.

The migration chain began when one of Brian's three brothers went to Canada as an international student in 1969, became a citizen, and sponsored his parents in 1990. The parents then planned for Brian, his wife, Wai-Yin, and their three school-age children to follow them and expand their Canadian businesses. Kinship ties can disrupt as well as support migration plans; the Wans' emigration project was not smooth, with unspoken and broken commitments and contradictory interests (Gold 2005). Their story thus highlights the different migration experiences and expectations of women and men and of various generations in the family, in particular of one generation having a family firm.

Brian Wan: The Son Who Is Left Behind

The emigration of the Wan family started in a small way. What began as the senior Wan's desire to improve a child's chances through foreign education resulted in a migration chain. As the son slated to run the family business in Hong Kong, Brian's place in the family migration chain would be the most complicated.

Brian Wan, the youngest of four boys in the Wan household, was born in Hong Kong in 1957. When third son Tony was in Form 2, his second year of secondary school in 1969, his parents worried over his poor school performance and involvement with a youth gang in the neighborhood. Hearing that several classmates were going to secondary school in Toronto, the Wans let Tony go along. Brian recalled, "He was sent to Canada then because Father worried he'd become a 'teddy boy' in those bad social conditions in late '60s. Chinese parents are good at saving money so that wasn't a big problem."[1] Tony followed the global school network, naturalized, and eventually pulled his parents and some of his siblings along.

Father Wan had worked in the restaurant business from the age of thirteen and was growing too old to serve as a chef. Soon after Tony's departure, he used his industry networks to open a store that would supply local dim sum restaurants with imported frozen meat. At that time, his eldest son, Lok-Tai, was working at a sales outlet, while his second son, Bun-Tai, had followed Father's footsteps and become a cook. So Father Wan counted on the labor of his youngest son, Brian, who began working in the butchery part-time when he started Form 1, the first year in a respectable English-language secondary school. This store was to feature centrally in Brian's life, as both a symbol of future prospects and constraints on his dreams.

Brian's schooling would normally have given him an advantage because few youths had opted for the English-school stream at the time. His education, represented by status symbols such as speaking some English and his Anglo-Saxon name (which a teacher gave him), might have made it possible for him to pursue his ambitions. Brian had expected to enter the lower ranks of the civil service. However, since his brothers had gone on to do other things before Father Wan even opened the business, upon graduation in 1974, Brian became the son who could carry on the family business, regardless of where his personal aspirations might have led him.

Brian's situation was not unusual. Chinese business families commonly deploy family members as low-cost but reliable labor. Employing their children draws on emotional bonds, obligations felt, and the economic strategies of the family head (Wong 1988). For Brian, this meant that although he had dreamed of becoming a police officer, he was obligated to step into the role of chief worker at the family firm, which he did without any outward complaint. Once there, his whole life became bound up in the business—even meeting his future wife, Wai-Yin, who drove a truck making deliveries for the store.

As part of his obligations, Brian worked hard and rarely took holidays. There was no rest for him even on his wedding day in 1981. "I had to deliver the merchandise before dressing for the wedding ceremony. The next day, my father phoned at six in the morning to remind me to start work," he recounted with a chuckle.

Wai-Yin recalled this incident as well. It was one of many that led this even-tempered woman to harbor a grudge against her in-laws for treating Brian poorly. "He has a strong sense of family and doesn't utter a word of complaint. No matter how his parents scorn him, he doesn't argue. He only expresses dissatisfaction behind their backs."

Wai-Yin also bemoaned Brian's meager salary; he earned no more than other working-class employees at the time and was not entitled to profit-sharing. But Brian expected to share in the family fortunes in the future and appreciated other opportunities that flowed from his parents. For example, when his son Siu-Kei was born in 1983, they were allowed to live rent-free in an apartment owned by his parents in the neighborhood of the store. Though Wai-Yin had hoped to buy a subsidized flat of their own, the government-built apartments they were offered were located far from the meat shop. Brian recalled that moving to their own flat would have been the same as finding new employment: "If I'd left my father's business, he'd surely commit suicide." Against Wai-Yin's wishes, they moved into a 900–square-foot space on the second floor of a building built in the 1940s in To Kwa Wan, sharing it with the family of Lok-Tai, Brian's eldest brother. They divided it into separate sections to accommodate the two family groups, each having two tiny bedrooms, a small sitting area, a kitchen, and a bathroom.

Unfortunately for Wai-Yin, demanding family firms are greedy institutions that require a total commitment from the employee, ranging from extended hours to work expectations that mix exploitation with paternalism as a management strategy (Edwards 1979).[2] For Wai-Yin, who had labored most of her life in manual jobs and felt entitled to the right to enjoy tea and mahjong with her friends after a hard day, Brian's inability to protect his own time, and worse, to protect their relationship, was a source of great frustration. Though Wai-Yin was close to her large family in Sha Tin and embroidered her kinship obligations with emotional warmth and mutual support, these placed second to the bonds between a son and his parents in the joint family firm.

Wai-Yin grasped the degree to which Brian's identity was tied to his place within his birth family but defended her own rights. This largely meant resisting the role of compliant daughter-in-law that Mother Wan, as an older woman, hoped for (Dai 1991). Mother Wan was not keen on Wai-Yin's desire to work outside the home, feeling that such employment was at the expense of her service to the wider family, such as cleaning their rooms and doing other small personal services (Yi and Chien 2006). The contestation of her rights would lead to Wai-Yin's steadfast resistance to Brian's migration plan and her perverse delight in its scuttling.

Migration Becomes a Family Affair: 1983–91

In 1983, the next step in their extended family migration occurred. Brian's second brother Bun-Tai fell in love with a Chinese Mainlander, who had kin in Canada. With little expectation of getting legal permission to enter Hong Kong herself, she instead was able to reunite with her parents in Toronto. Bun-Tai followed as a tourist. The couple had a son who had a slight developmental disability and could not care for himself. Bun-Tai committed to stay and support his family. For a decade, he worked in Toronto as a cook in a Chinese restaurant, using fraudulent work papers. He said, "No, the photo didn't look like me. But it seems that Westerners can't tell us Chinese apart." Now, two brothers—Tony and Bun-Tai—were in Toronto.

As Hong Kong neared retrocession, the major settler nations extended the chance to immigrate to those Hong Kongers who could generate the necessary resources. Tony, who had become naturalized, seized the opportunity to capitalize on his parents' business success by inviting them to immigrate. His parents agreed and joined Tony 1990 through family reunification. Father Wan sold his own apartment on Broadcast Drive. He kept his meat shop running, leaving son Brian in Hong Kong to continue managing the butchery and help finance the move, intending to bring him later to Canada.

With the ongoing cash flow from his wholesale meat store and the returns from the sale of the flat, Father Wan made several investments in Toronto. Although they operated their wholesale meat business for years, the elder Wans were not optimistic about doing the same in Canada. Instead, they capitalized on the construction boom in Toronto's Chinese neighborhoods resulting from immigrants escaping retrocession. They opened a small wholesale building supply firm that also did minor renovations. Tony took charge, teaming up with two former Hong Kong classmates.

Father Wan made a business plan around the hardware store to allow the two sons still in Hong Kong (Brian and his eldest brother Lok-Tai) and their families to qualify for immigration status as business investors. They were to add value to Father Wan's Toronto hardware firm. In 1991, Eldest Brother and his family migrated and began to work there.

At the outset, Brian had every reason to expect a place in the family businesses in Canada. Emigration seemed natural. As a son in the family trade, Brian believed he would have a claim to the fruits of the family's labor. The wholesale meat business, in which he had labored for years, had been profitable and had provided funds for the family migration efforts. Further, because his brothers had already settled in Toronto, there were helping hands to assist Brian's family—which now included his son, Siu-Kei, and daughters Po-Kei (born in 1984) and Yuen-Kei (born in 1986)—adjust to the new environment. That was important to Brian. "In Toronto, even opening the water taps is different," he said.

Several events foreshadowed the end of Brian's migration plans. Wai-Yin told us how, on the eve of his parents' departure for Canada, his father accused Brian of mismanaging the business. Reluctant to start an argument before they left Hong Kong, Brian did not clarify matters. Instead, he solicitously asked his mother what food she wanted to eat on their last night. Wai-Yin had stomped out of the room, outraged at the lack of trust displayed by his father and at Brian's refusal to defend himself.

Next, in 1991, Father Wan suddenly sold the meat supply store without taking into account Brian's view that the selling price could be much higher. Father Wan used the capital to invest in small eateries in Toronto, with Tony again in charge. Wai-Yin suspected Tony's strong part in such family politics and intimated that Tony, eager to have the capital moved into Canada where he could access it, must have convinced Father Wan to sell.

But Brian's deference was fueled by his strong sense of obligation and pride in fulfilling Chinese kinship norms. He remained convinced that he, too, would continue as a partner and in the end would join the family enterprise in Canada.

Evolving Migration Plans: 1991–93

Brian had always lived "under the ancestors' shadow," to bring to mind Francis Hsu's apt phrase (Hsu 1971). In this case, it was his parents' shadow. Even after emigrating in 1990, his parents expected Brian to continue running the store as an employee and to transfer profits over to the enterprises in Toronto. The senior Wans also planned yearly trips to enjoy Hong Kong's milder winters and be cared for by Brian's family. So Brian and Wai-Yin's home environment continued to reflect his familial obligations and deep involvement in the extended-family economy. Because Brian and Wai-Yin's home would host the elderly parents on their transnational visits, Brian and Wai-Yin never fully made it their own. Though the departure of Elder Brother's family left Brian's family alone in the divided flat, Brian made no major renovations, keeping the two residences separate in order to provide space and privacy for his parents on their visits.

Brian did take the opportunity to paint the entire flat a mild green and install fluorescent lights to add brightness, but his family continued to reside only in their half—four hundred square feet for five people. Space constraints forced them to furnish their home in a practical, space-saving style. A set of wardrobe closets served as a wall to separate Brian and Wai-Yin's bedroom from their children's. The three children shared one room, which Brian insisted was their choice—but it appeared that he was loath to move into his parents' side. In the dining room, each child had a writing desk with little cupboards on the top. Brian's collection of seven hundred miniature liquor bottles (no duplicates), which he started assembling as a teenager and knew by heart, was the special touch that made it home.

Wai-Yin, a frank woman used to speaking her mind, showed limited enthusiasm at having to care for—indeed, in her view, to respond to every whim of—her in-laws on their transnational visits. The experience also showed her what life would be like if Brian joined the family enterprises in Toronto where she would be under the constant scrutiny of her husband's family. She found the thought chilling, especially in contrast to the caring relationships she had with her own family. Hence when Brian's father sold the wholesale meat supply store, Wai-Yin was understandably concerned that without the need for Brian to maintain the family business in Hong Kong, they would surely be summoned to Canada. Their own part in the migration chain was about to materialize.

Instead of feeling cast adrift, Brian was both excited at the fruition of his migration plans and aware that for the first time in his life, he had the opportunity to look for work outside the family firm. While waiting for news of the next steps, he said, "I can do whatever I want and have no limitations."

Trying something different, Brian drove a taxi, then a large goods truck for the same television station that Uncle Chou (chapter 4) had driven for. His job turned into a time-consuming position, but he was used to having work take over his life. Wai-Yin complained, "The studio doesn't know the schedule until that day. He just calls home if he can't make it for dinner. Sometimes if he works late, he will stay at the studio, sleep there, and start working again the next day. And his salary is just HKD 6,000." Wai-Yin grumbled, without any effect, that Brian lived for his work. This time, however, he was not working for the extended family. His job took his time but not his undivided loyalty.

Brian also wanted to take the test to drive container trucks. "I've a friend that does it. It's a good job, because of the expansion of Hong Kong as an entrepôt. But it's hard to get a license. I tried once but didn't pass the parking part. I've already spent HKD 10,000 on lessons." He did not fear that the truck driving would be a heavier workload than his present job: "There's no such word as 'difficult' in my dictionary. Work! Work! Work—so as to make more money. Hard work is nothing to me!"

When he finally passed the test, he found he did not have enough personal connections to enter the field, in addition to being wary of cross-border driving. Wai-Yin, hearing about other cross-border drivers being charged with a range of infringements, pleaded with Brian not to attempt it. "You need to drive across the border to China. When you've had traffic accidents, you'd be in trouble. Nothing can help but to pay a HKD 50,000 bribe to those officials. People in the mainland are very troublesome." Brian agreed, saying "This is called 'out of risks come wealth and fortune.'"[3] However, being risk averse, he pulled out—tangles with the Chinese authorities were not worth the risk.

Scant Political Views

The Wans remained unfazed by retrocession. They were not beset by anxieties over changes to familiar social institutions or loss of social status under a new regime. As small-shop owners, their vision was fixed to the neighborhood. The elders had not passed on any sharp recollections of Communist excesses, and neither Brian nor Wai-Yin was sufficiently interested in politics for the reversion to have much of an effect on their plans. Instead, family determined the Wans' future as emigrants.

Although both were Hong Kong-born, the couple felt little patriotism and did not fight to preserve their Hong Kong identity. At the same time, like many we met, Brian had little confidence in China and was not sentimental about leaving Hong Kong. A man who spoke his mind (although, importantly, never to his parents), Brian stressed that personal freedom is important: "Without a lot of money, we can still live. The most important thing is freedom of speech and a carefree attitude. Hong Kong people are accustomed to speak freely. If you do not like the boss, you can yell at him. But in China, you cannot. You may commit a political error without any knowledge of doing it." He guessed that after the transition to Chinese hegemony, the civil service would suffer and in this way "disorder would appear." He said, "China does not have a real legal system at present. Although some people say that China is changing, if she changes, then I might come back from abroad. But let's see her change first."

Wai-Yin's views of a future in Hong Kong were fatalistic; given the impossibility of changing China, it was ridiculous to even try. She thought that much of the fear around retrocession was unwarranted. To demonstrate her point, she picked concrete examples, which she made to seem absurd, and punctuated her comments with peals of laughter: "Sometimes I wonder, why are people afraid to live here? There're so many people, hundreds of thousands. Why would any one person be afraid? Even thinking they'd punish us by sending us to the countryside is ridiculous; there's no farm here!"

When asked whether seeing the 1989 Tiananmen massacre on TV had frightened her, she responded, "Hey, it doesn't matter. Life is just the same, it passes. You can choose not to go out to the street. No one forces you to go out." About the troops firing on students? "I watched all night. It is like playing drama. It seemed rather inhumane, but it was real." When pressed, she admitted, "We are not the type to do politics. Smoothly and stably you live on. Let it be. People can die when crossing the road. It's meaningless to protest such kind of things. If you want to fight against them, you cannot win."

Since concerns over Hong Kong's future under China were not about to convince Wai-Yin of the benefits of moving, to ease the tensions arising from his emigration plans, Brian appealed to her sense of duty to her children. "He urges me to think about the children. He always says that 'the air is better, it's more quiet and spacious there. It's better for them.'" Thinking of the circumstances that led to his brother Tony's emigration, Brian said, "Children there are more pure and don't so easily turn bad. Hong Kong television screens Japanese cartoons which are too violent for the children; Canada has fewer of them. Also, the academic study there is easier, and the children can learn more English."

In the end, though, Wai-Yin could not think of any reason, political or otherwise, that would be worth leaving for. As a woman whose important ties were in her immediate area, emigration had never been a goal for her. In particular, family-dependent emigration was the last thing she wanted. Asked whether she would have wanted to emigrate even if Brian had not, she firmly replied, "No," and insisted, "If you have a day's life, just live it. Especially since it's not bad in Hong Kong. If you can work and can eat, let it be. I do not know English and other things. But Brian really wants to go."

More space, fresh air, and his children's education did figure in Brian's emigration plans. And yet his primary motivation was to rejoin his extended family, even to the point of overriding his wife's sentiments. Despite her protests, in reality Wai-Yin had little choice, tied as she was to her husband's future.

Tied Migration

Migration is a boon for those third-world women who cannot access opportunities to earn money at home (Foner 1986; Gabaccia 1994; Grasmuck and Pessar 1991). In contrast, in newly industrial Asia, women were the foundation of the manufacturing labor force (Salaff 1981; Pun 2005). Working-class women lose a lot by migrating to North America where jobs are harder to come by. Thus, although Wai-Yin's kin ties pulled her along in the family migration project, she was aware of the opportunities she would forego in earnings, as well as her personal freedom.

Although the term "reluctant emigrant" usually refers to those in the affluent middle class, Wai-Yin was just as much a reluctant emigrant as those we met in chapters 3 and 5. Working-class people like Wai-Yin had their own reasons for holding back from migration. With only primary 4 schooling, Wai-Yin had never studied English and had no formal credentials. Anyone could do the work she did; her ability to land a job and move freely from one position to another stemmed entirely from local contacts. Wai-Yin's active world in Hong Kong was bound by her kin circles and her To Kwa Wan neighborhood friendship networks. She changed jobs when she was unsatisfied and found new openings through her brother, husband, and other locals she knew. Whereas she had little trouble finding jobs in Hong Kong, Wai-Yin feared that she would not easily be able to rebuild these contacts abroad.

Kinship structures nuanced the Wans' tied migration with the result that the nature of obligation and reward that bound Brian and Wai-Yin differed greatly. Brian was the direct descendant of the patriliny and had contributed greatly to his extended family's economy. Though he did not phrase it in terms of rewards because he felt filial gratification from his compliance to the family's plans, he nonetheless hoped that his returns would finally come in the form of emigration. In contrast, as his wife, Wai-Yin had no claims to profits from the firm. Instead, she was tied to her husband who was tied to his parents' fate. Wai-Yin's rootedness in her local networks was as important to her ability to move around in society as was Brian's tie to his family. Both were rooted, but where Brian's ties might take him elsewhere, Wai-Yin's would have kept her in place. In the end, however, Brian's family ties let him down, dealing him out of family life in Canada.

Changing Plans: 1992–93

Still convinced of his place in Canada, Brian entered Toronto in early 1992 on a tourist visa to learn the ropes in the building-supply firm. His visit was only temporary, and he left behind his wife and children, although they came briefly to look around. By reading, he mastered enough to serve the customers knowledgeably. He did not have a sense of "second-class citizenship" (said in English punctuated by a proud laugh at his mastery of the idiom). Although this utterance showed his ability to speak colloquially, he admitted that communication was a problem. He did not consider this a serious issue, however, because the family had settled into an area where he could get by easily speaking only Cantonese. "Learning more English," he joked, "is so I can communicate with my children in the future."

On his return to Hong Kong in late 1992, Brian eagerly planned for the move, attending evening classes in English and Mandarin and studying industrial design in order to extend the family building-supply business. He even paid CAD 3,000 to consult a Canadian lawyer specializing in business immigration. However, after visiting Brian in Toronto, Wai-Yin became even more reluctant to emigrate. In a joint family all brothers are presumed equal but Wai-Yin uncomfortably noted her in-laws' favoritism. Along with the building-supply company, Father Wan had purchased houses in Scarborough with the revenues from the sale of the meat supply shop. Although nominally these properties were his, Father Wan did not actively work, because his connections and his expertise were lost in the foreign country. Instead, he had assigned the investment decisions and management to Tony. Referring to this situation, Wai-Yin told us, "The houses in Canada are now in the title of Third Son. Tony acts very smart, and even his wife looks like a high-class woman. Show offs. I also dislike how they treat Eldest Brother-in-Law Lok-Tai in the building-supplies company." She worried about Brian's place within the family hierarchy as well as her own.

Wai-Yin feared that she might not be able to work there and, because she had the lowest education of all the daughters-in-law, she anticipated having to take over the housework in Canada. "One of my friends has immigrated there but could not find any job. She had nothing to do but to wander around in snooker clubs and sometimes work part time. That kind of life seems boring and meaningless. The economy is bad in Canada—the living environment is better than in Hong Kong. Canada's too quiet. I found it very boring. I was almost bored to death." She joked, "My husband said if I couldn't find a driving job that his parents' house is very big and I'd use a lot of time to clean it." More seriously she added, "I'll worry when it really happens."

Wai-Yin knew what she could expect from life in Canada since she took care of Brian's parents when they returned to Hong Kong several times a year. Though Mother Wan had gradually begun to do more of her own housework, her irascible presence was apparent in her constantly voiced criticisms of her working daughter-in-law. She was especially unsupportive of Wai-Yin's homemaking style, chastising Wai-Yin for earning and spending without a plan or savings, for not being frugal as shopkeepers' wives are reputed to be. Their intertwined, multiplex roles gave Wai-Yin little freedom of decision making, especially when in the same city. Wai-Yin defended herself, commenting on Brian's low income and the support of her own family, saying,

> They always say that we spend a lot of money. I got really very mad. I knew they meant me. So what? That's my own money. But who knows whether it is my money, my husband's, or my own sister's? My sister and mother also buy things for our children. All my children's clothes are from my sisters. If they don't want a certain item, they usually give it to me. My husband cannot even give me enough to support the family. His mother also complains that I never shop around before I buy anything. How much can you save if you shop around? What about the time that you spend, the bus fares and so on?

More important for Wan-Yin than taking the time to shop for the best price was her need to juggle the responsibilities of her hectic family life. Mother Wan had never helped Wai-Yin out at home. Wai-Yin's own mother had made it easier for her. When the children were young, she cared for them off and on. Now she suffered from cataracts and could no longer help out. Wai-Yin tried to do it all, relying on shift work to get it done (Presser 2003).

After her night shift, she'd return home at dawn to briefly rest, cook lunch and dinner, and then take the children to school. "If I've the night shift, I'll do it all in the morning. I prepare the dinner beforehand; they'll heat it up themselves." The Hong Kong school system does not take into account parents' schedules when they organize school sessions, making it hard for working parents to handle child-rearing responsibilities. The Wans' son and youngest daughter attended the morning session at school and their middle daughter attended the afternoon session.

For a while, overwhelmed with the constant shuffling between work, home, and school, Wan-Yin quit her outside jobs. But after this short period of family devotion, "I came close to bearing it no more. It's very boring when I don't have a job. Maybe it is because I am used to working outside. I feel like a 'donkey woman,' spending the whole day washing, cleaning, tidying. Like losing a spirit." This experience made her even more resolute in her need for paid employment. She grew increasingly concerned about her likely inability to get a job after immigrating to Canada and the nature of her ties to the extended family.

Living in Hong Kong while Brian's parents lived abroad gave Wai-Yin some respite from their pressures on her. Anticipating her parents-in-laws' demands on her when they returned for visits, one summer, Brian and Wai-Yin hired Ah Si, an Indonesian maid—a fairly common practice. With little government-assisted child care or other family supports, working women, even those from the lower middle class, put their homemaking burdens on women from poorer countries in the region. The servants expect to have their own room, but often in the tiny apartments of the lower middle class they have to squeeze in with the children, or even worse, into spaces under tables (Constable 1997).

In the Wan household, although Ah Si slept in the second apartment, it was not hers, and the other family members expanded freely into it. Her salary at HKD 1,800 was less than half the government-set minimum wage for servants. Brian explained that Indonesians are cheaper because they can speak neither Cantonese nor English. To justify Ah Si's low wages, Brian downplayed her help, emphasizing how they were supporting her. They did not send her outside the home to shop, ostensibly because she did not speak Cantonese. In reality, they were trying to seclude Ah Si from other servants who might inform her of her rights. They thought she did not know that her wages were below par.

Wai-Yin thought Ah Si was a great help. She herself didn't mind cooking but washing dishes deprived her of the time to relax after dinner, the time of the day that she enjoyed most. Wai-Yin confessed that Brian no longer helped her with any housework now that he could enjoy his male privileges at home. The servant performed menial personal tasks, such as cutting his nails. She also peeled grapes for him, something Wai-Yin no longer had to do. But the main purpose of hiring Ah Si was to emancipate Wai-Yin from serving her mother-in-law when she visited from Canada. Wai-Yin looked forward to playing mahjong when her mother-in-law returned in December because Ah Si would take care of her.

Ah Si began to protest her low wages. Labor movement organizations have played a role in domestic labor politics since the early 1980s, and it was not hard for her to learn about her rights (Ford 2004). When they visited Wai-Yin's nephew's home, Ah Si encouraged his servant to request higher wages: "My nephew was very angry and had to add HKD 2,000 to her original wage in order to keep her. There's no protection to the employer!" snorted Brian. Then Ah Si asked for a termination of her contract. The Wans were unable to find some of their petty cash, and attributed the loss to Ah Si. Brian announced angrily,

> Ah Si has gone. Stolen our money. The red packet money of my son's and daughter's and my own money is missing. I have no idea what the total amount might be. We always suspected that we had lost some money but we thought it was only that we had forgotten how we spent it. But I won ten HKD 100 notes from playing mahjong and paid some attention to them and later found some missing. Even though she broke the contract, we still need to buy her air

ticket home. What will happen if we do not pay the air ticket? A lot of trouble. Those employment agents are fierce! I'd rather pay her off.

At that point it looked like Wai-Yin would be recruited back into home-making tasks both in Hong Kong and Toronto. As it turned out, Wai-Yin needn't have worried. After a set of somewhat unclear family decisions, Brian's emigration plans began to unravel.

Third Brother Tony, the first Canadian in the family and in charge of the immigration procedures, wanted to deal Brian out of the Toronto family businesses. There were problems with the government over their inadequate tax records (or even payments). The building-supply business had suffered setbacks with the downturn in Toronto's housing market in the early 1990s. Wai-Yin reported that Tony had cut Eldest Brother Lok-Tai's wages by a third. "Before, Tony told my husband that we could complete the procedures in November 1992. But it's now January 1993. Then he said that due to taxation problems, it could not be finished. There is no way but to wait. If it fails, let it be."

With emigration plans on hold, Brian tried to raise capital outside of the family for business migration. When his second brother Bun-Tai became estranged from his partner and returned to Hong Kong in 1993, the two brothers launched petty businesses. First, they opened two illegal video parlors. One small shop in an arcade had, as a cover, signed photos of television stars for sale, which Brian acquired from performers he drove for the station. Brian took us on a tour of the shop. A large ancestor shrine at the doorway blocked the view to the rear where the video games were found. There were a number of video games that entailed making wagers. The players bet on the horse-racing machine, and if they won, a crudely fashioned drawer popped open with money. Brian acknowledged the sub-terfuge: "That's illegal; it's gambling." Overall, this shop did not perform well. When the government more strictly prohibited students from going to video game centers, repeated police visits forced Brian to close it down.

The two brothers then used their vans to move goods such as bibles, computer supplies, and University of Hong Kong students' belongings; this became their second business. However, their profit was reduced by frequent parking tickets while delivering the goods. Brian complained, "If you get caught, it's very expensive. One day I had to pay HKD 700, caught three times! Once, my brother was trying to remove some cargo from the van and a policeman passed by. Issued a ticket, didn't even warn him; isn't this too much? At least if he tells you to leave, then you don't feel bad about it. Bun-Tai was really furious and even scolded the officer."

The businesses Brian set up required no professional or technical knowledge, only time. Wai-Yin insisted, "He's a workaholic. He can work from six in the morning to three in the morning and only rest for a couple of hours. He's willing to work for more than eighteen hours a day." In spite of his work ethic, Brian had difficulty establishing a business. His business performance was less impressive than his spirit. He blamed his failure on poor timing: "I opened the video store after the craze had peaked."

In late 1993, a final paternal blow ended Brian's migration project. Father Wan announced new family plans for Brian. Despite Brian's efforts to secure enough capital to migrate independently of his family, Father Wan told him that since he and his wife wanted to return home for several months a year, they needed Brian and Wai-Yin to remain in Hong Kong. Brian accepted that he'd receive no support from his family to pursue his own migration and, more importantly, that maintaining his obligations would mean remaining in Hong Kong. At this point, Brian told us resignedly, "It doesn't matter whether we emigrate or not." Brian and Wai-Yin still followed the dictates of Brian's parents despite the physical distance. Their emigration project had come to a halt.

Reframing Themselves As Nonimmigrants

Their views of themselves as future immigrants having ended, Brian and Wai-Yin reaffirmed their deep roots in Hong Kong. When the authors visited them in 1994, Wai-Yin had left all traces of anxiety over their family's future behind her. She had begun working as a driver for a fish market, a job that she acquired through local connections—one of her younger brothers was a driver at the Lo Sang market and learned that his coworker wanted to quit and was looking for a replacement. Wai-Yin was invited to tea to meet him. She happily reported, "It's a good job, fewer hours, more money, HKD 8,000, and more benefits—lunch and a snack." At the end of her day, she went to the teahouse with her pals or helped Brian transport goods for his sideline business.

During our visit, we joined Wai-Yin, waking up at sunrise in order to drive to the Yuen Long wholesale fish market pier, where fishermen and fisherwomen bring their catch from China. This was her beat, and she was clearly at home here in the fast-moving auctionlike world of fish vending, where knowledge of the fish, the future clientele, and the trustworthiness of the fishermen to sell unadulterated products all come together. We grabbed a quick breakfast of "yin-yang tea," a Hong Kong East-West mixture of strong English tea and coffee lightened with condensed milk (the tea's name is a play on words for mixing dark and light, male and female elements) in her neighborhood Lo Sang market in To Kwa Wan. We then stopped to pick up the cargo truck belonging to Wai-Yin's employer, a local fishmonger, whose whole family was in the fish trade. Wai-Yin climbed deftly up into the truck's cab. Two of her boss's sons loaded the back with metal containers filled with salt water and large wicker baskets to carry the fish they would purchase. They came along to help choose the fish to sell that day. Two more brothers stayed behind to tend the stall, one to sell, the other to scale fish for the customer.

The Yuen Long wholesale fish market was in the distant New Territories in Northwest Hong Kong. By seven-thirty in the morning the bustle was overwhelming to the outsider, but Wai-Yin knew what to do. Men and women from one Mainland company wore matching light-green T-shirts and green pants. Protected by rubber boots and a clear plastic outer garment over their cloth pants, they poured the catch from their boats with buckets into large aerated tanks on both sides of the street adjacent to the pier, creating an avenue of flopping fish. Fish sellers shouted out the prices of their wares using hand-held loudspeakers. An elderly man wheeled over a block of ice, divided it with a pick, and put it in the tanks in the truck Wai-Yin drove. Her two youthful helpers attached their aerated hoses to these tanks and wheeled their wicker carts on a dolly to the pier to choose their purchases. They scooped fish into their baskets and transferred them into the tubs filled with salt water in the truck. This particular morning they bought shrimp, inexpensive mullet, and mudfish. The boys said that because the income of the market customers is limited, anything more expensive would not sell: "From talking with them and being there a long time, we know what Lo Sang people buy."

With the wares loaded, Wai-Yin drove us all back to Kowloon to discharge her cargo. Her day's work done before noon, she went to the nearby tea house for a quick mahjong game with her neighbors. Like her job, mahjong and "yum cha" (morning tea) at the tea house were all neighborhood pursuits, underscoring the importance of the local place to this woman. It was clear that Wai-Yin enjoyed working not just because of the salary, but because she found it interesting. She used neighboring relations and had a lot of local knowledge. Finding work like this in Canada was unlikely.

Part of a working woman's identity was that she also took care of her family. Wai-Yin's class-based views of mothering balanced the nuances of choice and constraint (Duncan 2005). She defended the relevance of her working for the lives of her children, saying, "Work allows one to have greater exposure, meet more friends, and become livelier; it is good for the children too. If I work, my children can be more independent; they will concentrate better on their work."

Unlike middle-class mothers we met, who think their children will do better if they anticipate and monitor their activities (Devine 2004), Wai-Yin criticized mothers who hover around their children. After all, she did not have the time. Her best friend, a primary schoolmate, took on every aspect of her children's care. Wai-Yin felt this weakened the children. Wai-Yin encouraged her children use the neighborhood resources, for example to eat out to save her time. "Too much protection will only spoil the child. I let my kids buy food at street stalls. My friend said street food was dirty. But see how strong and fat my daughter and my son are. When I stayed at home that time, they became very dependent. They asked me to cook snacks, get drinks, simply treated me as a maid!"

Whereas many working-class mothers studied elsewhere feared for their children's safety, to the extent that they did not go out to work or in other ways curtailed the children's freedom, to Wai-Yin, To Kwa Wan was their familiar neighborhood (Dodson 2007). It mainly houses traditional shops and the Lo Sang wet-food market with its live chickens and fish. All around, open-air Chinese shops spread their goods on makeshift counters. Street stall owners sell cooked food to street diners, changing offerings with the hour of the day and season. In the morning the breakfasters sup congee (rice porridge); in the evening, chicken and rice bake in clay pots over traditional charcoal or gas hot plates. Wai-Yin's children, however, began to feel the pull of McDonald's and other air-conditioned chains that are encroaching on their neighborhood with their long menus of food from the East and West.

Eventually, the children's buying food in street stalls became a family issue. Brian confessed, "Our son had digestive problems. He always eats meals from McDonald's." Their son added his protests, "It's those damn instant noodles. It's because she [gesturing at Wai-Yin] doesn't cook meals." At this point, his sister Po-Kei muttered her agreement at Wai-Yin's motherly shortcomings. Brian took his wife's part saying, "You can always buy a lunch box outside or you can cook by yourself." Embarrassed, Wai-Yin excused herself: "I cook, but they don't eat it." The son retorted, "It's too hot in here!" To which Wai-Yin snapped: "Exactly. They said it's too stuffy here at home. They like eating in cafes. Every time, HKD 10 each. So it's HKD 60 a day for two meals. They think that a fried egg outside tastes much better that what's cooked at home. Very frustrating!"

Such an exchange was fairly typical of the Wans' permissive parenting style, which was not the traditional authoritarian approach of earlier generations, nor was it the highly planned approach to parenting of the middle class we met. We queried Wai-Yin, "How can your relationship be so easygoing? You don't insist on respect or anything like that?" Wai-Yin: "No such thing for this generation. We're close. You can't be strict; they're tougher than you!" But when it came to the larger issue of their children's school performance, their lenient attitude gave the impression that they had resigned themselves to failure. They were mainly relieved that the children were obedient and did not "go bad."

Although these were not academically or professionally aspiring folk, the Wans did feel the pressure for their children to get through school with good results. They were aware that as parents they affected their children's performance but they did not know what to do about it. And the measures they took did not bring about the desired results.

When we first met them in the early 1990s, two of the three Wan children had middling results in school. Siu-Kei, the eldest son, was struggling to enter junior secondary school, and youngest daughter, Yuen-Kei, was getting low grades in primary school. By the mid-'90s, it was becoming apparent to their parents that these two children might not attend a good secondary school or go to college. Their attitude toward schooling exhibited the culture and behavior of working-class parents, although they had slightly more resources than average.

There is much academic debate over why working-class children, whether in North America or Hong Kong, often have lower school performance than middle-class children and what parents from diverse backgrounds do to help their children achieve. Some scholars note that there are two family cultures. The school and family institutional cultures mesh seamlessly for the middle class while fitting poorly for the working class who do not provide a home culture that corresponds to what is valued at school (Lam 2005; Lareau 2003; Coleman 1988). These writers locate class differences in parents' reasoning about their children's abilities (Devine 2004).

Others put it more simply: it's not their culture. With less money and less time, working-class parents cannot help their children with school-related tasks (Chin and Phillips 2004). In Hong Kong, this debate is intensified by the British Colonial heritage, the foreign tongue, and the complex school allocation system that streams children into schools of different quality and "bands" within schools largely based on testing at an early age. The Hong Kong educational system measures students by the narrow standard of rote learning, penalizing those who perform poorly.

The Wans mirrored several aspects of the debate. They did not greatly value the written word that is central to the culture of schooling. Their home environment did not contain books or magazines; and as they went about their affairs, there was little discussion of the newsworthy topics of the day—signifying to their children that what the school promotes holds little value in the parents' daily lives. When asked if her children were interested in reading books, Wai-Yin replied, "Yes, but books are very expensive. That's why I don't buy them, and even so, they may not like the books that I buy. So usually I will just borrow from my relatives. The kids are only good at playing games, not their studies. I don't force them. If they like to do something, I just let them do it. I don't put pressure on them; they're still very young." We noted that neither Brian nor Wan-Yin did much personally to help their children with school-related tasks. As Wan-Yin told us, "I'm not qualified, and Brian doesn't have the time." They generally accepted their children's poor results, waiting to intervene when they saw that the children were really in trouble.

When young, their children went to poorly rated primary schools not far from where they lived. When son Siu-Kei was in Primary 6 and it was time to enter secondary school, Brian and Wai-Yin did not want him to choose the technical-school stream, thinking it was lower in standard. Perhaps because they expected the Canadian school system to reshape their children's academic paths, they confronted their children's schooling on the eve of important placement exams—later than middle-class parents did. With Canada out of the picture, the Wans blindly hoped that placement in a better school would be the solution.

With its focus on test scores, the Hong Kong education system co-opts parents into spending extra time and money on tutoring, cramming as much as possible into their children in a short time. All around them, where education was a consumption item, topping up the children's schooling was big business. Working-class parents could not escape the panic engendered by the competition for better schools. Even those inattentive to their children's homework or unable to pay much for tuition would take on what should have been the school's burden. In their worry, the Wans, too, tried to influence their children's ability to get higher grades on exam scores by hiring others to give private tuition at considerable sums. Nearing graduation from primary school, the two eldest got two hours of tutoring every day, at a fairly steep price: HKD 900 per child every month.

In contrast, the middle class (for example, the Luks in chapter 3, and the Gungs in chapter 6) developed study plans ahead of time to give the children a feeling that they could gain control over their schoolwork. Interestingly, these two families did not hire tutors, reasoning that by the time a tutor was needed, it was too late. The parents did the work themselves, mostly from an early age.

To Wai-Yin, the children's performance was inscribed in their personalities: "The girls are very poor in math and Chinese, even though they have private tuition. If they have some Chinese stories to read, they really find it difficult. They don't even ask questions anymore. I don't know why. Maybe it runs in the family. They just don't take it seriously. They don't listen to the teachers at all. So I think it is just their attitude. They are very stubborn." Wai-Yin summarized her view of the problem with her conjecture that poor results simply "run in the family," and gave up (Chan 2003).

Putting more stock in the influence of children's innate traits on their school performance than on the practice of teaching is worlds apart from the views held by the Luks and Gungs who actively shaped their daughters' learning process (Devine 2004; Lareau 2003). While the Wans understood the importance of education and were willing to spend money on it, they regarded educational excellence as something "inborn" and appeared helpless to improve their children's performances in Hong Kong. They felt unable to mentor their children and generally left them on their own.

Eventually, Siu-Kei got into an academically respectable school where he was busy at extracurricular activities. His grades remained low, however, and his parents' worries did not end. Older daughter Po-Kei was the best student of the three. She had been in an elite class for several years and ranked in the top quarter of her class of over forty pupils. Nevertheless, as she approached her school exams, Brian informed us in a frustrated tone, "She can't remember the formula of calculating the areas of square, triangle. But she tells me, 'You can't study maths for an exam. You should work hard on maths instead. If you don't understand something, you can't follow any further. It's like a house of cards, if the foundation is wobbly, all will fall.'"

Although Po-Kei had to wrestle with her exam scores, she presented the issue in ways suggesting that she understood education as a process. She took her exams in English and even though her comprehension and expression were limited, she apparently did all right. She selected a well-known convent school as her high school. Wai-Yin agreed to the choice, preferring single-sex to coeducational schools for Po-Kei, who she thought of as tomboyish. Again the vocabulary of innate qualities, in this case gender, percolated through her reasoning: "A girls' school may make Po-Kei more ladylike."

The school performance of Yuen-Kei, the youngest daughter, was the worst. She did not like studying and fell asleep in the middle of doing her homework. "Yuen-Kei can't follow. She's lazy." Wai-Yin dubbed her a "Filipino maid," someone who preferred doing housework to homework, saying, "She helps me a lot, even carrying things." Brian became so worried about Yuen-Kei that each day, no matter how tired he was, he found time to check that she had finished her schoolwork.

Computers were another means to improve the Wan children's results.

Working-class parents were not certain how machines would help their children get better grades. They were outside the debates in parenting magazines and books over computers' role in stimulating children's reasoning capacities. They only knew the children had to have a computer, even if they shared it. For years, Brian had tried to make deals through friends for a cheap machine, although he could not make them function. In 1996, after Siu-Kei entered secondary school, Brian told us, "Computers? Siu-Kei's school doesn't have one; we don't own one either. So he doesn't know them. I want to buy a computer, but I am confused about which one is good. I'm too old to learn this, but I did spend two weeks learning it a few years ago. I got rewarded for perfect attendance!" They finally bought a computer before Siu-Kei's exams, but Wai-Yin complained, "I don't know whether or not he knows how to use the computer; I just see him playing games all the time."

The Wans clearly tried and yet began on an uneven playing field when compared with middle-class families. However, their family business background gave them more opportunities than most blue-collar workers, and this finally became an out.

The Next Stage in the Wans' Family Emigration

Transnational moves are often time stamped. Exits and returns are associated with the life cycle, and the exits are linked to the institutions that manage these passages (Elder 1974; Ley and Kobayashi 2005). In the case of the Wans, the oldest and youngest family members continued transnational moves in concert with their ages. In 1996, during their summer holidays, the Wans' two daughters made their first trip to visit kin in Toronto. Afterwards, Brian remarked, "They loved Canada because most of the time they just played around. Yuen-Kei is really very lazy. But she wants to study in Canada. I say, 'Go ahead then!'"

In 2001, having given up on Yuen-Kei's abilities to pass in Hong Kong schools, they sent her abroad, the final option for desperate parents with resources. This institutionalized escape hatch defuses the pressure for local school reform, playing on parents' desires to give their children the best credentials—if not the best education—they can afford. Still a student, Yuen-Kei is poised to become the next in the Wan migration chain.

In a strange twist of fate, Brian's daughter was finally making a transnational voyage when, after over ten years in Canada, his extended family was making its way back—with Mother Wan leading the way. Caring for Brian's mentally challenged nephew was a factor. Brian's second brother,

Bun-Tai, had been in and out of Hong Kong frequently over the years looking for well-paying work and he now decided to bring his son back to live in Hong Kong without the boy's mother. With her dependent grandson in her charge, Mother Wan had high priority for a subsidized government flat. In a move that pleased Wai-Yin, they lived apart from Brian's family. Father Wan, Eldest Brother Lok-Tai, Tony, and their families remain in Toronto.

Summary: Limits to Working Class-Tied Family Migration

Brian Wan's migration story is tightly linked to his extended family who had emigrated to Canada to pursue global school and family networks. But petty business people who depend on their kin to migrate may find that family networks are not always reliable migration channels.

Kinship obligations are strongest where there is joint property to manage. Where the patrikin make migration decisions to fit the needs of the business, the senior male can demand compliance with these plans and can overlook the interests of other family members. As the only son who had been working in his parents' wholesale meat store, Brian was tied to his extended family's transnational migration plans and Wai-Yin, as Brian's wife, was also tied. Decisions surrounding migration were made by the extended family, leading to tensions within Brian's household.

Brian Wan was eager to join the family business in Canada. But when the business immigration application was scuttled, having no capital of his own, he was rejected. At any rate, Brian's parents preferred that he stay in Hong Kong to care for them on their transnational trips.

As a result of their different social fields, Brian and Wai-Yin were divided over emigration. Their story underscores the varied meanings of family-dependent migration to men and women and those of different generations. Emigration was the desired resolution for Brian, a compliant family migrant, but was resisted by his wife. Whereas Brian acquiesced to decisions made by his kin for him and his family, Wai-Yin had a different sense of living overseas. Wai-Yin's greater freedom in her own territory contrasts with the kinship restrictions she anticipated abroad. Her resistance was passive since she was not in control of her migration fate. She was subordinate to her husband who was in turn subordinate to the authority of his family. While she understood her family duty and didn't evade going abroad, her best place was in her neighborhood where her roots were. She felt her husband was best off there as well. In the end, without overt struggle, things turned out Wai-Yin's way.

PART THREE
WORKING CLASS FAMILIES: UNLIKELY EMIGRANTS

Kinship ties that reach abroad are the chief conduits for working class family exits, but poverty can block these channels (Massey et al. 1987; Wong and Salaff 1998). When we first met the three laboring families presented in this section, two considered emigration and one applied. However, economic restructuring and the demise of well-paying manufacturing jobs narrowed their options. Marginal economic positions made dependable personal networks all-important. Kin who were abroad drew others after them. If kin were close by, laboring families did not attempt to emigrate.

Hoping for their children to live in a democratic society, the Szetos (chapter 9) entertained emigration, but without funds or truly dependable contacts abroad, they could not follow through. The Hungs (chapter 10) pursued their application to join kin in Boston, but were beset by family problems and did not succeed. The Chias (chapter 11), having once illegally followed kin to whom they were closely connected from China to Hong Kong, did not consider going further afield. Without transnational social fields, the Chias were immune to the emigration fever that infected Hong Kong.

Similarly, few of the working class respondents to our 1991 random survey were emigrants: 24 percent of the well-off families, but only 6 percent of the working-class families had applied. Since their goal was to reunite with their dispersed kin, laborers with emigrant family members were more likely to apply than those without these ties. Of the working class applicants in our survey, two-thirds had kin who lived abroad; of the nonapplicants, under one third had kin abroad. We also learned from our qualitative study that siblings living abroad exerted a strong pull on working-class families (Salaff et al. 1999; Palloni et al. 2001). Nevertheless, their slim educational and career achievements disqualified them from current skill-based immigration systems. Hence, none of the laboring families we studied, including the three we meet in these pages, succeeded in moving abroad. Weak family economies negated migration plans and proved kin are not enough.

CHAPTER NINE

The Szeto Family
Nowhere to Run

When we met them in 1993, both Sonny and Sinying Szeto worked in the garment industry. Once the foundation of Hong Kong's industrialization, the decline of demand for textiles and garments undermined the Szetos' economic base. Their parents and grandparents before them had been well-off in China, but the loss of family property after the Communist revolution and flight to Hong Kong had fragmented their families. Albeit wary of Hong Kong's reversion to China (Bertaux 1997), since their kin could not take responsibility for them, and they were without a strong family economy, Sonny and Sinying could not act on their inclinations to leave. Instead of exiting, they expressed themselves through their political gestures (Hirschman 1970), which bonded them to others in Hong Kong's community of the poor. While these tight networks did nothing to aid emigration, they did relieve the Szetos' anxieties and helped them adapt to a changing Hong Kong.

The Family Heritage

Both Sonny's and Sinying's parents were from prosperous families in China, and through this advantage, had relatively good educations and modern views. According to Sonny, "People like them did not need to worry about their livelihood." Sinying divulged, "My parents-in-law were quite liberal in those days. They had a love match, not an arranged one. Mother-in-law said that she loved Father's good looks."

Sonny's father was a customs official in the Guomindang (KMT) government. In 1949, after the Communist revolution, he fled to Hong Kong, leaving behind Sonny's mother and two brothers. Sonny had not yet been born. Sonny recounted, "As a government employee, Father was afraid for himself. Even if you're not a soldier, just working for the KMT may send you to prison." His only recourse was to leave his wife and children behind.

Arriving in Hong Kong penniless, Father Szeto found work in the nascent film industry writing Chinese subtitles for English-language films. Alone in Hong Kong, this debonair man took a second wife. In Chinese society, men from wealthy families informally took a second wife, or concubine, to demonstrate their status and to provide sons. Their second wives also gave them a home abroad. The concubine was not married in a formal ceremony, had lower status than the first wife, and had no property rights of her own, but her children were socially recognized. Thus, when a man took a second wife, he was not necessarily deserting the first, and often hoped to recognize his obligations to both families (Tam 2005).

Since most of Sonny's extended family also fled overseas after the Communists confiscated their family property, Sonny's mother, faced with the task of raising two small boys without family support, went to join her husband: "Mother came mainly to reunite the family, not to run from China's politics. Many of my father's cousins who had been supported by his family's land holdings had fled to Taiwan or America. She was left with few relatives close at hand. She had only one cousin here, a senior staff person in Taiwan's China Airlines. He, too, later emigrated to the United States and couldn't help much." Although Mother Szeto found her husband with his second family, they did not become totally estranged. She bore Sonny, her last child, in 1954.

During this period of social chaos in Hong Kong, there were no legal or normative constraints, and Sonny's father only marginally took care of his children. Sonny and his family grew up poor and without crucial social networks to make it in the working world.

> At first Father did not give us any money, probably because that woman asked him not to. Mother did any kind of work she found, like sewing clothes at home, until she could no longer manage. She got fed up. Mother pushed us three onto them. I remember how we brought along our bedding and walked to their stone house on Diamond Hill from our shared room in Kowloon City. Mother took us to the front door of that house and then she left us! She's like that! This escapade lasted just one night. During that night my eldest brother had an argument with that woman. The next morning, Father brought us home to ask Mother to take us kids back. He also promised her money for us. As far as I know the amount Father gave Mother only covered rent, not much left for food. Yet there was nothing at all before that!

Sinying's background differed only in the details. Her grandmother was the second wife. The first wife's family made it possible for Sinying's father to obtain an English-language education, and he landed a highly sought-after civil servant post. This did not protect him during the Japanese occupation, and he was forced to work as a coolie (a manual porter) to support his family. The hard life damaged his health, and he passed away when his children were young.

Sinying's family, as dependents of civil servants, received some government compensation, but they were very poor. Because they were not in a direct line of descent from their grandfather, few in their family circle offered help. Sinying's mother and the three children eventually moved to Wong Tai Sin Resettlement Estate, one of Hong Kong's earliest subsidized public housing quarters.

Both Sonny and Sinying began working as youngsters to contribute to their families' economies. Sonny took up part-time labor and then left school midway through his lower secondary education: "My grades weren't so good, and Mother was badly off and couldn't afford the school fees. So I just stopped." Still, Sonny's schooling was modestly superior to that of many from his class background. Taken together with his intellectual curiosity, leadership qualities, and adaptability, he would achieve upward mobility in his later working years. For Sinying, her limited education could only gain her a working-class wage. Family would become her primary occupation.

Having fallen from a better life, the Szetos' heritage fostered family values overwhelmingly devoted to family survival. Their habits and family morals revolved around keeping their children safe (Dodson 2007). This survival-first script turned them against emigrating.

The Life of the Working Poor: 1970–89

Sonny As a Young Worker

Sonny packed cartons on assembly lines and did other jobs "even though factories claimed that they didn't hire children." Although they had little direct contact, Father Szeto helped arrange jobs for Sonny and his older brother in his artistic circles. Sonny's brother had an aptitude for this work and became a sound technician, mixing sound, voice intonation, and pitch for films. Sonny became an apprentice in an advertising firm for the film industry, but apparently lacked talent.

Despite receiving some assistance, Sonny noted a general shrugging off of paternal responsibility. "He really wasn't around. He simply found a friend to take me on; that was it." In the end, Father's intercession did not give Sonny much of a boost. Apprenticeships were personal, not rule bound, and he was not given an inside track to skill-building tasks.

> At first, when I was learning, I just watched the master, and cleaned up, but couldn't do anything myself. I was there for three years and found it frustrating. There's no set time for a traditional apprentice to become an artist. If you learn, then you learn. If you don't, then you move on. I tried and tried but still didn't make it. Only drawing the backgrounds on posters featuring films and commercials, I lost interest. I earned HKD 50 a month with board in the beginning, and HKD 100 three years later. Not enough to live on, but it reduced our family burden.

Unsuited for this line of work, Sonny left his father's peripheral sphere of influence and began to build up his own network to find jobs. He had to start in a laboring job from the bottom, without the protection of people to speak for him. Yet his abilities and modicum of secondary education allowed him to make gains beyond those of his working-class peers.

The community of the poor provided a surrogate family. Friends from his youth in a poor living environment seemed purer, untainted by material competition. Recalling the public housing dwelling where he met his long-term friends, Sonny said, "We grew up with each other. When we're young, we sometimes slept together on cots in the walkways, and talked into the summer night." This group of people retained their connections throughout the years and helped one another in minor ways. They were people the Szetos could take as confidants, ask for favors and advice, and share opinions. Through these connections, Sonny got most of his jobs.

Let's consider work in relation to other spheres (Pettinger 2005). Like other working men, Sonny's laboring career was embedded in other social relations, especially friendships. The industrial setting was itself rooted in Hong Kong's peripheral global economy, where bosses had little control over the market. In this unsettled economic climate and with no profession to protect them, bonds between workers were vital for survival. Workers helped each other when their organizations did not. They found jobs for each other and regulated the work flow themselves. Nevertheless, these tactics were purely defensive. In Hong Kong's subcontracting industries, factories opened and closed, orders either came in or did not, and workers went in and out of the workplace.

In the garment industry Sonny started as a cutter, cutting fabric to fit paper patterns with a ten-foot-long mechanical scissors. It took about six months to learn the basics, and he transferred what he knew going from factory to factory as workloads shifted with every contract won. He met Sinying at one of these factories; they married in 1978.

Sinying's Work: The Home Life and Family Identity of the Working Poor

In a poor family a woman must balance her assumptions about how to do her family work well with helping her family manage economically. Like most who grew up in impoverished backgrounds, Sinying was strongly committed to a unified family. Having her work as a wife and mother, and considering the low wages she received, Sinying could not always justify entering the job market (Duncan et al. 2003). She sometimes held a job, but other times did not. At an early age, she ended her primary school education to begin assembly line work in plastics and electronics factories (Dodson and Dickert 2004). When she transferred to garment seaming in San Po Kong, Kowloon, she received a decent working-class woman's wage. After marriage she continued to send money to her mother, while she and Sunny struggled financially.

At a time of scarcity, many of the poor doubled up with friends. For the Szetos, sharing housing was not just a natural way to reduce living expenses but also kept them within a circle of like people whom they saw as a good form of social support—their social capital. They first moved into a Kowloon apartment with Sinying's coworker, then rented a small house on Cheung Chau island with Sonny's childhood friends. Called the "outlying islands," Cheung Chau island had no roads, no large markets, and no shopping centers, and the ferry from Hong Kong took considerable time.

Considering the cost of commuting, Sinying quit her seaming job and devoted herself to her family work. "Village houses are good to live in if you can," she said. "Very cheap. No management fee at all. The only thing not so convenient is traveling to work and markets everyday. And the mosquitoes!"

In 1980 the Szetos welcomed their first son and moved into small rented quarters in Kowloon. When rental costs became too much to handle, Sinying returned to work, leaving their baby with Sonny's mother during the day, dining together, and returning home to their tiny quarters at night. This arrangement worked well for a few years, but when her second son was born in 1983, her mother-in-law could not handle both boys. Sinying found it impossible to balance outside work with her responsibilities to her family. She took in industrial outwork, but their living quarters were still too expensive. As a result, they registered for public housing and Sinying began looking after her small niece to help make ends meet.

Underdeveloped social services and poorly paid working-class jobs make mutual support a survival strategy. Better-paid career women, such as Aloe Gung (chapter 6), help their natal families with money and advice, but stop short of physical labor. For women without higher education, kin work is a recognized form of labor, for which they also earn pay. It is understood that they need even this small input for their family economy. When her brother divorced, Sinying took care of his daughter so she could help her brother and contribute the HKD 2000 a month she earned to Sonny's mother and her own family.

The path to public apartments was not straightforward. To move up in the long queue, families justified access by their size, by housing the older generation or a handicapped family member, and by their low wages. The Szetos registered for housing under Sonny's mother's name, hoping that housing a three-generation family would shorten the waiting time, and took the step of "moving in with mother to make it true." Within a few years they were allocated a 310–square-foot flat in Sha Tin, where they would remain for nearly twenty years, paying just HKD 900 rent per month (about half the cost of a private flat of similar size and quality at the time).

In the end Sonny's mother preferred her familiar neighborhood of San Po Kong. Luckily, she could afford to live on her own after the Chinese government returned her family property in the 1980s. Sonny filled us in, saying, "Although Mother's family's property was confiscated, her relatives had secretly saved their deeds. When their claims were recognized, they got five of the flats back, which they sold and shared out. Totally my mother got HKD 20,000. She supports herself on this and the small allowance each of us give her."

Even without Mother Szeto, the flat barely contained the five of them. They divided the sparsely decorated room with a wooden board stretching from floor to ceiling to create two bedrooms, and built a small cubbyhole for Sinying's niece. Because they had coped with rising costs and dropping income by withdrawing into their home, all the space was fully used. Sonny cut back on activities that the working class enjoyed. There were no Sunday dim sum breakfasts. They had no investments and did not gamble or play the horses. They rarely traveled. "Everything costs more. All we can do is spend less outside to save some money."

In an affluent society those with low earnings hide their poverty like a disfigurement, retreating into silence (Dodson and Schmalzbauer 2005). However at this time the large majority of Sha Tin District's half million people lived in public rental housing, so the Szetos felt poor among equals. They thought of neighborhoods as people rather than a place, and their life was enriched by a feeling of community around them. They came to know most of their neighbors, and the ties between neighbors, facilitated through everyday contacts, were important to them (Forrest et al. 2002). Sinying later analyzed the basis for their close feeling. "We know everyone on the same floor. We see each other daily. We often leave our doors open. When we take our children to school and pick them up, we use the same elevator. It's natural for us to chat while waiting outside the school. And we clean the corridor together. We do everything together. And most importantly, we all moved in at the same period. It makes all the difference."

Connected to those with whom they shared a common history and who participated in their daily routine, they felt at home. Sinying was primarily responsible for building bridges between neighbors. This helped give her a sense of purpose within the family, since for those who had fled war-torn China, having a place they could call home was key to their family script.

An Industry in Decline: 1990–95

The garment industry had allowed Sonny to apply his leadership abilities and move gradually up the career ladder to supervisory positions. In the 1990s the majority of manufacturing companies shifted production to China for low-wage labor. In this manufacturing decline, most workers accepted that they would have to change their trade. In 1993 when we first met Sonny, his earnings hovered around HKD 10,000 per month, including bonuses for meeting deadlines. This good working-class job was in a subcontracting trade that depended on orders and investment from outside Hong Kong. As the industry went into decline, workers relied increasingly on their networks to handle the fluctuating workloads. "In this trade, you hear about jobs from others. If this factory offers me work, I'll do it. If another factory has work, I'll go there. They may ask me to process 1,000 pieces and then I call people I know to help. If I don't have time, I'll pass the whole job on. If you work a long time in a field, you get to know more friends, and it's a good way of finding jobs. I've worked in at least thirty factories during these years. We all know one another."

Soon Sonny was holding down multiple factory jobs to earn a living: "Factories hire me for one job at a time. I may go to Kwun Tong today, Kwai Chung tomorrow, Castle Peak Road the day after. You can even work for eight or ten factories at once. I came here (Castle Peak Road) a couple of weeks ago. Now, I'm employed here for the whole summer, on one contract."

But conditions again changed rapidly. Instead of remaining the whole summer as he expected, two months later he had shifted factories.

There were two cutters in the previous factory, and when orders dropped there was only enough work for one. That guy stayed and I came here. We separate so that one of us has enough work. It's good for both of us. Still, because factories are moving to China, only about 20 to 30 percent of our former business remains here. Our work is labor intensive. It's hard to compete with China. It's cheaper to open factories in China, not only garments, but in almost anything, even if the quality isn't that good. Here, we mainly do the final processing, like packaging and labeling. No factories are left in a good shape the whole year. We're happy if a factory has orders even for nine months. This year, there were several months when we had only a few days work.

A few years earlier, Sonny turned down a chance to move to Fujian with his factory. He cited difficult labor conditions there as the main reason for staying in Hong Kong, but always lurking was his strong sentiment for protecting his family. Following his boss to China and separating from them was not a good solution.

It's common nowadays to have offices in Hong Kong and factories in China, to earn as much as possible. My garment factory has one factory here and one in Fujian. My boss is a Fujianese and he says labor costs are even cheaper there than in Guangdong. There was a chance to go. But I didn't like it much because I have my family here. Another reason I turned it down is the long working hours. There's no holidays or rest days. If there's overtime jobs to do, you work 'til midnight. You just stay at the factory. Further, we rarely get a permanent position in cutting. We're mainly piece workers.

By 1993, although there was little work in Hong Kong, he had already missed the chance because Mainland China's workers' skills were catching up. "Nowadays, factories in China no longer need our skills. We Hong Kong people went to China several years ago and trained a lot of Mainland supervisors. They've already learned it all. What's important is that you're happy with your job. What's the point of staying there if you can't live well?"

Sinying had strongly opposed his move to work in China. Drawing on memories of their past broken family lives, she reflected on the importance of family unity.

Why didn't I let him go? Every woman knows why! If my husband were to work on the Mainland, he'd have to stay there a long time. He'd become bored and lonely. Maybe he'd find another companion and have another family in China. People change easily when they find themselves in different situations. The temptation's great. I think it's not necessary to give the family up for the sake of money. My husband would also worry that the children would learn bad ways without him here. Anyway, there was no guarantee that he could earn much more. Even if he could, our life in Hong Kong wouldn't be secure. Still, although this is a decision made by both of us, if he insisted on going, I'd have no choice.

Strong Political Views

The political outlooks of professionals we met was sustained by Hong Kong's institutional environment in which they were elites. Their expertise fostered their sense of self so that, when threatened as it was on the eve of reversion to China, it triggered thoughts of emigration. For the laboring poor, however, an uncertain professional status was not the issue. While they had numerous other reasons to worry about the future—the most important of which was the decline of the manufacturing industry—they did not attribute this trend to reversion to China. Nevertheless, dislike of Mainland institutions, a sentiment voiced by many, fed Sinying's concerns. "Although I am Chinese, I don't like the social system and culture in China. I feel that there's a lot of social inequality and people are very greedy. I dislike it very much there."

The Szetos went further than their peers and worried over personal freedoms. This reflected their heritage from their liberal parents, with their good education and modern views. Such outlooks had imbued both Sonny and Sinying with the importance of living in a free environment, which led them to fear for their children's future after reversion. When we asked directly about reversion, Sonny piped up,

> Am I worried about 1997? Of course! I worry most about my children's future, like I can't be sure how the education system or the new system of government will affect them. Or even what will happen when they go out to work. All these things are not sure, and no one knows what's going to happen. I won't worry about myself that much. Of course, I still hope that the present situation will not change, but we can't be sure what will happen eventually. I hope that the freedom of expression that we have now will still exist. I worry whether my children can be free to say things that they want, to do things that they like to do. They are a generation that takes freedom seriously. They wanted a modernized, free society. But even if we worry we still can't do anything to change it. So for me, I take things as they come.

Emigration for political reasons might have appealed to the Szetos, who recalled their parents' past political hardships and who were uncertain of the future after the transition. Despite such fears, the Szetos could not leave. Sonny expressed their position, saying, "Well, there's nothing we can do except move elsewhere. Yet, there's no way for us to leave. Those who can, run, but for families like us with nowhere to run, worrying won't do any good.

With no way to exit, the Szetos expressed their anxiety over public affairs in the political arena. They participated in the major political events, starting with the pivotal June 4, 1989, protest march against the Tiananmen Square massacre. Joining others like themselves helped link them to their cultural milieu and bind them to Hong Kong. They belonged to a segment of people who wanted to stick together to make a difference in the changing political terrain.

Sonny closely watched political events for trends that could affect his family. The Szetos were believers in democratic participation and staunchly supported the controversial political measures passed by Chris Patten, the last Colonial governor:

> Although sometimes I don't understand Patten's style, and don't get all his ideas, I feel his method of running the government suits us Hong Kong people. What I understand of it, I support. I feel he is independent in the sense that when he decides on something, he won't change it because of immediate pressures. No matter what the outside forces are or what the situation is, he sticks to his decisions. In this way, he affects the whole system. I hope that he can adapt to new situations that arise. This will satisfy more people. For instance, reorganizing LegCo and ExCo.[1] The two councils have their different opinions, and that's good for both. Everybody is doing their part, each one has an equal share of decision making. And this is good. Since 1992, I've felt that Patten is good and that his system is going to be supported by the people.

The Szetos' politics were local. In the few electoral contests permitted them, they voted for those individuals who worked for the local community and for their class interests. Their votes reflected the dependency of the community of poor on basic social services. As Sonny explained, "Since living here, I've voted for those that work for our district. At least they can improve the bus service."

Like many of the working poor, Sonny was primarily concerned about competition from imported labor and tracked the records of representatives who opposed labor importation. Middle-class professionals also worried that they would lose their jobs to unqualified outsiders, but this issue was even more crucial for the working class who could easily be replaced by outsiders. In 1994 Sonny explained,

> Last time, I voted for someone who I felt can help in the realm of employment. I don't know a lot of things, and most of the things that I know, I learn from TV. I listen to television and radio and read newspapers, which give personal information about the candidates. Maybe I'm not all that involved, but I just want to be well informed. I saw this candidate on television, and that's when I decided to vote for him because he keeps saying that he'll help people like us.

I deliberately voted for a new face to see if there would be any change. He was a member of Civil Force.[2] My wife and I voted for different candidates. But all are democrats. Sinying's candidate succeeded, although mine didn't.

Sonny favored candidates who spoke up for popular suffrage. "I prefer independents, like Emily Lau. She's really smart! I met her canvassing at the bus stop. She's forceful and persuasive. As a radical she dares speak out. When we want change, compromisers may not be able to express their views as strongly as she does. A lot of Hong Kong people feel that voting is a waste of time. I think Hong Kong people should participate in elections, because that can help us improve our living conditions."

The Szetos discussed with their friends what to expect after 1997 and whom to vote for. Sonny stated, "When we're together, we sometimes discuss these things, and I ask their opinions. I might ask them who is better. If we are from the same electoral sector, then we could probably discuss who to vote for, but if we're in different sectors, then we have to make our own decisions."[3]

Work Life: Declining Industries

More pressing than politics in their daily lives was the declining industry in which Sonny was employed. He realized there was no great demand for his skills in Hong Kong. Despite years in the trade, he could not afford to be committed to it.

A lot of people I know are changing trades now. Those who can go to China and open their own factory. Those without money end up doing something else. Those with good English can find the best jobs. I don't have any other field I'm especially good at. Instead of changing, I go from factory to factory to find work. It's always been that way. Work as long as you can, and don't try new jobs unless you are well educated or in a stable field. I thought of changing fields once in the 1980s. But then the work in the garment factory was quite good, so I didn't change. Suddenly, late in 1994, no factory work! The most quiet period. Although I could be said to be among the busiest of my friends, 'cause I've been doing it the longest, even I had no jobs.

Like many others, Sonny had gotten a driver's license as a type of working-class "insurance." For a dismal ten days in 1994, Sonny tried his hand at driving a taxi. But he had not foreseen the high entry costs: "Although I already got the license, I don't know the routes. At least I should know how to go to places like the airport, hospitals." His friend lent him a car but at a time when he had no income, he paid several thousand dollars to learn his way around. Sonny said, "I drove the car around and the instructor told me where to go. He really earned a lot because many people come out to drive taxis when the economy isn't good." But he gave it up after less than two weeks, saying

> Driving a taxi's tough. The traffic's hard to handle. I worked under great pressure. There's only the morning or evening shift, so you need to work over ten hours a day. It's up to you whether you're hard working enough to earn some money from driving. But it's not really stable. It all depends on the street. If you are lucky enough, then you'll find lots of customers. If not, you won't earn enough. Normally an experienced driver can earn HKD 700 or 800 per day, it costs HKD 250 to rent a car for a shift, I also needed to cover other costs, around HKD 130 for gas, that's already HKD 400 a day, leaving HKD 300 to 400 net income. Then the front light broke on the third day. I hadn't earned anything, but had to pay HKD 1,000 for repairs!

Sinying grumbled, "He got less than HKD 100 a day. Useless. It wasted time and energy." Sonny countered, "Just then, the previous factory asked me to come back. There was work again."

During these hard years, Sinying's ties to kin, which she cemented with weekly visits and small services, remained her central focus. Sinying justified staying outside the formal labor force by the importance of her daily work with her children. "Since I need to look after my niece, I can't really get a full-time job. All three kids come back for lunch, and we eat dinner at home together at night." To her, family was more important than the small amount of money she could earn. "People of different ages have different functions in society. I can pass on my experience to the children!" Her choice seemed reasonable. Hong Kong's competitive examination system rests on the work women do to help their children study. The educational system changes often and even middle-class parents have to struggle to boost their children's test scores. Better-educated women who take on this tuition work can do without personal cramming. Having ended her studies at primary level, Sinying had to upgrade her own knowledge so that she could tutor her niece. "The competition to get into high school is so keen. I read books to help me with my niece's homework."

Despite wanting to help her children do better than her generation had, she did not send them to the private music and art lessons popular among the middle class. In this the Szetos were similar to American working-class families who know that their children should participate in sports and learning but rarely do so because these activities are far away and expensive (Chin and Phillips 2004). When low-cost alternatives were at hand, the Szetos' eldest son joined clubs at school and a nearby community center for drama, table tennis, and basketball. When he changed to a school without them, he switched to nearer pursuits.

The Szetos passed on their activist politics to their sons. A TV, their main consumer purchase, became the family's key leisure activity and was used for education. They studiously watched it, taping news programs aired when they were not at home to view later. During our visits, the television was usually with the volume turned down, the children keeping sight of the silent moving images. Reading was another family pastime. There was no hi-fi, laser, or compact disk player, elaborate toys, or computer, but there were always books and newspapers in their home. When their younger son was just fourteen, he knew the candidates his parents voted for, and gave the names of the members of the political bodies when we asked. In this way the Szetos found a place for themselves within Hong Kong's evolving institutions.

Landing On Their Feet: 1995–2003

As their industries underwent restructuring, working-class families' earning power dropped; many lost their jobs (Leung 2002). Sonny had developed complex technical expertise in cutting garments, exercised leadership skills, and had many working years ahead of him. When global economic factors disrupted his trade and ended his original line of work, he was prepared to take up any job he could find. Since he already had a driver's license, in 1995 Sonny supplemented his dwindling garment work by driving coworkers who did industrial cleaning after hours. "One of my friends got a second evening job in a pest-control company. After stores close, they need to do cleaning. He brought me in. A group of us work together, an hour in each place. Usually there's one pest control operation in each company every month. If there's a lot of work, they'll ask you to come back two or three times more. We don't earn much. About HKD 250 each for an evening's work."

Through this peer connection, Sonny began a new career in a novel organization, and within two years, left the garment business entirely. We wondered if he would become alienated, leave the scene, or join with others in seeking social change (Cheung 2005). When we asked about this dramatic career shift, he insisted pragmatically, "Am I wasting my garment-cutting skills? Hard to say. I can't really say that the present job is or isn't good. When the economy changes, there's no choice. It's just a way to survive!"

Sonny still saw himself as a worker, and leaving the occupation he'd undertaken for a significant period of his life did not threaten this identity since insecurity was a feature of working-class jobs (Cheung 1998). No political group advanced plans to change structures to help unemployed workers and their families, and the unemployed formed no social movements (Jasper 1997). The popular culture of the Hong Kong self-made man boasted that people should make their own way out of unemployment, even on this massive scale. And that is what Sonny did.

Sonny and Sinying approached their economic impasse differently than did other marginalized poor we met (Cheung 2005). Sonny's above-average education and wider outlook put him at an advantage. Their marriage bond was another resource. The Szetos were the only of our laboring couples who tried to work out joint solutions as a couple. The social arrangements of work also helped Sonny get ahead since his former coworkers, his social capital, pulled him into their sphere (Parry et al. 2005). He landed on his feet and his family benefited. With Sonny's new career in a growth industry, they were transformed over time from being part of the needy poor into members of the affluent working class.

Emigration: Not a Solution

Entering a profitable industrial service job did not lead the Szetos to emigrate. The main conditions preventing their exit were weak ties to emigrant kin and no marketable skills of their own. Personal networks were crucial alternatives that allowed migration for those without money. But kin ties gave the Szetos only weak support.

There had been emigrants in the Szeto families in previous years who departed for the United States and Taiwan after the 1949 Communist revolution. Few maintained contact, and they lacked any obligation to help the Szetos. They had broken the migration chain.

Sonny's oldest brother lived in Canada. Why didn't they pursue that claim and follow him? On the regulatory level, married brothers could not easily establish a legitimate claim to family reunion. Even more important, in Chinese tradition these were not claimable ties. Sonny's brother had followed his wife's kin (her mother, sister, and brother-in-law)—their family's first immigrants—to Toronto. Furthermore, the older brother could not get a job in Toronto. As Sonny explained, "It doesn't matter. His wife's side has money so he can stay at home without working." The couple built a house in Scarborough, home to many Hong Kong Chinese, where he was in the bosom of his wife's family. "My brother's sister-in-law's family lives next door. One is on the front and one is at the back. They could walk into each other's house through back doors." Sonny's brother suggested that their mother join them, but she had refused to leave her familiar San Po Gong neighborhood. If she had joined her eldest son in Canada, Sonny might have followed.

Like others in Hong Kong, Sinying also had emigrant kin, but their relationship was even weaker. The Szetos did not consider joining the emigration chain linked through Sinying's cousins. "We're not close," she said. "We've married and have little chance to see each other, except in family gatherings." The fact that friends who figured most directly in their lives were not emigrants further dampened the Szetos' interest in migration. Without supporting links, whether kin or friends, and without solid economic resources, the Szetos realized that going abroad was not a realistic option. Instead their unsettled past had shaped a family script dedicated to keeping their own small family unit intact and avoiding risks that an unsecured emigration would incur. Improvements to their family economy were enough.

Relaxing Their Political Guard As 1997 Approaches

Sonny was lulled by China's economic liberalization during the late 1990s and expected that China would modernize its political system. His relaxed political guard was most noticeable in his reframing of the 1989 Tiananmen incident.

> At that time, I really felt sad and depressed, couldn't believe the government could do such a thing. But as time went by, my bitterness lightened. I thought, the Chinese government concentrates more on developing the economy. They've become open to trade and commerce. Conditions in China in the economic realm are improving. So the situation now is much better than at the time of the June 4 incident. As for the political realm, no one really knows. Any improvement should include freedom, not only money. Yet these things are interrelated. I think when Mainland living standards improve, so will people's overall quality of life.

As 1997 approached, Sonny radically changed his viewpoint, becoming optimistic that retrocession would bring about the best of both systems. He emphasized the commonalities between the populations as Hong Kong became China (Mathews et al. 2008).

> There's nothing to be afraid of. After all, although we live in different places, we're all Chinese. So, I don't think they'll do anything to harm Hong Kong. I think there won't be much change in our lifestyle, the economy will shift more towards commerce. Politically it will stay the same—"Hong Kong people ruling Hong Kong people." There could either be a Chinese official from China or a Hong Kong official ruling the SAR. But the Mainland Chinese might not be as experienced as officials are now in Hong Kong. So, if there are some changes to be made, they should ask the opinions of Hong Kong officials. They should combine their opinions instead of arguing against one another, like they do now. Then they can get the best results.

Sonny was not alone. After the 1997 handover, Sinying noticed that "many people are not so concerned about democracy because the Mainland authorities treat us well enough. Although the Democratic Party often preaches democracy, many people seem to abandon that ideal and concentrate on economic development." This turnabout shifted views away from emigration, as Sonny stated, "Hong Kong people have changed their standpoint about June 4. Just after the incident, people wanted to emigrate, but nowadays they've changed their minds. My best friends haven't thought of emigration, but both thought of investing in China. My taxi driver pal wanted to start a business in China, but couldn't work it out. The other guy works as a hotel manager; his wife is a designer, has business in China. Hong Kong people behave according to their own interests. You can clearly see that it's a tendency of many people to go to the Mainland."

The dramatic turnabout of these friends who wanted to make money from the Chinese giant impressed Sonny. These close friends remained his role models. They were like him, but they had prospered. Their opinions counted for Sonny, who envisioned his own future actions in theirs. Sonny saw his friends as people like him, for whom leaving Hong Kong no longer made sense.

2000: *Their Home as Source of Pride*

Positive experiences shored the Szetos' commitment to Hong Kong. Sonny joined the affluent workers in a restructured economy. His work in pest control was in demand. Sinying, too, was able to return to work. Their family economy improved even more after their children became earners. In 1998 their eldest son was accepted into Hong Kong University's journalism department and went on to become a reporter. The youngest son found a job in an electronics firm and began to work his way to management in sales. In a few short years, as the ratio of earners to dependents improved and the family prospered. This overall sense of gain after so many years of poverty was gratifying.

In the late 1990s, the community of the poor began to fragment with economic change. The government offered subsidized housing for sale, and having their own home became a source of great pride for their working class friends. The Szetos' friends and neighbors who had already improved their earnings were first to buy their own apartments. But those without money to buy their own home felt bitter at being left out of the Hong Kong "miracle," fracturing the sense of solidarity undergirding the community of the poor.

In 2000 the Szetos held a family council and decided to buy a 660–square-foot apartment. Government assistance pushed the decision—they could borrow the mortgage money without interest when buying a second-hand government-built flat. The price of joining the mainstream consumer society was a monthly mortgage of HKD 4,000, over four times their previous rent. They took pride in being able to afford it. They furnished the home in white wall-to-wall carpets, a thick foam sofa, and shiny new white laminated tables and chairs from Ikea. A matching white cabinet housed their TV and hi-fi system. They now had the amenities they had denied themselves for years.

This move cost more than money; their loss of community was deeply felt. They did not integrate easily with new neighbors whom they did not know. No longer having young children, they could not meet other parents at the school gate or on other casual occasions. Status differences among these affluent working families were displayed, and people withdrew to avoid being looked down upon. Sinying reflected, "Now the neighbors are . . . It's hard to describe . . . it's weird. We rarely open the doors at the same time. It's very different to where we lived before. Here we are newcomers, and we did say hello to them but somehow are still unable to make friends." Nevertheless, old networks soon partially coalesced. They had learned about this apartment from friends who lived nearby, and other former neighbors followed. "A few months after we moved here, one of them phoned me excitedly, 'Sinying, I bought a place next to yours!'" Their old network was gradually reshaping itself.

Past their entry into the consumer society that their new home symbolized, most rewarding to Sinying was the achievement of her long-term desire— her family would remain together and prosper. The new home was the essential foundation of that family ideal. When we met with the Szetos in 2003, fortunes had shifted further in their favor. Demand for Sonny's pest control work had increased, even when others suffered downturns. "We work at shopping malls in the day, and office buildings at night, and that's counted as overtime. We do the cleaning for many housing estates, and we do the pest control at the same time. Never short of business! During the SARS outbreak, we were one of the few beneficiaries. Really busy! We had to cover up from top to toe all day to protect ourselves. This was steriliza- tion work, we charged extra. During that period, we worked at least three to four nights a week. I also drove the crew in the daytime."

The industrial cleaning business was strongly gendered and racially seg- regated, and he could not bring Sinying in (Cockburn 1983). "Mostly men do this kind of work. Our work isn't heavy physically, though. You use the machines and chemicals to help kill the pests. Simple as that! There're some women, mostly Filipino or Thai, but they do the heavy work, and don't get a good price." Instead Sinying, who turned fifty in 2003, stayed in factory work. With her children in the workforce, home tasks were easier to do. "There's still a few sewing jobs left. Something to do with the quota system.

Someone I once worked with recommended me; she knows I know how to operate a sewing machine. As long as you did it before, it'll come back to you after you start. There's nothing much else for older women who don't have school credentials."

At the same time, around them they saw the return of families from abroad, including Sonny's own brother and his wife after fourteen years in Canada. His wife's mother, their linchpin in Toronto, had passed away. Furthermore, Sonny told us, being abroad was costly:

> My brother lost money in the U.S. stock market downturn [after 2000]. So although he had a house and a car in Canada, he could only just manage to pay his expenses. Anyway he wasn't working and felt bored and wanted to lead a more enjoyable life. So he decided to cash in by selling the house because it had appreciated. Where he'll stay now isn't clear. First, he thought of going back to China to spend the rest of his days. He said that he would spend two years to find out whether life on the Mainland fits him. The cost of living is higher in Hong Kong and his savings will drain away quickly. For the moment, he rents a public housing unit from his wife's relative who's allocated it.

Although Sonny's brother had emigrated with an eye to the handover, his emigration more fundamentally had a family tone. He left Hong Kong through kin networks and returned when those networks brought him back; even now they house him. For him, like Sonny, politics receded into the background as family issues came to the fore. Sonny reflected, "Times are different now. When he left for Canada, it was just after 1989. Back then, China economy was not yet on the rising track. And the authorities sent troops to crack down on the students. People's view of China was different. That's why he chose to emigrate. We couldn't foresee China's development. Now China's economy is soaring."

Protecting Home

The Szetos remained alert to problems in their new affluent life; these came in the form of a political dictum—the threatened passing of Article 23 of the Basic Law for Hong Kong on political security. Hong Kongers had long distinguished their society from China's by macro-level institutional structures—their state, with its legal bodies. The process by which Article 23 was being passed invoked a theme important to Hong Kongers—legal process versus the arbitrary personal rule that long characterized Chinese history. The high-handed legislation renewed perceived threats to their way of life. The Democracy March on July 1, 2003, sent people to the streets to protest and was pivotal in the development of Hong Kong's political culture (Cheng 2005).

The Szetos joined a million others from various circles and perspectives in a day of protest. They noted that many marchers were newcomers to this kind of political event; couples, students, and young families arrived pushing strollers or carrying babies in their arms. Older people were brought by others, mobilized by organizations, or taken there by coaches. Group leaders held flags and members followed. The multitude walked from Victoria Park to the legislative buildings in Central Hong Kong. Normally, to get to the park from the entry at nearby Kingston Street takes five minutes. During this march, hemmed in by the throngs, the Szetos got to the starting point after four hours. Sinying enthused at the camaraderie: "We went on our own and just followed the procession. We walked to Victoria Park but couldn't squeeze in. So we walked to the central library, which overlooked the start of the rally. We joined in when the procession began. We followed the people but the procession was very slow. It was sardine-packed. We could barely move."

By two o'clock in the scorching afternoon sun they felt even hotter squeezed in among the people. A young religious man thanked God for every breeze. Sympathetic store owners handed out bottled water to the marchers. Many did not even make it to the end point. Despite the conditions, everyone seemed to understand that they were there for a greater reason, which set a tone of civility among marchers, two-thirds of whom were clad all in black. Sinying reported, "People behaved well. Didn't push and shove. It was very crowded but they were all considerate to each other. Usually a fight starts if some guy steps on another's foot. But this kind of thing didn't happen that day. Everyone was forgiving."

After moving slowly for several hours the Szetos left for home. Sinying confessed, "I nearly blacked out because of the heat. If the weather had been cooler, many more people would have shown up. As it was, the whole area was paralyzed. The earliest batch of people got to the march end point, the government headquarters, at about seven o'clock. We didn't get to it before we left. At five o'clock we were still in Wanchai, at the spot where the old Dong Shing Theater was located."

It was the first large-scale protest against the new Hong Kong government and, perhaps not surprisingly, many had concerns about joining it. Few had a history of active political participation under Colonialism. Some worried about violence or later retribution, yet set aside their fears in order to be heard. Sinying told us,

We went because we were disappointed by the economy and the government. And the law it proposed was sinister. We were pissed off by Regina Ip. Her remarks were really offensive, an insult to many citizens.[4] Bill 23 proposed to make many activities illegal. I think it'd give them an excessive power. They could enter and search your house whenever they want. My son's a reporter. He's also worried about it. There was already a case that reporters' activities had been restricted when they tried to cover stories. So personally, that law has great effect on us. Although some claimed the legislation wouldn't affect ordinary people, how could you know? So we thought it's unreasonable and fought for what we should have. They didn't consult people's opinions and just acted in an arbitrary way. We'd been kept in the dark about many of its details. You might find out later that many details were disadvantageous to you. So people got involved!

Like Tiananmen protesters before them, this event was their only means to express themselves. They hoped that their leaders and the world beyond would record their views, and in the end they were amazed at their power. Sinying recalled excitedly, "When I was there, I was thrilled by the magnificent sight. The atmosphere was impressive. When I got home and saw it on the TV, it's even more overwhelming, because they showed a bird's-eye view from a chopper of the entire Hennessy Road."

The march gave the participants a sense of belonging, which had been eroding since the handover. Sinying explains, "Before this, people seemed to lose interest in democracy, thinking more about the economy. After July first, people seemed to change. They're now interested in democracy too." The Szetos hope that their children can enjoy a better living standard and some freedom as well by remaining in Hong Kong. They feel vindicated by the turn of events.

Summary: Adapting to a Changing Hong Kong

The Szetos had no means to emigrate although they had reason to consider it during the long lead-up to 1997. Formerly well-off in old China, they had lost status and resources. The dreams of political franchise that their educated parents had passed on and the political turmoil they had suffered in the early Communist period created anxiety over their family's well-being after the impending reversion. At the same time, because of their forefathers' traumatic dislocations during the Chinese revolution they inherited few economic assets. Their working-class jobs gave them few internationally recognized resources, limiting their options; they wished to, but could not, leave. At the regulatory level, immigration was precluded.

While growing up, hardships strengthened the Szetos' belief in the importance of family. Because of their experience with fragmented kin ties, they wanted their children and others in their immediate circle to be able to depend on family. This belief led them to take certain jobs and turn down others, set certain housing goals, and reject an emigration trek that would disperse them.

Beyond valuing family, this working-class family was tightly networked with peers who comprised their social network. Remaining part of a community of the former poor was important. Peers took Sonny Szeto out of the sunset garment industry and into an industrial service job, thereby achieving a secure working-class level of comfort for his family. This employment environment was heavily indebted to his local networks. Since few colleagues went abroad, there were no available emigration chains. Leaving would rupture valuable ties. Finally attaining undreamt-of material goods in Hong Kong with Sonny's better work situation, the family was satisfied to remain.

Keen to keep their family together, the Szetos reasoned that emigration would cut them off from their work opportunities, well-established networks of friends, and closest family relations, central to their institutional framework. Their Hong Kong–entrenched identity established a personal security more attractive than the risk-laden uprooting of emigration. Staying in Hong Kong proved best for the Szetos' family script.

CHAPTER TEN

The Hung Family
Canceled Migration Dreams

The Hungs were part of a chain of migrants who tried to help each other make it to the new country. Chung dreamt of reuniting with her mother from whom she had become separated during the Cultural Revolution. The chance came in 1973. Chung's brother who had emigrated to Boston sponsored his parents first, and then in 1982 his siblings, including Chung and her husband Chak-Lui. But for two unexpected setbacks, Chung might have reunited with her family in America. Chak-Lui lost his skilled worker position, without which his family could not move forward in the immigrant queue. Later, in 1983, the birth of Ka-Man, their autistic son, shifted Chung's focus from planning for family migration to caring for a disabled child.[1] The whole family retreated from their migration project.

Through the Hungs' story, we learn how diverse identities and resources deter migration. Chung was not part of the global transnational fields in work or politics that enveloped middle-class emigrants. She was not promoting her daughters' cultural capital through sending them abroad for education. Chung was firmly tied to the family institution, which drew her abroad as it became transnational. But her sense of self, initially based on kinship ties to her extended family, shifted over time to obligations for her own special family. By accepting their fate in Hong Kong, the Hungs began to rebuild a modest life in which emigration would have no part.

The Early Years

The Hungs' careers followed the course of Hong Kong's industrial development. Like others in the community of the poor, as youths the Hungs left school for unskilled work so as not to burden their families. Gradually they picked up trades, climaxing at skilled manufacturing jobs. When industrial restructuring downsized their industries in the mid-1980s, they returned to unskilled work in the service sector.

Chak-Lui's parents ran a small shop selling food and sundries in Macao. In 1963 at age thirteen he left primary school. A few years later his kin found him an apprenticeship in a Hong Kong furniture factory. This should have led to mastery of the craft, but such small workshops did not provide stable employment (Cooper 1975). Chak-Lui said, "We carried the wood ourselves. I also had to cook and wash clothes. Then the furniture firm closed down—too many competitors. So I went to a workshop that made mirrors. Soon that company, too, went under." He next landed a plum industrial position dyeing fabric in Tsuen Wan where he worked for ten years. This was the high point of his career. "I added pigments to the dyes, and learned a few English words, like blue, black, yellow." Optimistic at earning a family wage, in 1973 his marriage was arranged to Chung, who moved to Hong Kong to join him.

The youngest of six children, Chung was born in Guangzhou, China. As a child she and four of her siblings crossed the border to Macao to escape the Cultural Revolution. Her eldest brother, Li-Liang, remained behind to care for their parents. It was Li-Liang who married an American immigrant and started the family migration chain.

Married Life, 1973–82

Chung and Chak-Lui were hopeful about married life. They rented a small room in a grotty area near the dying factory and while there welcomed their first daughter. It was important for both Chung and Chak-Lui to maintain the family economy, and Chung was as well organized as she could be. She carefully planned her reproductive life so that she could earn money. She recalled, "I was still young—only twenty-one—when I gave birth to Ka-Lei in 1974. I had to work even when I was pregnant. So I chose to space my kids because it's easier than taking care of several very small children at the same time. That's why there's a gap of nearly five years between their births." Chung took pride in balancing work and home life: "Many people at that time were in the garment industry, and I, too, started out in industrial outwork. I worked on high fashion at home and can make any part of the garment, a whole suit, by myself. Working at home made it easier to look after the children."

The Hungs' second daughter, Ka-Wah, was born in 1979. The daughters were obedient and keen at studying. Influenced by her life in the community of the poor, Chung did not set very high educational goals for them, hoping that they would quickly become independent wage earners. They could help earn money to support the sons Chung wanted to have.

In 1980 the Hungs moved into a public housing apartment in the outlying New Territories town of Tuen Mun. During the sixteenth century, Tuen Mun was a harbor for ships on international trade routes. Situated on the mouth of the Pearl River and on the route to Guangzhou, it was a strategic location for opposing forces; the Portuguese seized Tuen Mun in 1514, and China's Ming government took it back soon after. This outpost again became important in 1904 as a base for the revolutionary forces of Sun Yat Sen fighting the Ching Dynasty.

No longer the historical site it once was, the Colonial government developed Tuen Mun to house Hong Kong's large working-class and lower-middle-class populations, a catchment for the overcrowded central city area. The satellite city was plagued by poor infrastructure and widely viewed as an example of British Colonial folly. Originally supplying workers for the weaving and dying factories in nearby industrial Tsuen Wan (a bus or ferry ride away), when heavy industry moved to lower-waged China there were few local employment opportunities and no community services had been built. Laborers commuted daily by bus along stretches of narrow highway to work in other districts. Despite belated efforts to expand the limited recreational and service outlets, Tuen Mun was already known as an area of limited employment, impoverished services, drug traffic, crime, and desperate anomic working-class youths (Chow 1988; Lee 2008).

Luckily, the Hungs' own neighborhood had escaped this turmoil. Their neighbors were helpful and friendly, and they felt proud that they, as ordinary people, held good working-class jobs, were accumulating skills, had two lovely daughters, and had a place to call home. Such successes were the height of working-class family dreams. Without much more, they could still manage with the help of their friends (Tam and Rettig 1999).

The Hungs' Family Migration Chain: 1973–82

In 1973 Chung had another dream—her emigration dream. Eldest Brother Li-Liang, who was still in China, became engaged to a women whose mother had immigrated to Boston some years earlier. His fiancée's mother applied for her daughter to join her, and after reaching the United States, she sponsored Li-Liang. Within a few months of becoming a resident, Li-Liang sponsored his parents. Chung recalled the sequence of events, saying, "My parents were desperate to reunite with their children. They had already applied years back to come to Hong Kong where the rest of us children lived, but that reunion was much harder. They changed their plans and applied to go to the States and in a few months were accepted as new Americans."

Ironically, her parents were not permitted to cross the border to Hong Kong to live with their children. But going to the United States, where the political climate supported family reunification and immigration policies more congruently fit the reality of transnational kinship institutions, was easily accomplished (Kofman 2004). This was Chung's world, that of multiplex kin relations that happened to reach abroad. "Just after my mother arrived there, she started to apply for us. She wants to have all her children go so that we can have family reunion, instead of having 'some in the East and some in the West.' It's a family-oriented idea."

As Chung's parents pressed for their children to join them abroad, emigration became Chung's central wish. Thinking about life in the United States, Chung envisioned that entering through kin would be little different from their previous hope of bringing their parents to join them in Hong Kong. Chung did not consider life in the United States to be exotic or novel. She admitted, "No, I haven't been to America. The air ticket is expensive, and there's no reason to go there. I think the food is similar. You can still eat rice there. My mother can adjust, so it can't be hard. At first she didn't know English, but she's clever. She can go to the bank and get money now, much better than my father. She communicates with others quite well." Chung's vision of life in Boston was mainly a projection of her Hong Kong experiences, where kin, friends, and neighbors filled her social fields.

Around this time, Chak-Lui's younger brother also followed his wife to reunite with her family in Tucson, Arizona. However, Chak-Lui did not give serious thought either to following his brother or trailing his wife's family to Boston. He thought he would not prosper there. Emigration was entirely Chung's idea. Perceiving that the key determining features of their future were out of their hands, the Hungs did not work through their different views on migration. They thought they would decide what to do when the outcome of their application became clear.

Unexpected Blows: 1982–85

Despite sponsorship, it was hard for these working-class folk to gain admission as married sisters and brothers of a citizen. Chung knew that they would have to scrape together whatever savings they could if they were to qualify and so delayed her own application. Hence the first blow to Chung's hopes for immigration to America was economic.

This period began a transition for people like the Hungs. In their peak earning positions Chak-Lui and Chung held good workers' jobs. Within a decade of their marriage, however, as Chak-Lui recounted, "Dyeing factories moved away to China, even to Africa!" He lost his skilled job in 1983. Chung, too, suffered unemployment. "Now that even high-quality fashions all moved to China, there's no work for us here." Pushed out of their industrial jobs, the Hungs struggled to protect their Hong Kong family. They tried low-paid service jobs and applied for social assistance.

Chak-Lui never regained a footing in skilled labor, of which little was available. He first held a series of waiter jobs, but learned that he was not suited to the sophisticated restaurants. He recalled, "The first restaurant was a high-class place near Connaught Centre that Maxim owns. My brother-in-law cooked there. But they preferred people with better qualifications as waiters because lots of tourists go there. So no future for me. After that, I worked in local cafes in Sham Shui Po."

As the primary caregiver of two children, Chung balanced her mothering and work roles, but she did not have the money or know-how to assess her children's skills or cultivate their talents (Chin and Phillips 2004). As her eldest daughter turned nine, Chung did not arrange her daughter's schedule and did not consider sports, arts, or performances as programs that could develop her talents (Lareau 2003). She did not voice the middle-class belief that children needed to overexcel to do well in an increasingly competitive world. Her pragmatics centered on the concrete—a son to lead the family into the future. Without pensions, Chung and Chak-Lui would, as Chinese parents had done for eons, depend on their sons for this future support. Even today, substantial numbers of Hong Kong women with poor education believe a son is essential to their family (Wong 2007). Still, Chung also expected daughters to work hard and earn money for the family (Salaff 1981).

The son she had dreamt of was born in 1983. It was another blow when she learned that her dream would not be realized because he was autistic. Chung recalled, "He looked bright, beautiful, and was very active when he was a baby. But Ka-Man didn't talk even when he was one. He was already very different from his sisters, and I took him for an IQ test. The doctor asked me to wait a year to determine if he was really mentally retarded. But by the time he was two, I knew there was nothing to be done. I was very disappointed. I dared not have other children. What if I had a child that was even worse?" From then on, Chung's mothering became practical work that she must do to help her child survive. Although Chung's American kin pressed them to pursue their immigration application—even applying on their behalf and sending them the forms to fill in—after Ka-Man's birth, Chung dragged her feet.

The Decline of Skilled Labor
and Emigration Hopes: 1985–93

The Hungs turned from one position to another, each requiring fewer skills than the one before. They felt bandied about by economic conditions beyond their control, with their age making it harder to find jobs. As their careers went from best to worst, they lost their sense of optimism. Their emigration dreams faded as well. Chak-Lui recounted, "I became a furniture mover, high-class Finnish furniture, for a company. That job didn't demand lots of skill. For nine years [1985–93] I just went along with the truck, delivered the furniture, and assembled it for the customers. Just like a coolie. Anyone can do it. Then the owner made a bad investment in China and couldn't cover our company any more. We took him to court, but still couldn't get the salary owed us."

Demoralized, Chak-Lui made few future plans (Cheung 2005).

I'm fated to be a manual worker. I'm only suited for tough and low-paid tasks, like lifting and carrying heavy things upstairs. As for the future? I've no plan. Very unstable. But even being alive is not stable. You can't tell what will happen tomorrow. I just work as long as the job lasts. My daughters' generation is luckier; there are more opportunities and youngsters are sharper. They just quit if they feel unhappy. In the past we were dumb. Whenever apprentices were treated unfairly, we could only hide, depressed! I was never fired, but I lost my jobs because the company cut back or even disappeared. That's my life story from my time when I was a teenager to now.

Chak-Lui was never enthusiastic about an imagined future in the United States. He was already struggling in Hong Kong, a place he knew well, to support his special family and worried about his prospects abroad. Work instability, the lack of demand for skills from the earlier industrial period, and having no way to master the skills that were emerging under restructuring led to fatalism. The day-to-day life in Hong Kong was all Chak-Lui knew, and he did not expect that emigration would create a better scenario. He doubted his wife's dreams would materialize, and even if they did, it wouldn't matter much for him.

We wondered, "Since you're having trouble making a living here, don't you think you may have a better chance in the United States?" He replied,

It's not likely. More and more people are going there. How can the country, even a large one, offer jobs to all of them? My brother in Arizona told me that they don't have enough work. When he first went there, he worked in a restaurant. Now he's doing anything he can find. Too many competing for a place to live and work. In the past, with USD 100,000, you could start a restaurant business.

Now you need several hundred thousands. Like my wife's brother living in a town near Boston. Say there are four hundred to five hundred people working in the town. If there's just one restaurant, they'll have enough business. But with two, then not enough. Compared with Hong Kong, the place is vast, but population density is small.

We pressed further, asking, "Why are you worried that there are many immigrants there?" He explained it as a problem of migration chains—people would go where their kin went.

Take my wife's family as an example. At first, only Elder Brother-in-Law's wife went there, then she applied for him. They had several children, Brother-in-Law applied for his parents, then his sisters and brothers-in-law, and so on. One becomes more than ten! Then it becomes hard for all the new immigrants to get work. Li-Liang worked as a waiter in a Chinese restaurant when he first arrived in Boston. Then he saved some money to open a small cafe, a family business. To keep it competitive and the price cheap, you must do most of the work instead of employing people. Then think of Second Brother-in-Law. He went to work in Li-Liang's restaurant, but he had to leave because that small restaurant couldn't employ so many. He had to find work as a waiter somewhere else.

Basing his views in part on his projections of his own economic experience and in part on the experiences of others he had heard of, Chak-Lui concluded that it was not worthwhile to emigrate.

When we met the Hungs in 1993, Chung had not yet fully abandoned her dream of going to America. Like many others at the time, they were waiting for the slow state machinery to proceed as thousands of applicants, fueled by the retrocession, were filtered through the immigration gatekeepers. "We belong to Category 5, with the least priority. Still, we've all applied. . . . Mother suggested that I start the process. She said, 'You have an opportunity, don't lose it. When you're accepted, you can decide whether or not to go.'"[2]

Yet it was not only the immigration queue that stopped Chung in her tracks. Their shaky family economy gave her pause. Chung was already doubtful that they could meet the human capital–oriented immigration scrutiny; her working life had been disrupted by the birth of Ka-Man and Chak-Lui was struggling to find decent-paying work.

Her siblings, far more qualified than she, had already received green cards to the United States. "After First Brother Li-Liang, Second Brother applied. He's divorced, and as a single man both he and his son could immigrate easily." Chung's next two siblings to be accepted were her elder sisters whose resources through marriage gave them a boost. "One brother-in-law has a high rank in Maxim, a well-known Chinese restaurant; the other's a ship mechanic. His salary is quite high; he's got overtime work and didn't need to spend much. Sister's enthusiastic about immigration. She's got enough money to give to Li-Liang to buy a house for her arrival. He'll rent it out for her before then. Finally, Third Brother, who works in a shop, applied."

Chung emphasized the importance of having kin to look after them and expected Li-Liang to take care of everything if she were to immigrate.

> Li-Liang and his wife run a Chinese restaurant, near Boston, so he can offer us jobs. I don't know what they serve exactly, but I know the area is famous for lobsters. Chinese are known for their hard work and they do well. Second Brother worked in Li-Liang's restaurant in the beginning. Father also worked in the kitchen for over USD 1,000. He wrote to us that he could earn more in one month than several years in China. Mother helped there as well. It's the same for me too; if I go to America; I'll have to live near my brother so that he can take care of us.

At the same time, however, Chung was aware that such offers of mutual help did not always pan out (Menjivar 1995). "At first, Elder Sister-in-Law planned for Mother to live with her because she needed someone to babysit her children. But after a while, Mother didn't want to continue. Living together isn't easy." Chung had heard, though, that the state would step in if kin failed.

> Now our parents are old and they retired. The welfare for the elderly is good. Mother applied for a seniors home. Each old couple has its own flat, same size as ours. They also get a pension, more than USD 1,000. No need to be supported by my brothers in America. My parents adjusted well. Father's already in his seventies, so there are health problems. He's had a stroke. But the medical benefits there are very good. The government can really support them for the rest of their lives. The same for education; if you are intelligent, you get ahead. Like my brother's son—when he first went there, his English wasn't good but the school got a tutor to teach him English. After three years, he's now in University. I can educate my children in America too.

The birth of her disabled son redirected Chung's focus toward the practical concerns of caring for her family. So Chung waited until 1987, five years after her brothers and sisters, to file her family's papers. By then, she had already resigned herself to life in Hong Kong. Yet Chung was still ambivalent, hoping that apart from fulfilling kin duties, America could be a ticket to better her family's life. The government assistance that her elderly parents were receiving suggested that she and Chak-Lui could still be taken care of in their old age even without an able son. It also held out the possibility that there would be more help for Ka-Man beyond what they received in Hong Kong.

Dependency Mothering: 1983

The physical care and nurturing of a disabled child goes beyond everyday parenting (Kittay and Feder 1998). Like other mothers, Chung was expected to nurture her children, train them to become self-sufficient, and help them fit into the family and the wider society beyond while she contributed to the family economy. But dependency mothering had further challenges.

The first task was accessing state services. Hong Kong services are not organized around the caregiver's daily routines. As Pearson and Ning (1997) point out, the family, central to the work that is really done, is not formally integrated into the caregiving paradigm. In most cases, it is the mother who draws on the many strands of social assistance a family with special needs can get. Service providers take for granted that unassisted, the mothers will find and access them, giving scant thought to the schedules of hard-working mothers like Chung.

Chung enumerated the government allowances that she had received, most requiring frequent assessments of Ka-Man's eligibility. These repeated assessments and supporting letters were not only troublesome but shamed the parents (Wong 2007).

> The Social Welfare Department wrote a letter and we took it ourselves to the neurologist to sign. At that time they gave Ka-Man a psychological test, asked him things. They also explained things to me. They give us at least HKD 1,050 each month; if he has a more difficult problem, we get double that. We can use it as we wish. That doctor's visit takes me half a day. Luckily my son doesn't have to take medicine. Those that have to take medicine go more often. It makes me fed up! I've got to get off from work. I only get three days off a month and can't take more days off or I'll lose my job. Some don't even have to go at all. I said that, and the doctor replied, like a criticism, "Oh, you don't want to come so often?" Whereas in the beginning, I went every three months, now I can let half a year go [the doctor apparently relented]. Every two years I bring the forms up to date.

Viewing the primary purpose of these medical visits as registering for funds and not as working with the doctor to help her son, she calculated the costs of each and gave them up when they took more time than they were worth. "Besides free schooling, he also can get money for lunch and for the bus, but it's not so much; lunch costs only HKD 10 a day, and transport HKD 200 a month—together about HKD 400 monthly. They'll pay for half.

I don't try to get that money anymore. It's too much trouble to run around and fill out the forms for only HKD 200."

From age three to age seven (in 1990), Chung took Ka-Man to the training institute every day, where they taught him communication and self-care. They took two buses there and two more to return. Chung thought the care at the institute was good. There were occupational therapists, Red Cross teachers, and nurses with a ratio of almost one to one. "For two hours a day, he learned to care for himself and was taught to play with toys. That's as far as he could manage, although others learned more and could communicate like a normal child might." After this training Ka-Man went to a government-supported primary school for moderately disabled children; it had fewer staff. Chung was no longer responsible for bringing Ka-Man to and from school, and had only to meet his school bus, which gave her more time for other work.

As a second task, mothers are expected to help their children do homework. In dependent mothering the specialist teachers request mothers to keep up the exercises with their children so that the children do not regress. However, unlike mothering nondisabled children, it was hard to see results. Chung again weighed effort and effect. It seemed to her that Ka-Man was not benefiting from the interventions, and she didn't see any point in repeating the exercise programs without payoff. The speech therapist taught Ka-Man hand signs, but Chung didn't keep up the training. "It's hard for Ka-Man to learn. He doesn't look at people. He imitates signs like 'brush' and 'sleep,' but he needs you to ask him to do it. That's useless. So although I have been asked to continue the training at home, it doesn't help." Ka-Man lacked the capacity for spontaneous expression. Although it may have been rewarding for him to repeat known gestures, Chung did not gain satisfaction from his ability to mimic. Carefully organizing her mothering work within her time frame and funds, there was little leeway for attempting what she did not see as valuable to improving his condition.

We saw few specialized learning toys for Ka-Man in the home. He speedily completed simple puzzles and then was usually left with coins, marbles, and other things around the house. Chung believed her primary responsibility to Ka-Man was to keep him safe. Her approach toward his learning was like that toward her daughters, who were offered few learning opportunities beyond what was available at school. The difference was that the girls discerned what they needed from others and became able to argue for it (i.e., piano lessons, a computer), whereas Ka-Man could not.

Chung's inability to help her son become more normal did not sit easily with her. Dependency mothering work also involves managing impressions and handling stigma (Goffman 1963). As Chung viewed Ka-Man through others' eyes, she struggled against perceptions of him as a disabled child. She was quick to interpret others' comments as criticisms. Her association with a stigmatized offspring branded her as well, and she fought to normalize her son (Gray 2002). She interpreted the procedures for requesting financial help as disapproval. To Chung the term "Aid to the Disabled" signified that she had an "inferior" child, and at first she refused to take the allowance. She eventually accepted the money and even went on to fight for her rights to the full amount, although she had to present Ka-Man as severely disabled to get it. Playing up his disability troubled her a great deal because she wanted to be seen as a mother to a normal child.

The sisters also felt the stigma attached to having a disabled child in the family (McGraw and Walker 2007). Ka-Lei asked us why their brother was "like that." Was a disabled child a retribution for her mother's having done something wrong in a former life? Or, if he was the product of inheritance, would she give birth to a disabled child too? Chung defended Ka-Man to his sisters as well as everyone else. She found solace in a mothers support group, which gave her a sense of belonging and helped to shore up her self-worth (Brewer 1991). She learned that disabled children came from the full spectrum of family backgrounds. "Even the rich and the intellectuals have such children, and no one thing can account for it."

Meeting in the well-appointed Tsuen Wan Maxim Chinese Restaurant, Chung took these mothers gatherings as a perk to be enjoyed for a few more years while her son was cared for all day in the governmental institutions. Here, Chung could drop her defenses somewhat. "Our children went to the same preschool training institute in the past. We support each other and express our feelings. We all have our handicapped children in school now and can be free for a few more years." She was relieved to learn that Ka-Man was better behaved than many. She also learned that some parents resisted the stigma they felt by refusing to keep their child in day school because they got dirty there, saying that the institute didn't care much. These parents wanted a school that managed their children's behavior so that they looked normal and did not call attention to their disability. Chung appreciated that the school gave her much-needed "off" time, saying, "I think it's hard to take care of them. While we waited for him to be admitted, I kept him at home. That was very hard. Ka-Man gets dirty even at home."

Finally, mothering work usually lessens as children grow. However, a disabled child puts the mother's caregiver role permanently at the center of her life. Chung met the challenges of raising Ka-Man as best she could, but her goals narrowed. As she shouldered the family's daily maintenance, felt the blow that mothering a disabled child struck at her identity, and knew the pain of waiting for word from the immigration authorities (from whom they apparently never heard), her dream of reuniting with her family faded. Gradually she dropped her family emigration project. She accepted her family life as it was, as her fate.

Resigned to remaining in Hong Kong, she, like Chak-Lui, reflected that life would not be that different abroad.

> We haven't got much money. No matter where I go, I have to work. It's the same in foreign countries. Even if I were to go, I'd need to adjust. I'd be very anxious. I don't know how to start the whole family on a new way of life. Certainly, my brother will help us to find jobs and a place to live, but I still worry. Life here isn't bad. I've heard that many people in America are unemployed. Even in Hong Kong salary is low. You can hardly find a job here in the garment-making industry, let alone there."

She saw her choice as accepting reality. "It is not likely that a child like mine will be allowed to go. I can't leave him and he can't take care of himself. So I've given up hope. Sometimes I say to my husband 'I'll bring the two girls there, leaving him here with you.' But it's just a joke." The jest expressed Chung's sense that life had let her down. Her resignation was mixed with a palpable sorrow at the loss of her dream.

Resigning to Life in Hong Kong: 1993–2000

As Chak-Lui worked hard for his family, his fortunes improved somewhat. In 1993 he opted to drive a taxi full time, an option popular among laid-off workers. "I must meet my family expenses. I really had little choice—it's very hard to find someone to hire me at my age. In driving there's no age limit. You just hire the taxi and you can work for yourself. The cost for fuel and car rental is fixed. The rest depends on your effort. Even when you're sixty, you can still drive, though your insurance premium is high. By the time you're really not capable, you won't have the confidence to drive anyway." But Chung found fault with her husband's job choice, saying,

> He earns less than before. And driving is really draining. As a newcomer, he easily makes mistakes. During his first few weeks, he got caught driving in the wrong lane and had to pay fines. He's had accidents and had to bring the taxi to the shop to be fixed. He works long hours, but has to be alert. And they keep on changing the roads. At times he can't find his way. He even shows his passengers a map and lets them point out where they are going. His English

isn't good. He only knows words like "airport." Sometimes he won't pick up foreigners. He's like a foreigner himself!

Chak-Lui had trouble participating in home life. As a furniture mover, his hours had been regular and he helped with Ka-Man. Chung told us, "If there are no orders, he'll come back earlier and pick up Ka-Man for me." However, as a driver he tried to work as late as possible. He was also in an irascible mood. Chak-Lui had moved around as he delivered furniture, but now he was fixed behind the wheel. Tension gave him stomachaches, and he easily lost his temper. Chung commented, "Every evening when he's late, I think, did he have an accident? Was he stopped by police? Did he get fined? I always tell him to be careful." Ka-Lei protested at her mother's implied criticisms: "Father's a careful driver!" She was also pleased that her father was concerned enough to arrange a ride home for her from work at night. "When Father can't get me, the taxi station arranges for somebody to pick me up, though we still need to pay."

Gradually learning the ropes, Chak-Lui's earnings rose until, by our 1995 visit, long hours netted him HKD 5,000 a month. This was much below his wages as a skilled worker a decade before, but it was earning a living. Once again he was able to devote more time to Ka-Man. On one of our visits they went shopping in the mall for something Ka-Man needed. At another time Chak-Lui came back from work to take Ka-Man swimming. "I don't have hobbies. Whenever I have free time, I bring my son outdoors and play with him. We play ball and sometimes hike a few kilometers to the reservoir. He keeps up with me; I don't have to drag him. Autistic children need more activities. The girls are much older and don't like to play with him." Used to operating in the public sphere, Chak-Lui had no hesitation in bringing Ka-Man out and about, and was unembarrassed at being seen with him.

Chung's Activities

The bulk of caring for Ka-Man still fell to Chung. Although conditions are not identical, a survey of U.S. mothers of children with special needs found that one-fifth provided over twenty hours a week of home care and half reduced their hours of paid work or left work entirely (Leiter et al. 2004). This did not take into account their emotional work. Hong Kong's social services furnished little backup in these intimate family areas (Pearson and Ning 1997). Nevertheless, Chung tried to carve out activities for herself. She enjoyed an occasional mahjong game with her neighbors and tea with her support group. She also sought outside employment again late in 1993. "My neighbor who used to take garments home to work on together with

me is now a cashier in a Chinese restaurant. She found me a job there."
The most menial position on the floor, Chung carried cooked food from
the kitchen to the waitresses who served the customers.

> My salary's not so attractive, but I don't have a choice. After age thirty it's
> hard to find work. If we work part time at McDonalds, our salary would be
> less than HKD 12 an hour. For half a day, we'd only get a few dollars. They
> pay older women less. Here I get HKD 5,000 a month, lunch included. We get
> tips by rank. Four ranks for dim sum waitresses alone. Since I'm at the bot-
> tom, I get the smallest. If they didn't make much that day, I can't get any at all.
> That happens a lot. Restaurant business isn't so good 'cause of Hong Kong's
> economic problems.

She found her new line of work less demanding than garment making.
"Sometimes when we had to meet a production deadline and there were
many orders, we had to stitch without a pause until very late. In the restaurant, after you've finished your busy hours, you can relax a bit. Even when
it's busy, I can sometimes sit and rest." She also socialized more with her
coworkers. During one of our visits, she left to prepare for a coworker's
birthday party, excited to be in charge of ordering the cake. These activities
were part of her new life.

Scant Political Interest

The economic problems to which Chung referred relate to the roller-coaster
earnings of the working class that populated her restaurant as well as to low
public confidence in the Colonial government. Given the Hungs' dependence
on state services, we wondered if they might try to influence the public
sphere. However, they felt distant from political issues. Thoughts of 1997
were outside their concerns. Despite drawing on many strands of government assistance and resenting the amounts, Chung expressed little interest
in trying to use voting or community activities to shape the government that
so closely affected their daily lives. She left politics to the experts and felt
harassed at being urged to do more. Chung recalled that in previous local
elections, "Candidates knocked on our door, but I wasn't interested. I don't
know what they're doing. Someone visited our home and asked us to register.
So my husband did, but I don't know who he voted for." Looking after her
children and her other family tasks remained her core responsibilities.

The Hungs did not drop into the underclass. Both parents and children
followed their social networks, which led them into the new service sector:
Chung and Chak-Lui joined the manual services, and their daughters became white-collar clerks. Still, restructuring took its toll. With their income

halved, they became depressed, and when they pulled themselves up, their family roles had already gone separate ways.

Chung at Home

Most working parents have to juggle work and family tasks, and Chung's repeated travels with, and on behalf of, her disabled child made the time constraints of dependency care especially demanding. With only three days off work a month, she held to a strict time regimen. Chung's image of meeting her family responsibilities became measured in concrete terms, such as providing food and organizing pick-ups and drop-offs. Although she complained at her burden of housework, she saw it as "taking care of the family," which she considered her real work (DeVault 1991). "I set out the rolls and Horlick [chocolate drink] for my daughters at night. In the morning, I take Ka-Man to the school bus, go to work, then return home when he does." Chung scheduled everyone so that they all got out the door on time.

> My work shifts free me several hours in the middle. I go to the market, prepare the kids' dinner, which they'll later heat up in the microwave, and greet my son's school bus downstairs. At 6 P.M., one girl is at home and I'm at work again. Off at 10 P.M. Usually by the time I get home my family is asleep. Having three hours off is good so that I can do housework. My daughters find household chores tiring. They like things to be tidy, and yet they leave their books and other things on the table and don't put them back in the right place. Then they criticize me, saying that the place is like a garbage dump! They keep asking me to clean up, but though I feel it's their duty, I do it because I must take care of the family.

There was little dialogue in the family over responsibilities or goals in general and certainly not over housework. It was assumed that Chung would do it all. She felt mute before her better-educated daughters. "I can't argue with them. I don't know how to express myself. I am not clever. I let them decide their own way. Then there's no trouble."

Chung resented her family's poverty, but took solace in the fact that their public housing's open-air balcony, fenced in by a column of thin iron bars, faced the harbor, giving a spectacular view. From the living area, you could view brown and green sugarloaf-shaped hills and the blue-green sea. The sun shining in from the balcony brightened the rooms. Through the bars the family had witnessed the draining of the harbor as pieces of land around the typhoon shelter were reclaimed. Chung maintained that their luxurious view easily competed with the far more elegant dwellings and felt smug about her surroundings.

Chak-Lui had built wooden partitions to divide the 300–square-foot living space into two bedrooms (one for the girls and one for mother and son) and a sitting room. On summer nights he slept on a narrow plank bed on the exterior balcony to catch the breeze. Clothes dried from poles suspended horizontally from the balcony toward the horizon. A red shrine was poised in the middle of the living area.

They paid little attention to the appearance of the sofa, chairs, and cupboards in the living area, but up-to-date consumer items were important. Getting what Chung saw as the best brands made up for feelings of being restricted economically and socially (Mathews and Lui 2003). Even if their other plans did not work out, at least they participated in the wider consumer economy, a fact witnessed by a new 27–inch television set (topped by a video recorder), a new air conditioner, and an upright piano. "Second Daughter isn't outgoing, doesn't like electronic games, and seldom goes outside, so I bought a piano for her to play. It's Korean and cost us HKD 16,000. It's worth HKD 18,000 now!" Chung boasted.

Although it was not easily affordable, Ka-Lei had a computer. Her parents gave her HKD 13,000, and she decided on the model. Chung surveyed their accumulated goods, and commented, "Because we can't buy a place to live and we've no academic degrees, we buy things to entertain us. That's why so many Hong Kong people are willing to pay, buy, eat, and wear. Don't look so far into the future! Don't save so much! Now most people have an air conditioner, TV, video recorder, and we do too. It is the lowest, most basic living standard. That TV over there is new. The old one was broken so I saved up and bought a good one. I have to buy things to satisfy the girls." Chung's main complaint about their modest home was lack of private space for the girls. "When I see them holding books all the time, I feel tired for them. Studying is tough, especially since we don't have a room for them to study in. They work in the sitting room until late. We can't sleep because of their lights. Luckily it's quiet here because children around here have grown up and there's no mahjong playing at night."

Chung did not complain much about Tuen Mun's infrastructure, apart from occasional reflections on threats to her family's well-being. "The security of this area is so-so. Just a few days ago, my next-door neighbor was robbed in the lift. But they caught all four thieves in just two days! Still, we worry about teenage gangs in the corridors. We mainly stay inside at night." Thus Chung was enlarging her place in a narrow world through her outside work and social life, albeit mainly within her neighborhood.

Stigma: Circumscribed Social Spheres

Chung's sense of stigma led her to let go of her emigration dream. Parents of autistic children suffer the child's stigma themselves because of the contrast between the outward appearance of childhood normality and the child's socially inappropriate behavior (Gray 1993). Chung's lower status in society magnified how she perceived others saw her son, triggering extreme feelings of shame. Sensitive to strangers' views, she kept close to home (Gray 2002). In their familiar community, neighbors, shopkeepers, and others disregarded Ka-Man's actions as long as he was passive. Chung noted that "Ka-Man doesn't focus on much, so taking him to the market is not a problem, since he just follows along."

Afraid that his behavior would call attention to them, she seldom took Ka-Man on extended outings. "His appearance is not very different from others, but his behavior is very strange. It's hard to manage Ka-Man outside, now that he's getting older. He frightens others." Although Chak-Lui visited Macao yearly on his father's birthday, Chung rarely joined these excursions, embarrassed to travel in public with Ka-Man and aware of others' stares. "I haven't been to Macao for such a long time now I might not even recognize my husband's parents," she commented.

Chung was not able to deal with the unknown and could avoid the embarrassment of being out of place only in her home territory. As Probyn (2004) argues, the physiological experience of shame intersects with the physicality of place. Chung felt safer at home than in a strange place. However, by the mid-1990s Chung hoped people were becoming tolerant. "Times are changing. Few people understood autism before. Now that TV programs introduce this topic, people may accept him."

Obedient Daughters and Dependent Caregiving

The gendered system of dependent caregiving draws mothers and female siblings deeply into family care (McGraw and Walker 2007). Familistic ideology holds women accountable for moral conduct in families, gaining them virtue by being super-responsible. The Hung daughters understood themselves as good sisters to Ka-Man and were raised within this gendered sociocultural system to help out in the present and to adopt the family's burdens as their own in the future. They pledged to undertake Ka-Man's care, framing their role as meeting his needs (Harden 2005).

While young, the sisters' obligations were primarily limited to keeping an eye on their brother when their parents were out. They reported that they cooked, did light cleaning, and completed other simple chores, although Chung asserted the opposite. Eventually they should be able to support themselves, their elderly parents, and Ka-Man, if need be. They reassured Chung that they would take over their brother's care when she could no longer do so.

We asked, "Will your daughters console you by promising you they'll do well and repay the effort you've put out to bring them up?" Chung responded, "There's no need for them to say so explicitly. Certainly they'll repay when they grow up!" But she could not be certain and at another time expressed her ultimate concern about her own mortality (Kittay and Feder 1998). "I can arrange for my family okay now. I don't know what I'll do in the future, that's what I'm worried about. Still, it's useless to worry; it won't help." The girls' modest ambitions reflect the interplay between family resources, gender ideologies, the quality of schools, and their special caregiving role (Chan 2003). The Hungs hope to place the girls in modern service jobs, a step above their own blue-collar world. As long as the education department provided aid to them, they let the girls study. They did not direct their choices, letting the daughters choose their own paths. Since schools in their area trained youth for lower-level white collar jobs, it was taken for granted that this is what they would do.

It had occurred to Chung that the girls would benefit from family-tied migration. But sending them abroad to school alone in order to place them above their current station in life was beyond her expectations. Furthermore, given their special responsibility to their brother, they could not go unless all went together. In 1995 Chung reflected, "The next generation won't go into factory jobs like us in the past. Even those with only a few qualifications can go into sales. Like my elder daughter who has finished secondary education—if a higher institute admits her, she can continue; if not, she'll study in a college, even part time. Otherwise she goes to work. She is already twenty. I think that's enough education, but she replies to me, 'What's enough?' I am not clever in talking with them. I just let them to do what they like."

The eldest daughter, Ka-Lei, took a degree course in English translation. Chung applauded her efforts to save money: "My elder daughter is very good. She doesn't spend much and comes back for lunch. She also tutors and doesn't ask for spending money." While going to school, Ka-Lei worked in the office of a trading firm. She also earned HKD 100 per hour tutoring a Form 2 student. Her mediocre grades reflected these efforts. Her parents worried when, claiming to lack time, Ka-Lei revealed that she had reduced her tutoring to a few hours a week. "Boys are very naughty," she said. "It's tough to tutor. I want to quit." Her father counseled her, saying, "All students are the same. You should keep this one. He may be hard to replace." Unable to reason with her daughter, Chung expressed herself indirectly: "But you have time to gab on the phone!" she retorted. Ka-Lei's face fell at her mother's jibe, but she did not defend herself.

As long as they did their acceptable share at home and on the job, the daughters could choose their own friendships and activities. Studying in a Christian secondary school, the sociable Ka-Lei joined an evangelical Christian fellowship. She invited Chung to a fellowship meeting in order to lessen her mother's worries about this nontraditional group. Chung concluded that "church makes our daughter quite obedient."

Her school moved Ka-Lei forward on the white-collar track. In 1995 it covered each student's HKD 10,000 expenses on a six-week study tour to Australia. Classmates lived in private homes, had daily classes at the University of Melbourne, and went sightseeing. Ka-Lei enthused with vignettes of her first trip outside Hong Kong. "Students come back from the study tour with such good English. It's totally different there, the culture, the environment, and so on. You can really learn a lot." But she did not think of emigration, which was not taken up by those in her social fields.

After finishing her bachelor's degree in 1997, Ka-Lei continued working in the trading firm using her translation skills on faxes to clients. In 2000 she married a fellow churchgoer, a technician in the housing department, and was content to start her own family in Hong Kong.

Emigration: The Time Has Passed

Emigration is time-sensitive. The opportunities that family-tied migration might have opened greatly depend on the family life cycle. Waiting dampened Chung's desire to emigrate. In 1997 she summed up, saying, "The only reason to go might have been when the children were small so they could get good, free education. My parents suggested that I send my girls there for further education. But I won't go now; they've almost finished school. Also, Hong Kong's education is quite good and they can study well enough here. They get social assistance for school. There's no need to pay even for the matriculation course [to pass the exams to University]. Anyway, they're too young to live alone. They need to depend on others."

The Hungs had not passed the emigration torch to their children. Chung had not developed her daughter's ambition to go abroad, and Ka-Lei did not take emigration as her mission. Like her parents, Ka-Lei's ideas about life abroad were projections of the Hong Kong experiences she knew. Her study tour to Australia was not enough to kindle the flame. She limited her world vision to Hong Kong's mall life (Lui 2001). "What do I think about the overseas life style? It's very boring. I can't go to karaoke, shop, or do the things that people do here in Hong Kong. I'm almost finished with my schooling. Why should I go there? I wouldn't know what to do there."

Ka-Lei viewed her family's migration opportunity in terms of relationships, not as a response to global opportunities. Emigration was associated with joining a family she barely knew, and, unlike her mother, it was not a goal she valued highly. She could not imagine herself elsewhere. She would not sacrifice much for this emigration dream.

Thus not only had the time passed for emigration for Chung, it was no longer, if indeed it had ever been, part of her grown-up daughters' lives. Upon marriage, Ka-Lei no longer fit under the family umbrella in the emigration application. "That means, even if I can go, she can't go." Chung's deliberations reflect the strength of the family sphere for this laboring woman. Chung's emigration dream was that of drawing together her family, but she would not want to join her kin in Boston at the expense of those remaining in Hong Kong.

Summary

Chung's picture of emigration to America was grounded in family relations and bound up in kin feelings and ties rooted to particular institutions, places, and times. The desire for family-based emigration did not turn on anxiety over retrocession or competition for social status. A united family was more important to her than the promise of a higher station in life for her daughters. In her world, traditional institutions remained intact. She could not imagine that her family in Boston lived differently than she did in Hong Kong and expected that after moving to the other side of the world she would still live and work with kin and the immigrant community would support her.

In the end the goal of emigration was not easily attainable for the resource-poor Hungs. State regulations shut them out. Their application had low priority, and they were without funds or recognized skills to boost it. As the reality of dependency mothering took hold, Chung realized that not only could her family not overcome these political and economic barriers, but she could not go with a challenged son in tow. The Hungs' particular situation may have been special, but like other emigrant hopefuls without resources in our study, their application was not approved and they gave up migration as a pipe dream. Chung came to accept her modest family life as it was lived in Hong Kong's evolving community of the poor. She accepted things as they actually existed as opposed to having an idealistic or notional idea of them. The Hungs adapted to life as it is in the here and now of Hong Kong.

CHAPTER ELEVEN

The Chia Brothers
Constructing Hong Kong as the Place to Be

"Nowhere can we find a place better than Hong Kong"
—Bing-Kui, 1993

We have followed several laboring families as they negotiated the migration terrain, incorporating the "emigration fever" that swirled about them into the structures of their lives. The Wan (chapter 8) and Hung (chapter 10) families applied for immigration and the Szetos (chapter 9) considered applying to North America. None constructed a successful migration project. This chapter features nonemigrants—who represent the majority of Hong Kongers. Cross-border kin, work relations, and social networks tied the Chia brothers firmly to Hong Kong. Emigration was not part of their daily life. Hong Kong has often been described as a mobile city, and cross-border migration is part of its heritage. Those like the Chia brothers for whom Hong Kong was not their first home managed against great odds to rebuild their family economies in this new location but resisted another voyage.

Shy and junior, Bing-Kui consulted with his older brother Hon before agreeing to be interviewed. He often glanced at his brother to confirm his answer or simply commented, "the same opinion as my brother." Outgoing Hon dominated our visits, and over time his family came to occupy more of our story.

The Chias were a transborder migrant family. Escaping extreme poverty in China one by one, an uncle, an elder sister, and the two brothers took up illegal residence in Hong Kong during the 1960s and 1970s. We wondered, would they flee again because the place they had escaped with such difficulties was about to take over their new home? No, they had not run from China's politics. Their family script did not dictate their recouping lost status. Building a survival base for their kin group was their family goal. Having made it to Hong Kong, local as well as cross-border social relations dominated their lives. Hong Kong's reversion would strengthen their family relations and as the institutions surrounding integration with China evolved, their cross-border family ties became even easier to maintain.

Family Interdependence, Early Hong Kong Beginnings: 1962–79

The Chia family's migration history began when many people were leaving poverty-stricken Southeast China to seek work in Hong Kong. It was impossible to earn a living in their small hometown in Bao'an County (whose primary export seemed to be its own residents). The 1960s fishing industry in which the Chias were employed was experiencing a decline because of China's economic downturn after the Great Leap Forward (Jia and Chen 2001). Over a seventeen-year period starting in 1962 the oyster fishing boat belonging to the Chias dropped four of their family members off on Hong Kong's shores to find a better life.

At that time PRC migrants who succeeded in entering Hong Kong—legally or illegally—without being intercepted had the right to work and after seven years, to the right of abode. However, anyone caught by the authorities was immediately sent back. Uncle Tam, brother to Bing-Kui and Hon's mother, was the first to depart. Leaving his wife behind, he struggled for years to secure a foothold in Hong Kong's construction industry. Next came Kee-Lee, the eldest Chia sister. Her initial attempt failed; Kee-Lee was seized by authorities and returned to China. But she tried again and succeeded in 1972. Hon arrived in 1976, and younger brother Bing-Kui followed in 1979. He told us, "I was very young (sixteen years of age) and didn't want to leave, but my parents said it was for my own good. Life was harsh in China. My brother, sister, and mother's brother were already here. They'd take care of me." After arriving in Hong Kong, Bing-Kui depended closely on his two siblings and uncle. As was expected in this traditional patrilineal family, elder brother Hon took charge of Bing-Kui's care, both economically and psychologically.

Uncle Tam, who by this time had gained solid footing in the construction industry, took his sister's children under his wing. Hon recounted, "Uncle Tam took care of us. We lived in his house at first, and he found us jobs. We turned to him with any problems." Uncle Tam taught Hon and Bing-Kui the construction trade since they could not simply walk off the street and get a job. Kee-Lee moved rubble with carrying poles on Uncle Tam's subcontracted construction sites, and her husband taught Bing-Kui to pour cement and lay tiles for building foundations. Even with the support of their more established kin, learning the trade in this informal manner was not easy. Bing-Kui explained, "They don't hire people who are really inexperienced because it's a waste of time and money. New workers are just learning, don't finish on time, and you have to spend your time teaching them while paying them. As a fresh worker, I worked all over to learn, following those I knew. No one else will teach you."

From the start of their new lives in Hong Kong, the Chia brothers settled into building their own families and helping the fortunes of those relatives left behind, until their Bao'an community, on the outskirts of the city of Shenzhen, prospered.

Settling in Hong Kong, Depending on Ones' Own: 1980–92

Their networks were the means through which the brothers met their wives, the first step in building a family. Hon's wife, A-Ling, came from a neighboring village in China. Introduced through mutual contacts, they married shortly after he settled in Hong Kong. A traditional working-class woman, A-Ling believed that her main job was to have children, raise them to the best of her abilities, and provide a nourishing home for all. She also added to the family economy by taking on work, first as a seamstress and later as a cleaner, when such work existed. She and Hon welcomed the first of four children, a daughter they named Angel, a year after they were married.

Bing-Kui's marriage path was more tenuous. This shy lad had an arranged match to Eu-Yong, a lovely Hakka Chinese woman from Jakarta. She was only twenty years old when they met and did not speak Cantonese. Both she and her older sister had taken a kind of marriage tour. Eu-Yong reminisced, saying, "At home we have a tour to Hong Kong. My sister joined it two years ago, and someone on the tour recommended a New Territories village guy to her and they got married. I took that tour also. The guide knew I had a sister here and also that I wasn't married. Eventually someone introduced me to Bing-Kui. Even though I'm far from home, it's good because I have my sister here."

The brothers rented a small apartment together in Kowloon Bay until 1986 when the Hong Kong government requisitioned it to construct an overpass. They next purchased an apartment together in the neighboring Kwun Tong District. Hon was proud of meeting his family needs, and housing was central. "We could have waited for resettlement, but as a father I've a big responsibility. So we decided to get this place right away. The real estate agent helped us find a walk-up flat in this old building. The two of us paid a down payment of HKD 100,000 and we pay HKD 2,100 per month each for the mortgage. It'll take us a long time to pay it off."

Kwun Tong, one of Hong Kong's earliest industrial zones and most densely populated areas, does not look like other rebuilt areas with their high rises, condominiums, malls, and upscale European stores. Although most of the factories have moved to China, and flashy Hong Kong outlets have replaced the pushcart hawkers with factory seconds that Uncle Chou (chapter 4) plied in his early days, it still recalls its early factory origins. Buildings, streets, and air have a permanent gray cast. Aging buildings make Kwun Tong affordable to many of the city's poorest residents, although it is slated for redevelopment.

There is no doorbell on the main door to the Chias' building, so we phoned them to descend three flights of stairs to let us in. Despite the structure's shabby appearance, the brothers did not complain. For poor Mainland migrants, owning a family home in this area was an accomplishment. "Although the outside doesn't look so good, we renovated the inside to look better," Hon said, making clear his role in providing housing for them all.

During the 1980s Hon had extended his construction activities to include interior decorating and home improvements. He branched out into his own entrepreneurial business, which he registered although he did not have an actual office. He ran his company from cardboard boxes containing over one thousand neatly filed name cards, boasting that it was easy for his colleagues to contact him at home.

We first visited the Chias in 1992, six years after the brothers had moved into these quarters. To house the two families, Hon had put his skills to work, dividing the long 700–square-foot apartment into small domains. Bing-Kui's family, soon to have their first child, occupied a smaller 100–square-foot room. Hon, A-Ling, and their three daughters took two rooms. Each family had an air conditioner—the windows were rarely opened so as to keep out Kwun Tong's sooty air.

As he showed us around, Hon proudly pointed out the work he had undertaken over the years: kitchen floor tiles, the sizable chandelier hung from the living room ceiling, and the large stand that housed a koi aquarium, "not for better feng shui [fate], but just for fun, to make it more lively." Hon had also built an attractive teak wall cupboard in the sitting room, testifying to his craftsmanship, and finished the floors in a fine wood. To A-Ling's complaint that the cupboard looked worn, Hon retorted, "It used to be very good." He proudly stated that he had paid only HKD 100,000 for materials—a bargain—because he was recognized in the business. Furniture designed by Hon himself filled the space almost completely.

Their flat had been illegally enlarged. After their neighbor one floor above built a terrace for plants, Hon extended his living room underneath. The ceiling leaked constantly from the plant watering, and although he replastered often, it didn't help much. The electrical system also caused some problems. Because there were too few sockets for all their appliances, the air conditioner, refrigerator, rice cooker, television, and fan were plugged together with adapters. Once, when we attended second daughter Lucilla's sumptuous birthday dinner, water bubbled from the rice cooker onto the power supply, short-circuiting the electrical system. Luckily, Bing-Kui arrived and fixed the power supply just in time and cooking continued. Hon didn't acknowledge his wife's skeptical glances when he protested to us that his renovation skills had certainly improved from years before.

This apartment concretely manifested the link between kin and place in their lives, the importance of which was a great deterrent to further migration. By the way Hon dominated even this physical space, we could see that if he was not planning to emigrate, the thought would not cross Bing-Kui's mind.

Tangible Needs or Abstract Concerns? 1992–97

"1997? We don't talk about something so long term."
—Bing-Kui, 1993

The Chia brothers were part of a practical, tangible world in which personal relationships were paramount. They shared their lives with us because they considered us friends. They were less interested in our research than in the opportunity to have interesting chats. "You've come for a casual conversation with us, like the last time!" When our queries moved away from the here and now of their lives in Hong Kong, they looked puzzled and didn't understand the drift. Hon responded to our questions with repartee, swore when excited, and made innuendoes about our male college student assistant chasing girls (much to our assistant's embarrassment). He teasingly called Janet Salaff, "Gao Sao [Professor]—Gao Sao, why didn't you call us when you came to Hong Kong last time?"—to the point that A-Ling thought that "Gao Sao" was Janet's name.

Still, we saw that Hon, under his bravado and his repartee, and the more soft-spoken Bing-Kui did have real concerns about the future. They did not present these issues in terms of abstract analyses as did the better-educated people we met. Instead their discussions took a practical turn, divided into short- and long-term concerns. Their families' economies, which they thought most pressing, figured as short-term concerns. Long-term issues like politics that may have caused anxiety did not engage them at all. Less easily characterized was worry about their low social status, which arose often in their conversations. International migration was not part of their cognitive repertoire. They may have been aware of migration as part of the objective environment, but they would not act on it (Faist 2000; Brown et al. 1977).

Neither brother expressed worry over the political spinoff of reversion to China. Even though they knew that the Mainland government had some problematic policies, they did not know much about them. Bing-Kui and Hon's village was far from China's key political struggles, and they had never suffered politically. Having only gone as far as primary school, Bing-Kui had little occasion to study China's history. "Had your parents told you anything about the Cultural Revolution?" we asked. Bing-Kui retorted, "How dare we talk about China's policy!" Like other border crossers who fled poverty, an abstract loss of freedom was not one of their issues (Goodstadt 2005).

When asked about retrocession, Bing-Kui stated simply in 1993 that "we don't worry about it." What do their kin in Hong Kong say? "We meet or phone every week and usually discuss our life, not 1997. We don't talk about something so long term." What was worth chatting about were the immediate issues of the day.

Their mission in Hong Kong was reestablishing a vital family economy. Within this local context, they saw reunion with China largely positively. Like the Ongs (chapter 7), with their family divided by the border the Chias returned to China often to see kin as well as to get low-cost services. On one of our visits, Hon had just returned from his hometown where he attended his mother's birthday banquet. He brought back three chickens, which were cheaper there. He had seen a dentist and had a tooth extracted. The dentist told him that he needed ten visits to fix his dental problems. Hon told us that dental work in China costs only half as much as in Hong Kong, and he didn't have to wait as long. The time it took to return to China did not seem to bother him, since he could visit his kin at the same time. The Chias expected that reversion would ease family relations.

Neither brother was much interested in political participation. Hon insisted that "Politics is an insider's game," and as a common citizen, he couldn't know the "inside part." As usual, Bing-Kui echoed the opinions of others in authority. "I don't know anything about politics. I only can listen to the reports on TV and radio." He affirmed, "It's best not to take back Hong Kong," but expressed confidence in the future. The brothers had put behind them the deep poverty they had experienced while growing up and made material progress. Retrocession would not return them to a situation like that from which they fled as youths, and any change beyond that was not of great matter. Bing-Kui drew on the views of those close to him. "According to my friends, there shouldn't be a great change after 1997."

Economics hit home. Hon mulled over the panicked emigration of the affluent, which he reckoned had led to the downturn in the Hong Kong property market and depressed investment in housing and other projects on which he labored. He worried about the family economy, especially given his desire to have a son for their future. Their first three children were girls. "Do you think of having another one?" we asked in 1993. Hon weighed his answer: "We don't know. Actually having all these children is not that easy. Sometimes, if we're between jobs, things are difficult. And we also have to help them in their homework, so it's really tough." Despite his considered answer, Hon and A-Ling admitted to being traditional in trying for a son to the point of having one more child. The economics of raising a large family, investing in education, and even dealing with housing constraints would not deter them.

To help the family economy, A-Ling did outwork in the garment trade on her own industrial sewing machine. She worked hard and it entered her own private life. Hon's beeper once went off at the restaurant where we were eating dinner, announcing that A-Ling had to deliver finished garments. Their daughters, who knew the number by heart, rushed to the restaurant phone and called the contractor. Then A-Ling left before finishing dinner to deliver the sweaters. By the mid-1990s, when orders no longer came to Hong Kong seamstresses, A-Ling turned to part-time cleaning. Her loss of work greatly affected her, as she had few pastimes.

In contrast, construction prospered during the years leading up to retrocession in Hong Kong's pre-handover boom. But the Chias did not expect the good life to last, especially since the industry was based on bodily strength. Bing-Kui told us, "We work from our 'teens to our early forties. If you're forty-seven and look for work, a boss will assume that you're a slow worker because of your age and won't employ you. My brother-in-law is older than me, but he's been doing it for a long time now; that's why he can stay on. Besides, he's a 'boss' himself."

The job pushed the limits of physicality. "Last month the rainy season began, but we still worked a full week. Usually if it's just a shower, we continue working. If it's storming, then we cover and protect the outdoor work and continue with the indoor work. But we also have times where we work outside while it's raining. So, we're always wet!" Because their salary is calculated by the time worked—a day's pay in the mid-1990s was around

HKD 500—they couldn't go inside just to avoid a drizzle. "It's hard-earned money. Not really enough, but we can still survive. But we're always exposed to danger. Only office workers don't have to take risks."

Underscoring the physical danger in this work, Bing-Kui referred to a 1993 construction site accident when cables supporting a makeshift elevator broke and workers plunged to the ground. He was understandably disturbed at the loss of life, but then shrugged it off, "We are young; we just work hard. If you are educated, you can always find another job, but a laborer is different."[1]

Not surprisingly, given the physical nature of the construction industry, when they talked about the hardships in their work they focused on the body. Pun (2005) draws on bodily images to depict the immense changes that young country women undergo when they are roughly reshaped into attendants of a fast-moving assembly line. Like these women, construction workers immediately feel the work they do on and through their bodies with discomfort, danger, and physical fights. To escape this confining circle of physicality, workers must save money to start their own business. Because this option is constrained, workers at this level seldom leave the work site. Even so, Bing-Kui felt it was possible to "find a big project and save some money."

The brothers also dreamed of opening their own business together. Hon voiced a refrain similar to that expressed by the Detroit automobile workers Chinoy (1955) studied, the workers in Hong Kong's early industrial years Wong (1999) learned about, and others we interviewed for this book (including Brian Wan, chapter 8). "Hard work can maintain my family living, but being an employee is useless. You'll get nothing even if you work your whole life," pronounced Hon. Without much education the Chias had to work hard in a tough trade to make a family wage. "Our own business?— it's just a dream," Bing-Kui confessed.

Having gotten skills on the job without formal apprenticeship training and lacking a trade certificate, the Chia siblings could not become permanent employees. They constantly sought new work (Ip and Ng 2007). Hon pointed out that "a project in a new building lasts about six months. But we're not stable even in the middle. They fire people when they're displeased with their performance. Lots of unemployed people are applying for work every day. Even if you get a job, if you don't work fast enough, you go! Sometimes the boss stands behind you while you're working. You can't even rest; you don't want them to see you just sitting around. So you can't be sure how long you can stay."

Since they rarely stayed on a job site for long, they relied on personal relations to find jobs on other sites. In the mid-1990s Uncle Tam was still able to offer occasional employment to the Chia siblings, and they also counted on others. Bing-Kui said, "Brother-In-Law introduces me to jobs. Someone's needing a person, he'll phone me, 'Come over to work, help out.'" Bing-Kui boasted that his skills and personal networks would get him through. "Though some contractors prefer to import labor from China at half our wage for simple projects, I'm not affected. I'm skillful and I know many people." The instability of their work deepened the brothers' dependence on their local relations and strengthened their attachment to the community.

The Chias' low qualifications were obstacles to getting ahead in Hong Kong or abroad. Lack of English education, the painful sign of lower status that blocked them from the better jobs, came up at all turns (Chan 2002). Asked if they voted in the recent elections, Bing-Kui confessed, "I just randomly chose among the candidates. As most of it's in English, I don't understand anything. If I could understand it, then why should I work as a coolie, or as a construction worker, or at other hard labor? It's very simple, the more educated you are, the more pay you get." Hon escalated the topic, saying, "For instance, the airport, or other issues like hiring foreign workers—just because those mothers of a turtle egg can speak a few English words, they're able to get the high-paid jobs. And because we can't, we didn't get them and end up with a low salary." Hon's focus on knowing people kept him from voting. "I'm not so concerned with these things. When they sent me the form, I told my wife to throw it away. I don't know the candidates—how can I vote?"

Turning to migration, our discussion moved quickly to the topic of qualifications. The brothers were aware of their limited chances at success. "Migration overseas? How could we qualify?" Bing-Kui queried with strong emotions. If he went abroad, "I couldn't communicate with other people, couldn't even seek help! In Hong Kong, I can scold people as I like, and I can understand others' scoldings, because we have 'the same voice.'" This was important, because "here people take care of each other." Even if their new rulers were Mainlanders, he expected they would abide by the cultural norm of fraternity. "As we are also Chinese, there should be no mistreatment by each other." Clearly the Chias felt at home in their small niche in Hong Kong where they knew the ins and outs. Going abroad was another story.

"No money" was another reason for not pursuing emigration. Bing-Kui estimated that he'd need at least HKD 100,000 to emigrate (which was actually a fraction of the required amount). He was also aware of his dismal economic prospects abroad where he "might not even get a job cleaning dishes!" The brothers figured that those who emigrate have more money, and so for them getting jobs would not be so important. In the end, however, their lack of resources was not the main reason they rejected emigration. The Chia brothers' livelihood was intertwined with kin, and they were afraid to venture where they had no links with people on whom they could depend. Past his close ties with kin in Hong Kong were ties with those nearby in China. Bing-Kui asked rhetorically, "How can I emigrate? I don't know anyone. How could I find work? I have an uncle in the States whom I've never seen. If I passed him in the street, I wouldn't recognize him. There's no feeling between us. He couldn't help me at all. Among my close relatives, nobody intends to leave, so we never talk about it. Would my workmates emigrate? No, it's the same story."

The importance of their local relations turned the Chias decidedly against migration. Their network was characterized by multiplex relations so dense they permeated every aspect of the brothers' work and home lives. Rooted in place, they would not consider emigrating and leaving Hong Kong, the place they had worked so hard to get to and where they built up local reputations. Not only would they not be eligible to immigrate legally to the West, but their lives would not make sense to them outside this setting. Any immediate difficulties they faced, whether social or work related, could be alleviated through somebody they know. Other issues that could not be so handled got pushed aside. Their economic and social relations, ease of communication, and quality of life made Bing-Kui certain that "nowhere can we find a place better than Hong Kong."

Post-handover and Beyond: 1997–2006

In early 1997 the height of the property boom, Hon's labor was suddenly in demand. He juggled several projects at once, earning HKD 800 per day. However, the recession that came at the end of the year underlined the inherent instability of construction. On a personal level, clients who were aware of Hon's desperate fix demanded a lower price. Hon had renovated a restaurant that, according to his original quote, should have brought in over HKD 30,000 profit. Half done, the owner argued him down, and in the end Hon figured he only earned a laborer's wage. When asked if he would work on interior design for the Jockey Club where Bing-Kui and his sister were trying to get work, he retorted, "Not only do I want to work for the Jockey Club, I want to 'remove the turf' [clean up, or win money from gambling] there."

Gambling

> When races were on you could hear the crowds—a funny
> sound—loud, almost frightening, it seemed to surge after you
> down the streets like great waves of invisible water.
> —Waters 2006

Hong Kong has long been obsessed with gambling—whether horse racing, buying lottery tickets, or investing on the stock market—as part of the popular dream of making it. The Jockey Club rakes in USD 11 billion yearly from the million people who bet on horses (Landler 2001). The sport is organized to look like clean fun for the family with colorful circus tents and food fairs where Big Macs are renamed to fit the scene. People from all walks of life gather in the main betting hall and race area, the excitement of the game bridging social gaps for a short while. Races are boisterously social. The Chias go for the entertainment, thrill of winning, and a desire to escape reality. With no one concerned about credentials, they can boast of their accumulated racing knowledge and strategies. If they win big, they can quit manual labor and perhaps finance a business for themselves and their kin across the border.

This passion drew in everyone. One evening in 2006 as we reached with our chopsticks into the bubbling hot pots on the dining room table, we took a break while all joined in and enthusiastically discussed the "Queen's Plate" scheduled for the next day. The brothers planned to go to Sha Tin together, each with his own favorite in mind. Alongside others dressed in rough construction-worker garb, Hon and Bing-Kui lined up at kiosks to place bets on the Hong Kong Long Distance Horse Championship, with bets starting at HKD 1,000. Silent Witness, the most famous horse Hong Kong had produced, had won every start and was slated for the Kentucky Derby. Wild with enthusiasm, spectators crowded the cement ground floor and rushed to line up to get souvenirs in the horse's colors, trampling and injuring each other. Meanwhile, in the owners' carpeted luxury restaurant upstairs, guests sipped champagne, unaware of the melee below.

A-Ling gambled as well. Her sport was mahjong, which she played two or three times a week. On a mid-June afternoon in 1997 she lost several hundred dollars in a neighborhood mahjong game. She confessed that when she did not have work, she spent more on the game because she was bored and had time to play.

The Chias rarely won at gambling, and their hard-won earnings flowed out as a result of their addiction. Although they did not live deeply in debt, and the outcome of racing fervor was not as serious as with some (Wong

2001), gambling disrupted family life. Family quarrels centered on gambling. A-Ling once seized her turn in the dinner conversation to complain that Hon spent too much money and time betting, saying it was not good for him or the family. "He reads the racing news while eating dinner. It's a very bad example for the children. On racing day he turns up the TV volume very high. It disturbs the children who are doing their homework." She then attributed the children's mediocre school results to their noisy home environment. Hon responded emotionally, "I can't give up my hobby for the children. I work very hard and want entertainment after work. If it's forbidden, I'd rather die!" A-Ling protested, "But you can turn the volume lower." Emphasizing that gambling was his self-expression, Hon retorted, "It wouldn't be fun! I have the right!"

Hon then chastised A-Ling for losing more than HKD 100,000 on the stock market, implying she had no right to blame him. He added almost proudly, "Mother of a turtle egg, I lost HKD 50,000—almost my whole savings—on Pacific Century Cyberworks."[2]

Gambling reflected their living in the here and now. It was something they could do with those around them, and it bonded the brothers. In their circles after a hard day's work, discussions about racing accompanied tips on future jobs. In other circles, such networking might have included thoughts on emigration, but the Chias' networks remained local. They also thought that gambling was something best done in Hong Kong.

Improved Family Living

Their constant toil improved their livelihood. When we visited in 2000, Bing-Kui, his sister, and his brother-in-law finally had a "big project." Their work group was renovating the Happy Valley Jockey Club. With a tight deadline the Jockey Club paid a premium of HKD 640 a day. Bing-Kui relied on his network to get into this project, claiming to know 90 percent of those on this site. "I usually follow my group. When they tell me the place, then I go. I also find projects by going to a certain teahouse in the morning, where people look for workers."

In 2006 Hon was working on a team laying marble in the renowned Mandarin Hotel. He landed this job through his social networks, which were not confined to his neighborhood but ranged around the territory. He had established a reputation that held, specific to Hong Kong. These ties bound the Chias to Hong Kong.

They relaxed, assured that their hometown, Bao'an, had emerged from poverty and kin no longer needed their ongoing remittances. In fact, the Mainlanders were doing even better than they. Three of the Chias' younger brothers and sisters had left fishing to become pork butchers in the market, a business introduced by a sister's husband. Bing-Kui protested that his work was tougher than his Mainland siblings' "more stable" employment. "For us, everything's unstable. We don't know how long we can work in this field. If it rains, we have to stop and aren't earning. Unlike us, they can go and open their stalls or they can just stay at home if it rains." Nevertheless, the Chia brothers' hard-gained reputations were not portable. Not surprisingly, neither considered a return move.

With his livelihood improving, Bing-Kui moved his family out of the brothers' shared flat when his second child (a son) was born in 1999. He, Eu-Yong, and their two children now lived in government housing in Tin Shui Wai, a considerable distance away.

With housing and work secured—the main goals of laboring families— they brushed off the idea of returning to China to live. "Go back to live? Don't bother me!" snorted Bing-Kui. So far, their success proved that Hong Kong's economy was good to them, and they felt they could not do better elsewhere. "It's the only place I can raise my family," said Hon. Furthermore, the border became less of a social demarcation when the SAR government extended tourist visas more freely to Mainlanders. On New Year's Day in 2005 the Chias excitedly planned to show around their brothers and sisters who would visit Hong Kong for the first time. To the Chias the meaning of reversion at an everyday level was making it possible to get closer to kin.

The Next Generation

A-Ling was pregnant again. She was nearly forty, and Angel, their oldest daughter, was a teenager. The Hong Kong hospital authorities refused to reveal the ultrasound information about whether she was carrying the precious son she and Hon wanted. "The doctor said we don't have to know," she reported. After consulting with her friends, A-Ling guessed she would have a boy by the way the child moved. It was a common practice for women in their circles to try to influence the baby's gender by practicing a kind of brainwashing. Eu-Yong had done this successfully when she was expecting her second child. She had kept talking to herself and others saying, "It must be a boy." A-Ling surely did the same.

When we returned in 2001, A-Ling beamed as she showed us her infant son. On our next visit in 2003, their daughters carried the boy around like they did their pet Pekinese. It was clear that the son was the new king of the home; Hon let him do whatever he wanted. As his mother, A-Ling's status had also risen.

When considering their children's future, the Chias' approach resembled that of the Wans or Hungs. They mainly thought that children learned according to their abilities, a capacity set at birth. Hon said his daughters were not good at school—they were born like that, he said. He worried about their examination results and bemoaned that they did not understand their classwork, got poor grades, and were asked to repeat courses. Although Hon knew that education was the basis for higher-level jobs, he did not reflect on how to make that happen. Helping with schoolwork was beyond him. He was reluctant to pay for tutors, whom he believed would not help much. He drew on those better educated that he knew, his cultural capital. Would Gao Sao (Janet Salaff) help Angel come to Canada for a bachelor's degree? Angel nearly died of embarrassment, her face turning bright red at her father's call for personal assistance. He pressed our research assistant, who lived nearby, into coaching Angel in his spare time. It was not enough. Angel took the certificate exam (the public examination for all school children in Hong Kong), passed only one subject, and was told to repeat the course.

The height of their expectations was that their daughters would get into office or sales jobs with the new economy. These were not strenuous or dangerous jobs, yet they were low paying because they are dominated by women without higher education. "Don't work as hard as we did!" they warned Angel to encourage her to complete her degree.

Luckily, Angel had a good relationship with her teacher, who arranged a job for Angel as a receptionist in a Japanese trading company, so she joined Hong Kong's growing nonmanual workforce. Angel's career fulfilled her parents' hopes. With minimal skills she began at HKD 6,000 monthly, more than her mother had ever earned. She answered clients' inquiries, stamped envelopes, and typed simple documents—all easy work. She felt luckier than her classmates who didn't have connections to get a job. Nevertheless, since communication had to be in English—one of her poorest subjects—working in a foreign firm was painful. She didn't know how to translate her words and ideas from Chinese and made grammatical mistakes with her "Chinese-style" English. She got confused if her colleagues spoke too fast or used complicated sentences while telling her what to do. Nevertheless, she passed the three-month probation period and received a HKD 1,000 raise. To meet her employer's expectations Angel continued her studies in evening school. Even though she had always been worried about her math ability, she studied accounting, paying for it herself. Her grueling regimen tired her out by the time she returned home at night.

Second daughter Lucilla left school and became a sales clerk in Causeway Bay. Now both daughters held service-sector jobs. When Lucilla returned late in the evening, tired after working long hours at the boutique, her mother fussed over her dinner, ensuring Lucilla would not miss out on choice pieces of seafood and meats.

Hon was relieved that his girls did not need to ask for money from their parents anymore. About their jobs, A-Ling said, "So so, not too good, not too bad." In one generation, the Chia family had moved from fishing to arduous but adequately waged construction work and then to the new service sector, in step with working-class careers. They were satisfied with what Hong Kong had given them. In their view, emigration would not improve their lives.

Summary

"Nowhere can we find a place better than Hong Kong." The self-congratulatory theme of the Chia brothers expresses the importance of locality in their lives. Research has found that Mexican working-class immigrants to the United States depend on social networks that reach to labor jobs in other locations (Palloni et al. 2001; Massey et al. 1987). Since the Chias' social relations, their main resource, did not reach past China, they remained interdependent with those they could rely on in Hong Kong. Ever since their arrival, penniless and literally "off the boat," their family members luckily honored their obligations, thus reaffirming that the brothers could not move beyond their embrace. Hong Kong's property and construction boom gave Bing-Kui and Hon earnings they had not dreamed of in their fishing village, with which in turn they supported village kin. They helped each other enter the construction industry and shared housing and advice. Risk cemented their personal ties. They lived well and spent freely, their livelihood turning on the short-term demand for their brawn. Their world was peopled with ties to kin and coworkers—often the same individuals. With their relations remaining local, they had no network pulling toward emigration and they did not fear that reversion would jeopardize these bonds. Even after retrocession and the steep drop in the housing market, they did not perceive emigration as improving their economic position. They still had work and homes of their own.

Years earlier their family script had led them to Hong Kong to work together to improve the family economy; they were successful at that. Their personal reality, including their decision-making processes, were collectively oriented. Since their access to jobs did not span the seas, they had little notion of a life outside their familiar group of personal contacts. They made sense of their local setting by emphasizing that only in Hong Kong had they been able to form successful families—something undreamt of in their poverty-stricken past. Thoughts of emigration did not provide a lens through which they could enact a future scenario of family betterment.

Without large international bodies to take notice and recruit them, without kin or workmates abroad, this existence grounded in the local did not spur an interest in moving or an ability to emigrate. At these institutional levels, these people are not family migrants. For the Chias, the boat stops in Hong Kong.

CHAPTER TWELVE

CONCLUSION
Movers and Stayers

When we began our study in 1991, well after plans for Hong Kong's retrocession to China were finalized, 12 percent of the 1,552 people we interviewed had plans to emigrate. Extrapolating this finding to a population level underscores the significant impact migrants would have both on Hong Kong and on receiving countries. The 1997 handover positioned Hong Kong on the brink of what could have been a mass exodus. But this was not the case for all.

We followed the course of a cross-section of our survey respondents to see what happened as retrocession approached. Would those who planned to leave follow through? Would more decide to leave as 1997 drew nearer? What shaped their migration trajectories?

This book introduces nine of these Hong Kong families from diverse social backgrounds, some of whom planned to leave, others of whom committed to stay. Asking what motivated them to exit, we distinguish three levels of social institutions: large-scale regulatory institutions, intermediate-level social relations, and more personal cognitive-cultural frames. We learned from the families we talked with how social class shaped the ways institutions affected migration decisions and outcomes. As well, the meaning of the handover differed greatly among families. Although retrocession spurred the migration of many, others had begun their migration journeys—if only in thought—long before 1997 had become an issue. For still other stayers, the handover was a welcome event, signaling a return to the homeland. To understand how a family's migration trajectory was shaped, we need to understand the family's place in the range of institutional structures.

Below we summarize how the institutions in which families were embedded figured in who left and who stayed, and the reception that movers encountered. We then spotlight the critical role of the Chinese family in migration. Finally, we compare the experiences of other family regimes to provide a broader context to Hong Kong family migration.

Social Position and Migration

Professional and Business Classes: Doors Open for Immigration

Business and professional families were embedded in structures at each level that prompted emigration, resulting in the high proportion of families from these classes (17 percent) who applied to emigrate. For many with resources, the shifting institutional terrain in Hong Kong was powerfully felt on a personal level and often sparked thoughts of exiting. Having invested a lifetime in their vocations and valuing the orderly progression of their careers, professionals such as Luk (chapter 3) and Francis Kwong (chapter 5) feared that China's poorly developed legal frameworks would distort the internationally respected standards their occupations had achieved. This concern was echoed among businessmen like Uncle Chou (chapter 4) who prided themselves on the quality of their work and feared that they could not remain competitive given Mainland China's reputedly slipshod manner of conducting business. They also anticipated greater competition from Mainland firms having the advantage of cheaper labor.

Threats to their professional success and integrity, felt on a personal level, were crucial in motivating these classes to consider emigration. People mobilize to protect their identities—which at the cognitive level are strongly linked to their careers. Professional and economic institutional structures shaped their identities as people who could live and work elsewhere. Working in a firm with branches in distant locales, holding membership in international societies, training abroad, and travel for pleasure introduced them to their foreign counterparts and familiarized them with the operations of their jobs abroad. They had a sense of their place as well-positioned Hong Kongers who could afford to expand their options abroad in the face of an uncertain future in Hong Kong. As the middle class shared their concerns with associates, the idea that it was advantageous to emigrate spread and paths abroad became institutionalized.

Once motivated, they applied through the point system that rewarded human capital, bringing into play state institutions that determined their acceptance. Professional and business-class applicants were pressed to immigrate. Gatekeepers promoted an image of the "ideal" immigrant with whom the elites in our study could identify. Lawyers, bankers, and immigration specialists jumped in to support their applications, swelling their numbers.

Further fueling their sense of comfort with the international scene, Hong Kong organizations in which such people were elites lobbied on their behalf to secure them the Right of Abode in Singapore, Great Britain, and other nations. Such strategies to keep their hard-to-replace skills built confidence in their success in moving abroad. But, as each mover would discover, the surface similarities they saw hid fundamental differences between the professional worlds in Hong Kong and internationally.

Our elite families had established themselves in Hong Kong, where local structures ensured their success, but once abroad structures clashed unexpectedly, with unhappy outcomes for them. Despite being part of the global reach, structures could not ensure a family's smooth integration into the foreign country nor their ability to earn a living wage. When they tried to relocate their global occupations and memberships, their credentials, training, and experience went unrecognized. The professionals learned that they could not project their Hong Kong contacts into the host country.

Local investments qualified them as immigrants, but because their social fields did not give them access to reliable information, they failed to locate a profitable niche. Uncle Chou, Luk, and Leung (Chou's kin), each of whom had anticipated that they could successfully invest in Toronto, turned from one short-lived business to another and then revised their plans. Finding that they could not count on overseas earnings, Uncle Chou, Francis Kwong, and the Leungs commuted for years to support their families. Astronaut life was an extreme example of clashing social structures at home and abroad.

Hong Kong's elite emigrants stayed strongly connected to colleagues back home, and these networks generated return migration to Hong Kong and a transnational status for the breadwinner in the family. Ultimately, they ended their cross-Pacific journeys by seeking less profitable work in Toronto (Francis Kwong and the Leungs) or retiring (Uncle Chou). Luk received his Canadian citizenship while still in Hong Kong, where he opted to remain in the end.

Over the years many professional families altered their perceptions of the future, no longer associating massive institutional change with the handover. As the institutional environment changed, and the structures that once appeared to support migration later did not, they brought their personal identity in line with Hong Kong's evolving institutional environment. Many cancelled plans to leave, while others who left returned (Salaff et al. 2008).

Lower-Middle-Class Families
Lower-middle-class families had less contact with global institutions or international social fields that prompted thoughts of migration or enabled

success. The less affluent they were, the harder it was to pass the resource test. Thus few met the state's immigration criteria.

In the 1991 survey, only 4.6 percent of the lower middle class had applied to immigrate abroad. Our book documents the narratives of two lower-middle-class families. The Gungs (chapter 6) and the Wans (chapter 8) had learned that their applications were unsuccessful. The occupations they had undertaken for a significant period of their lives did not reach outside Hong Kong, and none demanded specialized formal education. Additionally, no foreign colleagues (potential channels to international jobs) entered their daily routine. As a white-collar worker at the time of application, Aloe Gung was rejected for British Right of Abode. Although her income and education would later rise, she was pessimistic about her chances of finding another civil service job and transferring her expertise to England. Mr. Ong (chapter 7) lacked formal credentials altogether. With jobs relating exclusively to a particular area, these families viewed emigration as risky.

Moreover, these families were not networked with social fields that linked abroad. The daily activities of Wai-Yin Wan and the Ongs were situated in multiplex relations that would not transfer outside the neighborhood, let alone the region. True, Brian Wan was linked to kin abroad, but his parents controlled their business capital, and his application was stymied. Regional work ties were important to Kai Gung and to Mr. Ong. Neither could envision working outside South China. Their ties to family and kin—extremely important to them—remained local, further deterring migration.

The worldviews of these particular families were not threatened by reversion. They had never owned—let alone been dispossessed of—family property in China. Hence they had not inherited family scripts featuring emigration to avoid Communism and to regain honor for the patriliny. Instead, for the lower-middle-class members who had worked hard to get out of poverty, emigration posed a threat to family stability. Although concerns over increasing corruption and the disrupted social order threatened their identities as parents able to protect the family, such influences did not lead these ordinary families to exit. Ultimately, they did not expect that the institutions affecting the core of their family lives or their daily routines would undergo change after reversion to China. Instead of leaving, they retreated into the activities of work and family. Mr. Ong, a committed patriot, even celebrated reversion, his sense of historical continuity feeding his identity. This combination of embedded structures figured in these medium earners' horizons and did not provide an overpowering desire to exit. The ordinary families we met felt they had little to lose by staying in Hong Kong and much more to lose by moving.

Laboring Families and Migration

Hong Kong's working class had experienced economic and job uncertainty due to restructuring, which began before retrocession was announced. Frequent career disruptions left them uncommitted to a single occupational line, and they did not commit to professional identities. Since they had already experienced job loss, they did not see reversion to China as a particular threat to their work identities.

The migration literature tells us that laboring people follow their personal ties abroad, and we also found that social relations were key migration determinants for working families. These families were integrated into multiplex personal relations that they wanted to maintain. Without money or human capital, those few workers who applied to leave (3.15 percent of those surveyed) depended on family and close peers for support. Sponsored by kin, they expected that after arrival their relations would house them and find them work. Chung and her husband, Chak-Lui Hung (chapter 10) had many emigrants in their families, which sparked efforts to reunite. However, kin had little power to help them. Chung's application to join her family in America did not come to fruition since she could not meet regulative demands. These laboring people, who depended on family work roles, faced a situation similar to that of family entrepreneurs. Thus, the Leungs (chapter 4) or Brian Wan could only emigrate when their father and brothers delivered promised resources.

Laborers without close relations in the West rarely applied to exit. The relatives of the Chia brothers (construction workers, chapter 11) resided in Hong Kong and China. Hong Kong's reunification to China eased their access to cross-border family. The Szetos (chapter 9) had most (although not all) of their close kin—and all their friends—in Hong Kong. They considered emigration to North America less important for their family development than remaining close to those who cared for and supported them.

The ultimate immigration fate for blue-collar families who chose to apply was decided by official gatekeepers outside the family council. Migration was not a topic that generated family discussion, agreement, or plan. Family members rarely shared information about migration or even the goals of migration. Compliance was behavioral, not in terms of intent or meaning. Although Chung was committed to family reunion abroad, her husband and daughters barely acquiesced and were relieved when her migration project faltered. The Hungs drew together in their demanding Hong Kong life more than they had in the emigration dream. Hence overt compliance with the emigration plan masked differing agendas, goals, and desires of various family members. In fact, we do not know whether the emigration leader would have ultimately unified other family members' views around emigration, since none of the applications of the working-class and lower-middle-class people we met were approved.

The impending reversion to China challenged very few of the workers to think about life as it would unfold. The family script of the working poor was to keep their families together. The Chias and Szetos, both nonemigrants, had experienced greater poverty in the past. Their life in present-day Hong Kong was as good as it could be. Even the Hungs pulled themselves up into the lower levels of the service economy, gaining skills as they worked. They owed this improvement to neighborhood contacts and state support services and were loath to leave.

The activist Szetos had inherited an agenda of seeking modernity and democracy from their parents. They were suspicious of the PRC authorities who had confiscated their ancestral property, forcing their parents to flee and shattering their families. Eager for political change, the Szetos voted, debated with their friends, and marched with their children. However, realizing they were unacceptable to foreign gatekeepers, political concerns did not augur an attempt to leave. The Szetos could not envision themselves living abroad.

These narratives reveal the power of social institutions that motivated (or dampened) Hong Kong's migration fever and directed whether people wanted to leave and how they settled on arrival. In particular, these migration stories reveal the workings of the Chinese family institution, to which we now turn.

The Chinese Family Institution and Migration

The family prompts migration and affects the processes of adaptation in the new country, and family roles are themselves related to social structures. Early push/pull arguments reduce migration motives to the search for a better standard of living. In these views, people decide to migrate through rational deliberations. Having arrived, immigrants adapt to local cultures as part of the process of "pulling themselves up by their bootstraps." When this upgrading did not come about, newcomers were charged with hanging onto their traditional culture. However, this individual-centered paradigm has shifted. Studies find that ethnic institutions support people in stressful situations and can also promote social mobility (Zhou 1997). In the following discussion, we focus on those features of the Chinese family institution that eased our families' migration and adaptation to the new community.

These are the centralized family economy, goals of family unity, co-residence, transnational helping connections, and control over family members. At the same time, we trace how people's resources affect how they experience these structures.

Business families in our study were not the super-rich who built family empires through migration (Ong 1999; Orrù et al. 1997; Wong 1985). Nevertheless, their joint family economies enabled them to sponsor their family migration venture. The Leungs' and Wans' paterfamilias drew from—and eventually depleted—their Hong Kong businesses by transferring money and people abroad. The resources and expectations of a patrilineal family determined how they lived, worked, and emigrated. Members worked together to expand family property. Women were obligated to support the family firm, to maintain the reproductive base, and to work and contribute to the family economy. The husband's kin dominated household decision making. Brothers aligned to save money for migration, establishing migration as a family script. On arrival in the host country, the firms they set up, like those left behind, controlled who would be trained, who would work there, how others would contribute, who would move, and when it would happen. In the Wans' case, when kin later feuded to limit migration as a bounty, Brian acquiesced. His wife was not consulted. In these ways, business families strongly threw their institutional resources behind the family migration project.

All participants in our study had experienced the disruption of their families during World War II, the Chinese Civil War, and the consolidation of Communist power. The separation of kin prompted a desire to reunite—through migration if necessary. Chung's brother's Boston family restaurant sponsored his parents and preferred family reunification options to all brothers and sisters (unsuccessfully for Chung, as it turned out). Sonny Szeto's brother also followed his wife's kin to Toronto and urged his mother to reunite there as well.

Maintaining racial and ethnic group boundaries through marriage indicated family control, which enabled the seniors to attain their wishes. Marrying within their ethnic subgroup of Cantonese-speaking Chinese was easy in Toronto with its concentration of Hong Kong Chinese (Lee and Boyd 2008; Rodríguez-García 2006). There were subgroups, such as partners chosen from Cantonese-speaking churches or imported from Hong Kong. Marrying outside this group would have violated family norms.

Our immigrant families found that Toronto's suburban houses accommodated co-residence or living nearby relatively easily, a feature of familism that eased settlement. In the Leung family adult sons and daughters and their children all lived under one roof, facilitating a complementary division of labor and involvement in the family firm. Uncle Chou's son Elic also lived with him. Elic oversaw Chou's small shops, and after his divorce Elic's mother cared for his daughter during the week. Francis Kwong lived with his brother's family in Toronto, while complaining over their lack of reciprocity. The Hungs and the Szetos reported that their emigrant kin combined households in North America.

It has been argued that migration changes family roles and power structure. When households need dual incomes or when distance loosens patrilineal oversight, women can earn more, ease their household settlement, and view themselves apart from their family roles, gaining independence (Pessar and Mahler 2003; Cohen 2000; Erman et al. 2002). However, this may not be the case for the tied migration in patrilocal families as when brides move into the husband's family orbit and sacrifice cherished social support from those at home (Davin 2005a). This was exemplified by Wai-Yin Wan. Subordinated to her mother-in-law when both women were in Hong Kong, she was happy when her patrilineal kin emigrated to Canada without her. Loath to be retied to them abroad, she weakly protested family reunification, lacking the authority to take an open stand against Brian's family's emigration project. When Brian gave up this goal, Wai-Yin developed her own modest place, gaining scope to live and think in ways that suited her family roles and continue the cherished support of her natal kin.

Transnational family social support networks eased the costs of migration. The professional and business families migrated mainly to protect and advance their nuclear family. But they did not overlook those left behind and they also took care of the needy in their family circles. Luk and Francis Kwong helped their brothers locate jobs and bought apartments for their parents who remained behind in Hong Kong. Ching Luk continued her kinship support work during her migration stint (Salaff 2002; Mahler 1999). As elsewhere, there were long-distance conjugal relations, spatial ruptures in mother-child relationships, and shuttling of members of the family across locations (Landolt and Da 2005). Astronauts visited their Toronto families. Wives traveled the other direction and fulfilled their responsibilities to Hong Kong–based kin. Emigrant children with family residences in the country of origin were most likely to travel back and forth (Salaff et al. 2008).

The working and lower middle classes, although resource poor, nevertheless contributed to kin economically, practicing a partially collaborative family economy. The Chia siblings depended on each other in their construction work. The brothers lived together for a decade. The Chias and Mr. Ong had migrated from the PRC to Hong Kong to earn enough to help finance their families across the border and remitted as long as needed. Their lives were densely intertwined with kin and they stayed in Hong Kong to maintain these ties. The experience of growing up poor and relying on social support networks motivated the Gungs, Szetos, Chias, Ongs, and eventually the Hungs to remain in Hong Kong.

Familism as an ideology motivated action. External institutions and family norms strongly supported choosing one spokesperson as the family migrant representative. This spokesperson saw things in certain ways, set goals for the family, and brought about compliance. For those in this book, it was usually the employed husband, although he deferred to his father's authority. However, there were diverse interests, and the spokesperson's decisions did not always suit those in different family positions (Wolf 1996). Thus not all believed they would benefit from moving and not all stood behind the immigration application. Under the family umbrella they couched their opposition in terms acceptable to family values.

Resistance also shaped migration outcomes. We saw the contained dissension in the Luk family. Ching initially worked toward her husband's migration project, which was presented as benefitting the family and fulfilling family scripts. But ultimately their positions shifted. Ching negotiated behind the scenes, making alliances with Ruby to redirect emigration from father to daughter, to whom the migration baton was passed. Only by working in Hong Kong could Luk afford his daughter's boarding school abroad. Migration no longer signified carrying out the patrilineal family script of survival, but rather the advance of the daughter's cultural capital. Both scripts were compatible with the family concept. In another case, the three Kwong family members were not all committed to the emigration project to the same extent. Their son felt at home in his familiar Hong Kong setting but lacked the resources to resist the move. Francis eventually imposed emigration on his son for his own good, hoping to expand the lad's opportunities.

In these narratives, we found that movers and stayers rehearsed Chinese family precepts. The many forms of commitment to the family group enabled the family spokesperson to carry forward migration projects. These promised opportunities to advance the family, but also offered the chance to challenge family roles.

Comparisons: Family Migration

The structures that motivate Chinese family migration and shape settlement efforts are not unique. Other families aim to cohere and advance through migration and turn their family institutions toward these ends. They, too, practice mutual economic assistance and pool earnings, co-reside, marry within their group, and have transnational support systems.

Mutual economic assistance and co-residence especially point to immigrants' familistic orientations. To access kin-based emigration networks and their resources, the migrant needs to enact proper roles. Migrants and their kin in the home country engage in numerous mutual exchanges and obligations, and the ability to achieve and sustain family roles after migration confers status on both sides. Remittances are an important example. Remittances build linkages between the emigrants and their nonmigrant families reflecting not only the senders' income, but also their continued embeddedness in social ties back home (Piotrowski 2006). Remittances not only reflect the commitment of the poor to mutual assistance; remittances symbolize the migrant's proper playing out of family and community social roles and affirm their membership in their community of origin. English-speaking Filipinos stem from middle-class households, although they engage in domestic labor abroad. Their remittances enable them and their children to maintain a middle-class life at home (Kamiar and Ismail 1991; McKay 2005). In exchange, relatives back home care for the migrants' children, help build their homes, and get new homes themselves (Menjivar et al. 1998; Keezhangatte 2006).

Migrants convey cultural images of appropriate role behavior, in particular gender role expectations. In culturally distinct places such as Irish workers' communities in London in the 1930s, the contemporary Chinese catering industry in England, and Mexican communities in California, migrants maintain family roles at a distance through communication about and oversight of children and other kin (Ryan 2002; Song 1999; Malkin 2004; Parreñas 2005). Through such performances, migrants produce an image of a "respectable person," which legitimizes their leaving home.

Immigrant entrepreneurs from diverse cultures also rely on family labor power, although vast differences occur in the ways the family and firm are mutually embedded. Korean immigrants—who exhibit one of the highest rates of self-employment among all U.S. immigrant groups—launch family firms as a safety net. Seen as a stepping-stone to intergenerational mobility, they expect their children to obtain a higher education and abandon the ethnic enclave for professional employment (Kim 2006). In contrast, Italian second-generation youths continue to advance their parents' businesses, while keeping abreast of changes in the marketplace as a sign of loyalty. (Schmitz 2006). Asian-Indian Gujaratis built the budget motel business in North America, through chain migration and mutual assistance. A comparative study found that both East Asian and Eastern European family firms in Canada hire coethnics and kin, but the different kinds of industries they enter determine their probability of doing so (Froschauer 2001). In another form of transnational cooperation, Indians and Taiwanese educated in the computer field became embedded in the economies of more than one country. They use migrant family and friendship ties to establish labor, capital, and supply lines (Assar 1995; Froschauer and Wong 2006; Saxenian et al. 2002).

Mutual help between kin is not costless. Fulfilling their family obligations led migrant Irish daughters to do without food (Ryan 2002). Many researchers found that because small businesses depend on unpaid family labor, the urgency of family survival severely constrained the educational and occupational choices of second-generation Chinese in Britain (Tong 2005; Kim 2006; Song 1999; Suarez-Orozco and Qin 2006). The continued fulfillment of kin obligations is not calculated by a cost-benefit analysis.

Co-residence also reflects family cooperation among settlers. The overall rate of U.S. immigrants' co-residence was 35 percent in 1990, exceeding the 23 percent in the local populace (Glick 1999, 746), although there was considerable variation among groups. Living with family members may be seen as traditionalism, giving priority to the immediate and extended family's goals over the individual's. But co-residence is also a social support strategy that provides financial and social resources to dependent kin. The family contract is especially important for older people, who are usually embedded within family systems. In Canada, immigrant women are also more likely than native-born women to have extended family arrangements in later life (Boyd 1991). Multigenerational residence reflects their preferences as well as a lack of other resources (Wilmoth 2001).

Large-scale structures in the receiving society affect the ability of immigrants to fulfill norms of reciprocity. As a result, the hardships incurred in migration contribute to even higher levels of co-residence than in the homeland. Recently arrived Mexican immigrants to the United States are more likely to live with kin than they had in Mexico. Co-residence declines among the second generation not because of the spread of individualism but with their improved living conditions (Van Hook and Glick 2007). Menjivar (1997) compared the joint family economies of immigrant Vietnamese, Salvadorians, and Mexican working-class people in California. She shows that communities with more economic opportunities, social service counseling, and nonpunitive immigration law enforcement could better provide their families with mutual assistance (see also Haines 2002).

Immigrants' practice of marrying within their own group maintains their culture and is also influenced by many factors. To meet labor shortages in the post-World War II period, Belgium and Germany recruited workers from Turkey and Morocco. In the mid-1970s these countries curtailed labor immigration and family reunions became the main immigration criterion. This immigration regulation encouraged homogamy (Lievens 1999). Immigrants faced strong transnational pressures to bring in eligible cousins from back home as spouses. Further, second-generation immigrant men wanted to import traditional wives from the source country. Yet in-marriage was not solely a bow to tradition.

On their part, second-generation women opted to import better-educated and more modern spouses than they found locally. The geography of migration space had empowered second-generation immigrant women (Levitt and Glick Schiller 2004). When a woman married she was expected to live patrilocally and obey her husband's parents—but the parents of a husband brought in from the country of origin were far away. Moreover, as the one familiar with the local language, economy, and culture and the one who offered the desired migration opportunity, the wife could influence the patriarchal balance of power in the marriage. In these ways, families strategized around migration regulations to maintain social structure while at the same time migration experiences modified these structures and their meanings.

Resumed migration from the PRC provides our final example of institutional continuities in family migration despite change. For decades until the 1978 economic reforms, Chinese policies discouraged emigration to the West. Those few who managed to exit were branded as unpatriotic, which truncated their network ties. Global institutions that promoted migration spread only after China broadened relations with other nations and work and university structures encouraged study, training, and experiences abroad. Returning migrants were now rewarded as heroic modernizers (Nyiri 2001). These changes at the regulative level triggered a migration revival, and emigration and return migration increased. The earliest migrants to arrive in North America after this opening to the West had weak immigrant networks (Salaff and Greve 2006), but gradually kin networks emerged. (Salaff and Greve 2004).

Europe, though not a traditional PRC migration destination, has also seen a rapid expansion of Chinese populations (Laczko 2003; Benton and Pieke 1998). One example testifies to the importance of family in migration. Through transnational relations, former entrepreneurial families from Chejiang Province have established a foothold in the Italian garment industry that feeds labor, capital, and social support into the ventures (Ceccagno 2007). Because family and firm are one, as firms construct new managerial forces and workforces, migration follows. Chinese wives in Italy rely on their Mainland kin to support their reproductive roles, sending their infants home to them for early childhood care. A key feature of this new transnational investment is "the close links maintained by migrants with their Qiaoxiang (region of origin) and with other new Chinese communities in Europe. Such links are based primarily on family ties and other social networks that create, but are also a result of, migration strategies, and form a closely knit and dynamic migration system between China and European destinations" (Guerassimoff 2003, 146).[1]

It is not only that the physical distance between Mainland China and Europe can be forded more easily now or even that more can afford the crossing, and not only that the media-spread images transport people in their imagination to distant shores. The institutions surrounding migration streams also reduce social distance. In the PRC, as in the Hong Kong families we studied, global institutions now cross the seas, large-scale political and economic structures support moves, middle-range social networks and social fields offer examples of migration as appropriate, and kin networks abound. Cognitive accounts frame positive migration perspectives.

Fifteen years marks a long period in families' lives. Those people we met in 1992 as toddlers and youths are now finishing secondary school or marrying and having children of their own. Some advanced their careers. Others lost their jobs and started again. Seniors retired, with some moving to China and others to Canada. Social fields recombined. Journeys in people's imaginations changed faster still. These all figure in the migration trajectories of families in our study and enable us to view how institutions matter. Some of our families, especially those organized around family property, adhered to parochial, long-standing Chinese family norms, while others accommodated to a less restrictive version of these family norms. In all cases, the family was important.

Hong Kong migration has a rich institutional and personal heritage but it is not unique. Migration does not destroy the family institution. Although by moving, relationships inevitably change, these do not all go in the direction of weakening the family. Around the globe, families strategize migration projects to advance their goals, revealing the interactions between local regulations, family structures, traditions, and cognitive understandings.

NOTES

ACKNOWLEDGMENTS

1. The original project was titled "Emigration from Hong Kong Study, Correlates, and Causations" (Skeldon 1995).

CHAPTER 1. INSTITUTIONAL THEORY AND FAMILY MIGRATION

1. Mandarin, tai-kong ren. The Chinese characters are a word play on a homonym for astronaut, referring to the many miles the husband logs in the air. This term originates from the Chinese words "tai kong ren," with "tai" referring to wife, and "kong" meaning nonpresence, that is, the husband being without his wife in an empty nest.

2. Other writers who have distinguished institutions into levels by their scope and the behavior they control include Faist (2000) and Smelser (1995).

3. The United States passed the Chinese Exclusion Act in 1882, Australia passed the Immigration Restriction Act in 1901, and Canada passed the Chinese Immigration Act in 1923.

4. Currently, skilled immigrants applying to Canada are awarded points and assessed on six criteria: education; abilities in English or French, Canada's two official languages; experience; age; having arranged employment in Canada; and adaptability (which emphasizes employment and education of the applicant or their partner). Investors, entrepreneurs, and self-employed applicants are expected to invest CAD 400,000 or to own and manage businesses in Canada. See http://www.cic.gc.ca/

5. The family reunion class is still sizable in the United States (Triadafilopoulos 2006; Meyers and Yau 2004).

6. Correspondence between Angela Shik and former Vice Principal of Bishop Strachan School, May 25, 2008.

7. Portes and Borocz (1989, 183) estimate that the proportion of ethnic populations who are entrepreneurs with transnational links in major U.S. cities is as high as 18 percent.

8. Siu-lun Wong was an investigator for the project "Emigration from Hong Kong Study, Correlates and Causations" (Skeldon 1995). The 1991 random population survey represented the Hong Kong population, as found by comparing the distributions of sex, age, marital status, education, and occupation with the 1991 Hong Kong Population Census. Interviewers visited 3,098 randomly sampled addresses and listed all people who were Chinese over eighteen years of age living there. They randomly interviewed one person at an address, resulting in 1,552 completed files for analysis. See Skeldon (1995) for more information on the survey.

CHAPTER 2. HONG KONG'S INSTITUTIONAL BACKGROUND

1. Funds are in Hong Kong dollars unless otherwise specified, at the fixed rate of exchange, HKD 100 = USD 12.90.

2. Three questions in our 1991 survey mapped people's political attitudes. Only 12.5 percent surveyed were optimistic about the political future; 38 percent had little confidence in Hong Kong's political future, while 65 percent lacked confidence in the Chinese government (Wong 1995).

3. The size of the civil service fell to 160,000 people in 2004.

4. Since Colonial prerogatives permitted those from Great Britain to work without employment permits, their numbers are underestimated.

5. The proportions of applicants by broad occupational group were as follows: professionals and semiprofessionals, 17.9 percent; managers and administrators, 15.1 percent; clerks, 5.9 percent; workers and operators 3.9 percent; service workers, 2.7 percent; and unskilled laborers, 1.7 percent. By sector, those who applied were public servants, 14.9 percent; private sector, 7.2 percent; or self-employed, 8.1 percent.

6. Because they applied to many countries, and many countries do not distinguish the origin of immigrants applying, no overall statistics are available as to how many people left.

CHAPTER 3. THE LUK FAMILY

1. Secondary schools are divided into five bands roughly according to the primary school leaving exam results. Band 1 includes the highest scoring students. There is a complex method of matching children and schools, in which test scores, neighborhood, and family school ties play a part.

CHAPTER 4. THE CHOU AND LEUNG FAMILIES

1. At that time, they invested a minimum of CAD 250,000 in a business, and there were other requirements (Citizenship Immigration Canada 2006).

2. According to the 1991 Canadian census, 10 percent of the population in Richmond Hill as a whole were of Chinese ethnic origin. However, in the census tract where Chou bought his home, over a third were Chinese.

3. Vietnamese, Taiwanese, and Mainland and Hong Kong Chinese celebrate Lunar New Year in Toronto at the same time but in different places, styles, and languages. In North Toronto in 1993, Hong Kongers created the ambiance.

CHAPTER 5. FRANCIS KWONG

1. The Hang Seng Index, started in 1969, is a capitalization-weighted stock market index in the Hong Kong Stock Exchange. It is used to record and monitor daily changes of the thirty-four largest companies of the Hong Kong stock market and as the main indicator of the overall market performance in Hong Kong. These companies represent about 65 percent of capitalization of the Hong Kong Stock Exchange.

2. "Water Margin Chronicles," popular English translation: All Men are Brothers.

CHAPTER 6. THE GUNG FAMILY

1. The once poverty stricken Bao'an County has been transformed into the modern city of Shenzhen, Guangdong Province, China.

2. Performance appraisal is a regular review of employee performance within an organization. Here their assessment by the public is taken into account.

CHAPTER 7. THE ONGS

1. A Chinese historical novel written by Luo Guanzhong in the fourteenth century, expressing dismay over the division of his country. It is based on events in the turbulent years at the end of the Han Dynasty and the Three Kingdoms era of China, ending with the reunification of the land in 280.

CHAPTER 8. BRIAN WAN

1. Teddy boys refers to the British term for teenagers who dressed in a caricature of the foppish style of Edward, Queen Victoria's son. Teddy boys were Britain's first self-consciously styled teenage group. They identified closely with the American film *Blackboard Jungle,* raising a ruckus whenever it was screened.

2. According to Coser (1974), greedy institutions seek exclusive loyalty and attempt to reduce the claims of competing roles on those within their boundaries. Their demands are omnivorous.

3. "Out of risks come wealth and fortune." 富貴險中求

CHAPTER 9. THE SZETO FAMILY

1. The Legislative Council and Executive Council advised the Chief Executive. Limited elections were instituted for the members of "LegCo."

2. A local organization whose base is mainly in Sha Tin.

3. Voters register as members of functional or occupational constituencies and choose candidates who contest in that occupational sector.

4. Regina Ip Lau Suk-yee, 葉劉淑儀, a prominent government official of the Hong Kong Special Administrative Region (HKSAR), the first woman to be appointed as secretary for security to head the disciplinary service. Ip became a controversial figure for her role advocating Article 23. At a 2002 forum against Article 23, Ip made an infamous statement against democracy in Hong Kong: "Hitler was elected by the people. But he ended up killing seven million people. This proves that democracy is not a cure-all medicine." After the march the legislation was withdrawn, and Ip resigned from Tung Chee-hwa's administration.

Chapter 10. The Hung Family

1. Asperger's syndrome is a form of autism. Those with this condition have impaired social relations, obsessions, language delays, stereotypic behaviors and tantrums. Over 7,000 individuals diagnosed with autism were registered for social services in Hong Kong in 2000 (Mak et al. 2007).

2. Brothers and sisters of citizens can wait up to ten years to have their U.S. applications reviewed (Triadafilopoulos 2006).

Chapter 11. The Chia Brothers

1. Thousands of people are involved in industrial accidents in Hong Kong every year of which construction employees incur nearly half. The annual accident rate per 1,000 workers in the construction industry in 1998 was 248.6 (Siu et al. 2004).

2. Pacific Century Cyberworks is owned by PCCW, the largest telecommunications company in Hong Kong and headed by the son of billionaire Li Kah Shing (Ong 1999). As a result of acquisitions, its high debt caused the stock price to drop sharply in 2003.

Chapter 12. Conclusion

1. In southern France, PRC Chinese have bought up three wine terroir (vineyards); Chinese laborers work in other vineyards as well. Personal communication, Judith Nagata, research anthropologist, September 17, 2008.

REFERENCES

Alba, Richard D., and Victor Nee. 2003. *Remaking the American Mainstream: Assimilation and Contemporary Immigration.* Cambridge, MA: Harvard University Press.

Aldrich, Howard, Linda Renzulli, and Nancy Langton. 1998. *Passing on Privilege: Resources Provided by Self-Employed Parents to Their Self-Employed Children.* Edited by Kevin Leicht. Greenwich, CT: JAI.

Anderson, Benedict. 1983. *Imagined Communities: Reflections on the Origin and Spread of Nationalism.* London: Verso.

Anderson, Kay. 1991. *Vancouver's Chinatown: Racial Discourse in Canada, 1875–1980.* Montreal and Kingston: McGill-Queen's University Press.

Appadurai, Arjun. 2006. The Thing Itself. *Public Culture* 18 (1): 15–21.

Assar, Nandini Narain. 1995. Indian-American Success Story of "Potel"-Motels: Immigration, Tradition, Community, and Gender. In *Current Research on Occupations and Professions,* vol. 10. Edited by Helen Z. Lopata. Amsterdam: Elsevier.

Aydemir, Abdurraham, and Chris Robinson. 2006. *Return and Onward Migration Among Working Age Men.* Ottawa: Statistics Canada.

Bailey, Adrian, and Paul Boyle. 2004. Untying and Retying Family Migration in the New Europe. *Journal of Ethnic and Migration Studies* 30 (2): 229–41.

Baker, Hugh D. R. 1979. *Chinese Family and Kinship.* London: Macmillan.

———. 1983. Life in the Cities: The Emergence of Hong Kong Man. *China Quarterly* 95: 469–79.

———. 1993. Social Change in Hong Kong: Hong Kong Man in Search of Majority. *China Quarterly* 136: 864–77.

Bambrah, Gurmeet. 2006. "Final Report Survey of Immigrants with Engineering Backgrounds Settling in Ontario, Engineering Employers and Community Supports." Toronto: Council for Access to Professional Engineering.

Bell, Daniel A. 1998. Hong Kong's Transition to Capitalism. *Dissent* 45 (1): 15–23.

Bellah, Robert Neelly. 1970. *Beyond Belief; Essays on Religion in a Post-Traditional World*. New York: Harper & Row.

Benton, Gregor. 2007. *Chinese Migrants and Internationalism: Forgotten Histories, 1917–1945*. London: Routledge.

Benton, Gregor, and Frank Pieke, ed. 1998. *The Chinese in Europe*. New York: St. Martin's Press.

Benton, Robert D., and David A. Snow. 2000. Framing Process and Social Movements: An Overview and Assessment. *Annual Review of Sociology* 26: 611–39.

Berger, Peter L., and Hansfried Kellner. 1977. Marriage and the Social Construction of Reality. In *Facing Up to Modernity: Excursions in Society, Politics, and Religion*. Edited by Roger L. Berger. New York: Basic Books.

Bernstein, Richard. 1989. Vast Hong Kong Crowd Protests Beijing's Action. *New York Times*. June 5.

Berry, John W., J. S. Phinney, D. L. Sam, and P. Vedder, ed. 2006. *Immigrant Youth in Cultural Transition: Acculturation, Identity and Adaptation Across National Context*. Mahwah, NJ: Lawrence Erlbaum Associates.

Bertaux, Daniel. 1997. Transmission in Extreme Situations: Russian Families Expropriated by the October Revolution. In *Pathways to Social Class*. Edited by Daniel Bertaux and Paul Thompson. Oxford: Oxford University Press.

Bertaux-Wiame, Isobel. 1981. The Life-History Approach to the Study of Internal Migration. In *Biography and Society*. Edited by Daniel Bertaux. Thousand Oaks: Sage.

Bird, Gloria W., and Abrina Schnurman-Crook. 2005. Professional Identity and Coping Behaviors in Dual-Career Couples. *Family Relations* 54 (1): 145–60.

Blair-Loy, Mary. 2003. *Competing Devotions: Career and Family Among Women Financial Executives*. Cambridge, MA: Harvard University Press.

Bloemraad, Irene. 2006. *Becoming a Citizen: Incorporating Immigrants and Refugees in the United States and Canada*. Berkeley: University of California Press.

Bott, Elizabeth. 1957. *Family and Social Networks*. London: Tavistock.

Bourdieu, Pierre. 1981. Men and Machines. In *Advances in Social Theory and Methodology: Toward an Integration of Micro- and Macro-Sociologies*. Edited by K. Knorr-Cetina, and A. V. Cicourel. Boston: Routledge and Kegan Paul.

———. 1984. *Distinction: A Social Critique of the Judgment of Taste*. Cambridge, MA.: Harvard University Press.

———. 1986. The Forms of Capital. In *Handbook of Theory and Research for the Sociology of Education*. Edited by J. G. Richardson. New York: Greenwood Press.

Boyd, Monica. 1991. Immigration and Living Arrangements: Elderly Women in Canada. *International Migration Review* 25 (1): 4–27.

———. 2000. Matching Workers to Work: Asian Immigrant Engineers in Canada. *Working Papers* 14.

Boyd, Monica, and D. Thomas. 2001. Match or Mismatch? The Employment of Immigrant Engineers in Canada's Labor Force. *Population Research and Policy Review* 20 (1–2): 107–33.

Bray, Mark, and Ramsey Koo. 2005. *Education and Society in Hong Kong and Macao: Comparative Perspectives on Continuity and Change.* New York: Springer Publishing.

Breton, Raymond. 1964. Institutional Completeness of Ethnic Communities and the Personal Relations of Immigrants. *American Journal of Sociology* 70 (2): 193–205.

Brewer, Marilynn B. 1991. The Social Self: On Being the Same and Different At the Same Time. *Personality and Social Psychology Bulletin* 17 (5): 475–82.

Brinton, Mary C., ed. 2001. *Women's Working Lives in East Asia.* Palo Alto, CA: Stanford University Press.

Brown, Lawrence A., Edward J. Malecki, and Susan Gustavus Philliber. 1977. Awareness Space Characteristics in a Migration Context. *Environment and Behavior* 9 (3): 335–48.

Brown, Susan K., and Frank D. Bean. 2006. Assimilation Models, Old and New: Explaining a Long-Term Process. *Migration Information Source.*

Carr, Deborah. 2004. "My Daughter Has a Career; I Just Raised Babies": The Psychological Consequences of Women's Intergenerational Social Comparisons. *Social Psychology Quarterly* 67 (2): 132–54.

Carrasco, Pia, Rose Damaris, and Johanne Charbonneau. 1999. La Constitution De Liens Faibles: Une Passerelle Pour L'Adaptation Des Immigrantes Centro-Americaines Meres De Jeunes Enfants a Montreal. *Canadian Ethnic Studies* 31 (1): 73–87.

Carroll, John M. 2005. *Edge of Empires: Chinese Elites and British Colonials in Hong Kong.* Cambridge: Harvard University Press.

———. 2007. *A Concise History of Hong Kong.* Lanham, Md: Rowman & Littlefield.

Castells, Manuel, L. Goh, R. Y. W. Kwok, and T. L. Kee. 1988. *Economic Development and Housing Policy in the Asian Pacific Rim: A Comparative Study of Hong Kong, Singapore, and Shenzhen Special Economic Zone.* Berkeley: Institute of Urban and Regional Development, University of California at Berkeley.

Castles, Stephen. 2003. *The Age of Migration: International Population Movements in the Modern World.* New York: Guilford Press.

Ceccagno, Antonella. 2007. Compressing Personal Time: Ethnicity and Gender Within a Chinese Niche in Italy. *Journal of Ethnic and Migration Studies* 33 (4): 635–54.

Chan, Anita Kit-wa. 2003. The Making of Gender in Families. In *Gendering Hong Kong.* Edited by Anita Kit-wa Chan, and Wai-ling Wong. Hong Kong: Oxford University Press.

Chan, Annie Hau-nung. 2006. The Effects of Full-Time Domestic Workers on Married Women's Economic Activity Status in Hong Kong, 1981–2001. *International Sociology* 21 (1): 133–59.

Chan, Elaine. 2002. Beyond Pedagogy: Language and Identity in Post-Colonial Hong Kong. *Journal of Sociology of Education* 23 (2): 271–85.

Chan, Kwok Bun. 1997. A Family Affair: Migration, Dispersal, and the Emergent Identity of the Chinese Cosmopolitan. *Diaspora* 6 (2): 195–204.

Chan, Kwok Bun, and Sing Seet Chia. 2003. Migrant Family Drama Revisited: Mainland Chinese Immigrants in Singapore. *Sojourn* 18 (2): 171–202.

Chan, Kwok Bun, and Odelia M. H. Wong. 2005. Introduction: Private and Public: Gender, Generation and Family Life in Flux. *Journal of Family and Economic Issues* 26 (4): 447–64.

Chan, Ming K. 2003. Different Roads to Home: The Retrocession of Hong Kong and Macau to Chinese Sovereignty. *Journal of Contemporary China* 12 (36): 493–518.

Chee, Maria W. L. 2005. *Taiwanese American Transnational Families: Women and Kin Work*. New York: Routledge.

Cheng, Joseph, ed. 2005. *The July 1 Protest Rally in Hong Kong*. Hong Kong: City University Press.

Cheung, Chau-kiu. 1998. Impacts of Class on Hong Kong People's Well-Being. *Human Relations* 51 (1): 89–119.

———. 2005. Rational or Demoralized Responses to Work Restructuring in Hong Kong? *Human Relations* 58 (2): 223–47.

Cheung, Gordon C. K. 2004. Chinese Diaspora as a Virtual Nation: Interactive Roles Between Economic and Social Capital. *Political Studies* 52 (4): 664–84.

Cheung, Siu-keung. 2000. Speaking Out: Days in the Lives of Three Hong Kong Cage Dwellers. *Positions* 8 (1): 235–62.

Chiang, Frances Shiu-Ching. 2001. "The Intersection of Class, Race, Ethnicity, Gender and Migration: A Case Study of Hong Kong Chinese Immigrant Women Entrepreneurs in Richmond, British Columbia." Unpublished Ph.D thesis. Vancouver, BC: Sociology and Anthropology, University of British Columbia.

Chin, Tiffani, and Meredith Phillips. 2004. Social Reproduction and Child-Rearing Practices: Social Class, Children's Agency and the Summer Activity Gap. *Sociology of Education* 77 (2): 185–210.

Chinoy, Ely. 1955. *Automobile Workers and the American Dream*. New York: Doubleday.

Chiu, Stephen, Susanne Choi, and K. F. Ting. 2005. Getting Ahead in the Capitalist Paradise: Migration From China and Socio-Economic Attainment in Colonial Hong Kong. *International Migration Review* 39 (1): 203–27.

Chow, Nelson W. S. 1988. "Social Adaptation in New Towns: A Report of a Survey on the Quality of Life of Tuen Mun Inhabitants." Hong Kong: University of Hong Kong, Department of Social Work and Social Administration.

Chu, Pricilla. 1996. Social Network Models of Overseas Chinese Entrepreneurship: The Experience in Hong Kong and Canada. *Revue Canadienne des Sciences de l'Administration/ Canadian Journal of Administrative Sciences* 13 (4): 358–65.

Chung, Kan-chi 鍾柬芝. 2005 Disclosure News. *Star Magazine* 38–41. May 15.

Citizenship Immigration Canada (CIC). 2006. *Facts and Figures: Immigration Overview Permanent and Temporary Residents*. Ottawa: Research and Evaluation Branch, Citizenship Immigration Canada.

Clausen, John A. 1968. *Socialization and Society.* New York: Little Brown and Company.

Cockburn, Cynthia. 1983. *Brothers: Male Dominance and Technological Change.* London: Pluto Press.

Cohen, Myron. 1976. *House United, House Divided: The Chinese Family in Taiwan.* New York: Columbia University Press.

Cohen, Rina. 2000. "Mom is a Stranger": The Negative Impact of Immigration Policies on the Family Life of Filipina Domestic Workers. *Canadian Ethnic Studies/ Etudes Ethniques au Canada* 32 (3): 76–88.

Coleman, James S. 1988. Social Capital in the Creation of Human Capital. *American Journal of Sociology* 94 Supplement S95–S120.

Collins, Randall. 1979. *The Credential Society: An Historical Sociology of Education and Stratification.* New York: Academic Press.

Constable, Nicole. 1997. *Maid to Order in Hong Kong: Stories of Filipina Workers.* Ithaca, NY: Cornell University Press.

Cooper, Eugene. 1975. *The Social Evolution of Craft Production: The Wood Carvers of Hong Kong.* New York: Columbia University.

Coser, Lewis A. 1974. *Greedy Institutions; Patterns of Undivided Commitment.* Glencoe, IL: Free Press.

Dai, K. 1991. The Experience and Status of Chinese Rural Women Over Two Generations. In *Next of Kin: An International Reader on Changing Families.* Edited by L. Tepperman and S. J. Wilson. Englewood Cliffs, NJ: Prentice Hall.

Das Gupta, Monica. 1999. Lifeboat Versus Corporate Ethic: Social and Demographic Implications of Stem and Joint Families. *Social Science and Medicine* 49 (2): 173–84.

Davin, Delia. 2005a. Marriage Migration in China: The Enlargement of Marriage Markets in the Era of Market Reforms. *Indian Journal of Gender Studies* 12 (2, 3): 173–88.

———. 2005b. Women and Migration in Contemporary China. *China Report* 41 (1): 29–38.

Delmar, Frederic, and Jonas Gunnarsson. 2004. "How Do Self-Employed Parents of Nascent Entrepreneurs Contribute?" Paper read at First Annual Clemson/Kauffman Symposium on the PSED, at Clemson, SC.

Desai, Kiran. 2006. *The Inheritance of Loss.* New York: Atlantic Monthly Press.

DeVault, Marjorie L. 1991. *Feeding the Family.* Chicago: University of Chicago Press.

Devine, Fiona. 2004. *Class Practices: How Parents Help Their Children Get Good Jobs.* New York: Cambridge University Press.

DiMaggio, Paul J., and Walter W. Powell. 1983. The Iron Cage Revisited: Institutional Isomorphism and Collective Rationality in Organizational Fields. *American Sociological Review* 48 (2): 147–60.

Dodson, Lisa. 2007. Wage-Poor Mothers and Moral Economy. *Social Politics* 14 (2): 258–80.

Dodson, Lisa, and Jillian Dickert. 2004. Girls' Family Labor in Low-Income Households: A Decade of Qualitative Research. *Journal of Marriage and Family* 66 (2): 318–32.

Dodson, Lisa, and Leah Schmalzbauer. 2005. Poor Mothers and Habits of Hiding: Participatory Methods in Poverty Research. *Journal of Marriage and Family* 67 (4): 949–59.

Donkor, Martha. 2005. Marching to the Tune: Colonization, Globalization, Immigration, and the Ghanaian Diaspora. *Africa Today* 52 (1): 26–44.

Dubin, Lois Shaw. 2004. *The History of Beads*. London: Thames & Hudson.

Duncan, Simon. 2005. Mothering, Class and Rationality. *Sociological Review* 53 (1): 50–76.

Duncan, Simon, Rosalind Edwards, Tracey Reynolds, and Pam Alldred. 2003. Motherhood, Paid Work and Partnering: Values and Theories. *Work, Employment and Society* 17 (2): 309–30.

Edwards, Richard. 1979. *Contested Terrain*. New York: Basic Books.

Elazar, Dahlia S. 2002. "Engines of Acculturation": The Last Political Generation of Jewish Women in Interwar East Europe. *Journal of Historical Sociology* 15 (3): 366–94.

Elder, Glenn H. 1974. *Children of the Great Depression: Social Change in Life Experiences*. Chicago: University of Chicago.

Erman, Tahire, Sibel Kalaycioglu, and Helga Rittersberger-Tilic. 2002. Money-Earning Activities and Empowerment Experiences of Rural Migrant Women in the City: The Case of Turkey. *Women's Studies International Forum* 25 (4): 395–410.

Faist, Thomas. 2000. *The Volume and Dynamics of International Migration and Transnational Social Spaces*. Oxford: Oxford University Press.

Fanon, Franz. 1970. *Black Skin, White Masks*. London: Paladin.

Faure, David. 2003. *Colonialism and the Hong Kong Mentality*. Hong Kong: Hong Kong University, Centre of Asian Studies Monograph.

———. 2008. Rethinking Colonial Institutions, Standards, Life Styles and Experiences. In *Hong Kong Mobile: The Making of a Global Population*. Edited by Helen F. Siu, and Agnes S. Ku. Hong Kong: University of Hong Kong Press, 231–46.

Fawcett, James T., and F. Arnold. 1987. The Role of Surveys in the Study of International Migration: An Appraisal. *International Migration Review* 21 (4): 1523–40.

Feldman-Savelsberg, Pamela, Flavien T. Ndonko, and Song Yang. 2005. The Effects of Legends, Rumors, and Related Genres on Audiences. In *Rumor Mills: the Social Impact of Rumor and Legend*. Edited by Gary Alan Fine. New Brunswick, NJ: Transaction.

Festinger, Leon. 1962. *A Theory of Cognitive Dissonance*. Palo Alto: Stanford University Press.

Findlay, Allan M., and F. L. N. Li. 1998. A Migration Channels Approach to the Study of Professionals Moving To and From Hong Kong. *International Migration Review* 32 (3): 682–703.

Findlay, Allan M., F. L. N. Li, A. J. Jowett, and R. Skeldon. 1996. Skilled International

Migration and the Global City, a Study of Expatriates in Hong Kong. *Transactions, Institute of British Geographers* 21 (1): 49–61.

Foner, Nancy. 1986. Sex Roles and Sensibilities: Jamaican Women in New York and London. In *International Migration: The Female Experience*. Edited by Rita Simon and Caroline Brettell. Totowa, NJ: Rowman & Allanheld.

Ford, Michele. 2004. Organizing the Unorganizable: Unions, NGOs, and Indonesian Migrant Labour. *International Migration* 42 (5): 99–119.

Forrest, Ray, Adrienne La Grange, and Ngai-Ming Yip. 2002. Neighbourhood in a High Rise, High Density City: Some Observations on Contemporary Hong Kong. *Sociological Review* 50 (2): 214–40.

Freedman, Maurice. 1958. *Lineage Organisation in Southeastern China*. London: Athlone Press.

Froschauer, Karl. 2001. East Asian and European Entrepreneur Immigrants in British Columbia, Canada: Post-Migration Conduct and Pre-Migration Context. *Journal of Ethnic and Migration Studies* 27 (2): 2003–223.

Froschauer, Karl, and Lloyd Wong. 2006. Understanding Immigrants' Initiatives in the New Economy: The Case of Western Canada. *Canadian Ethnic Studies/Etudes Ethniques au Canada* 38 (2): 86–103.

Fung, Anthony. 2004. Postcolonial Hong Kong Identity: Hybridising the Local and the National. *Social Identities* 10 (3): 399–414.

Gabaccia, Donna. 1994. *From the Other Side: Women, Gender, and Immigrant Life in the U.S. 1820–1990*. Bloomington: Indiana University Press.

Gabaccia, Donna, Franca Iacovetta, and Fraser Ottanelli. 2004. Laboring Across National Borders: Class, Gender, and Militancy in the Proletarian Mass Migrations. *International Labor and Working-Class History* 66 (1): 57–77.

Gates, Hill. 2004. Coming and Going in Sichuan Households, 1978–1994. *Urban Anthropology* 33 (2–4): 357–87.

Giddens, Anthony. 1990. *The Consequences of Modernity*. Stanford: Stanford University Press.

Glenn, Evelyn Nakano. 1983. Split Household, Small Producer and Dual Wage Earner: An Analysis of Chinese American Family Strategies. *Journal of Marriage and the Family* 45 (1): 35–46.

Glick, Jennifer E. 1999. Economic Support From and to Extended Kin: A Comparison of Mexican Americans and Mexican Immigrants. *International Migration Review* 33 (3): 745–65.

Glick-Schiller, Nina, Linda Basch, and Cristina Szanton-Blanc. 1992. Transnationalism: A New Analytic Framework for Understanding Migration. *Annals of New York Academy of Sciences* 645: 1–24.

Goffman, Erving. 1963. *Stigma: Notes on the Management of a Spoiled Identity*. Englewood Cliffs, NJ: Prentice-Hall.

———. 1974. *Frame Analysis*. Cambridge, MA: Harvard University Press.

Gold, Stephen J. 2005. Migrant Networks: A Summary and Critique of Relational Approaches to International Migration. In *The Blackwell Companion to Social*

Inequalities. Edited by Mary Romero and Eric Margolis. London: Blackwell: 285–257.

Goodstadt, Leo F. 2005. *Uneasy Partners: The Conflict Between Public Interest and Private Profit in Hong Kong.* Hong Kong: Hong Kong University Press.

Goss, Jon, and Bruce Lindquist. 1995. Conceptualizing International Labor Migration: A Structuration Perspective. *International Migration Review* 29 (2): 317–51.

Grasmuck, Sherri, and Patricia R. Pessar. 1991. *Between Two Islands: Dominican International Migration.* Berkeley: University of California Press.

Gray, David E. 1993. Perceptions of Stigma: The Parents of Autistic Children. *Sociology of Health & Illness* 15 (1): 102–20.

———. 2002. "Everybody Just Freezes. Everybody is Just Embarrassed": Felt and Enacted Stigma Among Parents of Children With High Functioning Autism. *Sociology of Health & Illness* 24 (6): 734–49.

Greve, Arent, and Janet Salaff. 2003. Social Networks and Entrepreneurship. *Entrepreneurship: Theory & Practice* 28 (1): 1–22.

———. 2005. A Social Network Approach to Understand the Ethnic Economy: A Theoretical Discourse. *GeoJournal* 62 (1): 7–16.

Guerassimoff, C. 2003. The New Chinese Migrants in France. *International Migration* 41 (3): 135–54.

Haines, David W. 2002. Binding the Generations: Household Formation Patterns Among Vietnamese Refugees. *International Migration Review of* 36 (4): 1194–217.

Hamilton, Gary G. 2006. *Commerce and Capitalism in Chinese Societies.* London: RoutledgeCurzon.

Hamilton, Gary G., and Cheng-shu Kao. 1990. The Institutional Foundations of Chinese Business: The Family Firm in Taiwan. *Comparative Social Research* 12: 95–112.

Hardie, Edward T. L. 1994. Recruitment and Release: Migration Advisers and the Creation of Exile. In *Reluctant Exiles or Bold Pioneers: An Introduction to Migration From Hong Kong.* Edited by Ronald Skeldon. Hong Kong: Hong Kong University Press.

Harris, Karen L., and Jan Ryan. 1988. Chinese Immigration to Australia and South Africa: A Comparative Analysis of Legislative Control. In *The Last Half Century of Chinese Overseas.* Edited by Elizabeth Sinn. Hong Kong: Centre of Asian Studies, University of Hong Kong.

Hays, Sharon. 1996. *The Cultural Contradictions of Motherhood.* New Haven, CT: Yale University Press.

Hiebert, Daniel, and David Ley. 2003. *Characteristics of Immigrant Transnationalism in Vancouver.* No. 03–15, Research on Immigration and Integration in the Metropolis Working Paper Series. Vancouver: Vancouver Centre of Excellence.

Hirschman, Albert O. 1970. *Exit, Voice and Loyalty.* Cambridge, MA: Harvard University Press.

Ho Yu Chun 何友暉 and Sze Ching Ying 彭泗清. 2006. 趙志裕世道人心：對中國人的心理探索 (*Sociology and Psychology: An Inquiry towards Chinese People's Psychology*). Hong Kong: San Lien.

Ho, Wing Chung, and Yat Nam Ng. 2008. Public Amnesia and Multiple Modernities in Shanghai: Narrating the Postsocialist Future in a Former Socialist Model Community. *Journal of Contemporary Ethnography* 37: 383–416.

Hochschild, Arlie Russell. 1990. *The Second Shift*. New York: Avon Books.

Hondagneu-Sotelo, Pierrette, and Ernestine Avila. 1997. "I'm Here, But I'm There": The Meanings of Latina Transnational Motherhood. *Gender & Society* 11 (5): 548–71.

Hong Kong Federation of Industries. 1993. *Hong Kong's Industrial Development in the Pearl River Delta*. Hong Kong: Hong Kong Federation of Industries Industry and Research Division.

Hsu, Francis L. K. 1971. *Under the Ancestors' Shadow: Kinship, Personality, and Social Mobility in China*. Palo Alto, CA: Stanford University Press.

Hughes, Everett C. 1958. *Men and Their Work*. Glencoe, IL: Free Press.

Hyun, On-Kang, Wanjeong Lee, An-Jin Yoo, and Bok-Hee Cho. 2002. Social Support for Two Generations of New Mothers in Selected Populations in Korea, Hong Kong, and the United States. *Journal of Comparative Family Studies* 33 (4): 515–28.

Imber-Black, E., J. Roberts, and E. Whiting, ed. 1988. *Rituals in Families and Family Therapy*. New York: Norton.

Ip, Olivia, and Sek Hong Ng. 2007. "Social Connectedness of Occupational Community and Work Behavior: A Study of the Social Relations of Construction Workers in Hong Kong." Paper read at International Sunbelt Social Network Conference, at Corfu, Greece.

Jasper, James. 1997. The Art of Moral Protest: Culture, Biography, and Creativity in Social Movements. Chicago: University of Chicago Press.

Jia, Jiansan and Jiaxin Chen. 2001. *Sea farming and sea ranching in China*. FAO Fisheries and Aquaculture Department, PRC. FAO Series title: FAO Fisheries Technical Paper—T418. http://www.fao.org/DOCREP/005/Y2257E/y2257e04.htm.

Johnston, Ron, Andrew Trlin, Anne Henderson, and Nicola North. 2006. Sustaining and Creating Migration Chains Among Skilled Immigrant Groups: Chinese, Indians and South Africans in New Zealand. *Journal of Ethnic and Migration Studies* 32 (7): 1227–50.

Judd, Ellen R. 2008. "Families We Create": Women's Kinship in Rural China as Spatialized Practice. In *Chinese Kinship: Contemporary Anthropological Perspectives*. Edited by S. Brandtstädter and G. Santos. London: Routledge.

Kamiar, M. S., and H. F. Ismail. 1991. Family Ties and Economic Stability Concerns of Migrant Labour Families in Jordan. *International Migration* 29 (4): 561–72.

Kee, Pookong, and Ronald Skeldon. 1994. The Migration and Settlement of Hong Kong Chinese in Australia. In *Reluctant Exiles or Bold Pioneers: An Introduction to Migration From Hong Kong*. Edited by Ronald Skeldon. Hong Kong: Hong Kong University Press.

Keezhangatte, James J. 2006. "Transnational Migration, Resilience and Family Relationship: Indian Household Workers in Hong Kong." Hong Kong: Social Work, University of Hong Kong.

Kim, Dae Young. 2006. Stepping-Stone to Intergenerational Mobility? The Springboard, Safety Net, or Mobility Trap Functions of Korean Immigrant Entrepreneurship for the Second Generation. *International Migration Review* 40 (4): 927–62.

Kim, Phillip H. and Howard Aldrich. 2005. Entrepreneurship and Social Capital. *Foundations and Trends® in Entrepreneurship* 5 (4): 211–340.

Kittay, Eva Feder, and Ellen K. Feder, ed. 1998. *Love's Labor: Essays on Women, Equality, and Dependency.* London: Routledge.

Kofman, Eleonore. 2004. Family-Related Migration: A Critical Review of European Studies. *Journal of Ethnic and Migration Studies* 30 (2): 243–62.

Komarovsky, Mirra. 1971. *The Unemployed Man and His Family—the Effect of Unemployment Upon the Status of the Man in Fifty-Nine Families.* New York: Octagon Books.

Kotchick, Beth A., and Rex Forehand. 2002. Putting Parenting in Perspective: A Discussion of the Contextual Factors That Shape Parenting Practices. *Journal of Child and Family Studies* 11 (3): 255–69.

Kraar, Louis. 1995. The Death of Hong Kong. *Fortune* 131 (12): 118–27.

Ku, Agnes Shuk-mei. 2004. Immigration Policies, Discourses, and the Politics of Local Belonging in Hong Kong (1950–1980). *Modern China* 30 (3): 326–60.

———. 2006. "Changing Perceptions of Citizenship and Governance in Hong Kong." Paper read at Conference on the role of government in Hong Kong, at Hong Kong.

Ku, Agnes Shuk-mei, and Ngai Pun, ed. 2006. *Remaking Citizenship in Hong Kong: Community, Nation and the Global City.* London: Routledge/Curzon.

Laczko, F. 2003. Introduction: Understanding Migration Between China and Europe. *International Migration* 41 (3): 5–19.

Lam, Ching Man. 2007. *Not Grown Up Forever: A Chinese Conception of Adolescent Development.* New York: Nova.

Lam, Lawrence. 1994. Searching for a Safe Haven: The Migration and Settlement of Hong Kong Chinese Immigrants in Toronto. In *Reluctant Exiles or Bold Pioneers: An Introduction to Migration From Hong Kong.* Edited by Ronald Skeldon. Hong Kong: Hong Kong University Press.

Lam, Oi Yeung. 2005. "Family Dynamics and Educational Outcomes." Unpublished Master of Philosophy Thesis. Hong Kong: Department of Sociology, University of Hong Kong.

Landler, Mark. 2001. Web Comes Up Fast on the Outside. *New York Times.* March 18.

Landolt, Patricia. 2001. Salvadoran Economic Transnationalism: Embedded Strategies for Household Maintenance, Immigrant Incorporation, and Entrepreneurial Expansion. *Global Networks* 1 (3): 217–42.

Landolt, Patricia, and Wei Wei Da. 2005. The Spatially Ruptured Practices of Immigrant Families: A Comparison of Immigrants From El Salvador and the People's Republic of China. *Current Sociology* 53 (4): 625–53.

Lang, Graeme. 1994. Empowering the Passenger: Mass Transit Research in Hong Kong. *Journal of Applied Sociology* 11: 23–40.

Lang, Graeme, and Lars Ragvald. 1993. *The Rise of a Refugee God: Hong Kong's Wong Tai Sin*. Hong Kong: Oxford University Press.

Lang, Graeme, and Josephine Smart. 2002. Migration and the "Second Wife" in South China: Toward Cross-Border Polygyny. *International Migration Review* 36 (2): 546–70.

Lareau, Annette. 2003. *Unequal Childhoods*. Berkeley: University of California Press.

Lau Cho-Yam, Joseph. 1998. Urban Developments and Mobility Inequality of the Disadvantaged. *Southeast Asian Journal of Social Science* 26 (2): 45–64.

Lau, Siu-kai. 1982. *Society and Politics in Hong Kong*. Hong Kong: Chinese University Press.

———. 2003. The Rise and Decline of Political Support for the Hong Kong Special Administrative Region Government. In *Hong Kong Government & Politics*. Edited by Sing Ming. Hong Kong: Oxford University Press.

Lau, Yuk-King, Joyce L. C. Ma, and Ying-Keung Chan. 2006. Labor Force Participation of Married Women in Hong Kong: A Feminist Perspective. *Journal of Comparative Family Studies* 37 (1): 93–112.

Laxness, Halldór. 2005. *Under the Glacier*. New York: Random House.

Lee, Everett. 1966. A Theory of Migration. *Demography* 3 (1): 47–57.

Lee, Frances Wing-lin, and Fanny Miu-ling Ip. 2003. Young School Dropouts: Levels of Influence of Different Systems. *Journal of Youth Studies* 6 (1): 89–110.

Lee, James, and Ngai-ming Yip. 2006. Public Housing and Family Life in East Asia: Housing History and Social Change in Hong Kong, 1953–1990. *Journal of Family History* 31 (1): 66–82.

Lee, Michael H. 2006. The Development of Private Education in Hong Kong and Singapore: A Comparative Study. *Education & Society* 24 (2): 25–48.

Lee, Ou-fan Leo. 2008. *City Between Worlds: My Hong Kong*. Cambridge: Harvard University Press.

Lee, Sharon M., and Monica Boyd. 2008. Marrying Out: Comparing the Marital and Social Integration of Asians in the U.S. and Canada. *Social Science Research* 37 (1): 311–29.

Lee, William K. M. 2002. Gender Ideology and the Domestic Division of Labor in Middle-Class Chinese Families in Hong Kong. *Gender, Place and Culture: A Journal of Feminist Geography* 9 (3): 245–60.

Leeming, Frank. 1977. *Street Studies in Hong Kong*. Hong Kong: Oxford University Press.

Leicht, René, Markus Leiss, and Silke Fehrenbach. 2005. Social and Economic Characteristics of Self-Employed Italians in Germany. *Studi Emigrazione / International Journal of Migration Studies* 42 (158): 285–307.

Leiter, Valerie, Marty Wyngaarden Krauss, Betsy Anderson, and Nora Wells. 2004. The Consequences of Caring Effects of Mothering a Child With Special Needs. *Journal of Family Issues* 25 (3): 379–403.

Leung, G. S. M. 2006. "A Study of the Effects of Parental Support and Children's Resourcefulness on the Academic Stress of Senior Primary School Students in Hong Kong." Hong Kong: Social Work, University of Hong Kong.

Leung, Hon Chu. 2006. Politics of Incorporation and Exclusion: Immigration and Citizenship Issues. In *Remaking Citizenship in Hong Kong: Community, Nation and the Global City*. Edited by Agnes S. Ku, and Ngai Pun. London: Routledge/Curzon.

Leung, Vivian Hiu-tung. 2002. Gender Embeddedness and Family Strategies: Hong Kong Working-Class Families During Economic Restructuring. In *Transforming Gender and Development in East Asia*. Edited by Esther Ngan-ling Chow. New York: Routledge.

Levitt, Peggy. 2002. The Ties That Change: Relations to the Ancestral Home Over the Life Cycle. In *The Changing Face of Home: The Transnational Lives of the Second Generation*. Edited by Peggy Levitt, and Mary C. Waters. New York: Russell Sage Foundation. .

Levitt, Peggy, and Ninna Nyberg-Sørensen. 2004. The Transnational Turn in Migration Studies. In *Global Migration Perspectives*, No. 6. Geneva: Global Commission on International Migration.

Levitt, Peggy, and Nina Glick-Schiller. 2004. Conceptualizing Simultaneity: A Transnational Social Field Perspective on Sociology. *International Migration Review* 38 (3): 1002–39.

Lewin, Kurt. 1935. *A Dynamic Theory of Personality: Selected Papers*. Translated by Donald K. Adams and Karl E. Zener. New York: McGraw-Hill.

Ley, David. 2006. Explaining Variations in Business Performance Among Immigrant Entrepreneurs in Canada. *Journal of Ethnic and Migration Studies* 32 (5): 743–64.

Ley, David, and Audrey Kobayashi. 2005. Back to Hong Kong: Return Migration or Transnational Sojourn? *Global Networks* 5 (2): 111–27.

Li, F. L. N., A. M. Findlay, and H. Jones. 1998. A Cultural Economy Perspective on Service Sector Migration in the Global City: The Case of Hong Kong. *International Migration* 36 (2): 131–57.

Li, Peter S. 1992. Ethnic Enterprise in Transition: Chinese Enterprise in Richmond, BC, 1880–1990. *Canadian Ethnic Studies* 20 (1): 120–38.

———. 1994. Un-Neighbourly Houses or Unwelcome Chinese: The Social Construction of Race in the Battle Over "Monster Homes" in Vancouver, Canada. *International Journal of Comparative Race and Ethnic Studies* 1 (1): 14–33.

———. 2001. Chinese Canadians in Business. *Asian and Pacific Migration Journal* 10 (1): 99–121.

———. 2005. The Rise and Fall of Chinese Immigration to Canada: Newcomers from Hong Kong Special Administrative Region of China and Mainland China, 1980–2000. *International Migration* 43 (3): 9–34.

Lievens, J. 1999. Family-Formation Migration from Turkey and Morocco to Belgium: The Demand for Marriage Partners from the Countries of Origin. *International Migration Review* 33 (3): 717–44.

Lin, Angel Mei Yi. 2000. Lively Children Trapped in an Island of Disadvantage: Verbal Play of Cantonese Working-Class Schoolboys in Hong Kong. *International Journal of the Sociology of Language* 143: 63–83.

Lin, George C. S. 2002. Hong Kong and the Globalisation of the Chinese Diaspora: A Geographical Perspective. *Asia Pacific Viewpoint* 43 (1): 63–91.

Loh, Christine. 2004. Personal Communication.

Lubbers, Miranda J., Jose Luis Molina, and Christopher McCarty. 2007. Personal Networks and Ethnic Identifications. *International Sociology* 22 (6): 721–41.

Lui, Tai Lok. 1994. 呂大樂著][Lü, Dale] *Waged Work At Home: The Social Organization of Industrial Outwork in Hong Kong.* Aldershot: Avebury.

———. 1997. *"Wu Gai, Mai Dan!" yi ge she hui xue jia de Xianggang bi ji ("Check please!" A Sociologist's Notes on Hong Kong)* 唔該, 埋單 : 一個社會學家的香港筆記. Hong Kong: Xianren Hangyou Xian Company.

——— 2001. The Malling of Hong Kong. In *Consuming Hong Kong.* Edited by Gordon Mathews and Tai-Lok Lui. Hong Kong: Hong Kong University Press, 23–46 .

Lui, Tai Lok, and Stephen Wing-kai Chiu. 2007. Governance Crisis and Changing State-Business Relations: A Political Economy Perspective. *The China Review* 7 (2): 1–34.

Luxton, Meg. 1980. *More Than a Labour of Love: Three Generations of Women's Work in the Home.* Toronto: Women's Press.

Ma, Eric Kit-wai. 1999. *Culture, Politics and Television in Hong Kong.* London, England: Routledge.

———. 2007. Grassroots Nationalism: Changing Identity in a Changing Context. *China Review* 7 (2): 149–67.

Mahler, Sarah J. 1999. Engendering Transnational Migration: A Case Study of Salvadorans. *American Behavioral Scientist* 42 (4): 690–719.

Mak, Anita S. 1997. Skilled Hong Kong Immigrants' Intention to Repatriate. *Asian and Pacific Migration Journal* 6 (2): 169–84.

———. 2006. Career Relocation Issues and Repatriation Dilemma: Skilled Hong Kong Immigrants to Australia. In *Experiences of Transnational Chinese Migrants in the Asia-Pacific.* Edited by D. Ip, R. Hibbins, and W. H Chui. New York: Nova Science, 103–16.

Malkin, Victoria. 2004. "We Go to Get Ahead." Gender and Status in Two Mexican Migrant Communities. *Latin American Perspectives* 31 (5): 75–99.

Man, Guida. 2004. Gender, Work and Migration: Deskilling Chinese Immigrant Women in Canada. *Women's Studies International Forum* 27 (2): 135–48.

March, James G. 1994. *A Primer on Decision Making: How Decisions Happen.* New York: Free Press.

March, James G., and Johan P. Olsen. 1989. *Rediscovering Institutions: The Organizational Basis of Politics.* New York: Free Press.

Massey, Douglas S. 1990. The Social and Economic Origins of Immigration. *Annals of the American Academy of Political and Social Sciences*.

Massey, Douglas S., Rafael Alarcon, Jorge Durand, and Humberto Gonzalez. 1987. *Return to Aztlan: The Social Process of International Migration From Western Mexico*. Berkeley: University of California Press.

Massey, Douglas, Joaquin Arango, Graeme Hugo, Ali Kouaouci, Adela Pellegrino, and J. Edward Taylor. 1993. Theories of International Migration: A Review and Appraisal. *Population and Development Review* 19 (3): 431–66.

Mathews, Gordon, Eric Kit-wai Ma, and Tai-lok Lui. 2008. *Hong Kong, China: Learning to Belong to a Nation*. New York: Routledge.

Mathews, Gordon, and Tai-lok Lui, ed. 2003. *Consuming Hong Kong*. Hong Kong: Hong Kong University Press.

McBride-Chang, C., and L. Chang. 1998. Adolescent-Parent Relations in Hong Kong: Parenting Styles, Emotional Autonomy, and School Achievement. *Journal of Genetic Psychology* 159 (4): 421–36.

McCracken, Grant David. 1988. *The Long Interview*. Beverley Hills: Sage.

McGraw, Lori A., and Alexis J. Walker. 2007. Meanings of Sisterhood and Developmental Disability: Narratives From White Nondisabled Sisters. *Journal of Family Issues* 28 (4): 474–500.

McKay, Deirdre. 2005. Migration and the Sensuous Geographies of Re-Emplacement in the Philippines. *Journal of Intercultural Studies* 26 (1, 2): 75–91.

McLaren, Arlene Tigar, and Isabel Dyck. 2004. Mothering, Human Capital, and the "Ideal Immigrant." *Women's Studies International Forum* 27 (1): 41–53.

McLoyd, Vonnie C., Ana Mari Cauce, David Takeuchi, and Leon Wilson. 2000. Marital Processes and Parental Socialization in Families of Color: A Decade Review of Research. *Journal of Marriage and the Family* 62 (4): 1070–93.

Menjivar, Cecilia. 1995. Kinship Networks Among Immigrants: Lessons From a Qualitative Comparative Approach. *International Journal of Comparative Sociology* 36 (3–4): 219–32.

———. 1997. Immigrant Kinship Networks: Vietnamese, Salvadoreans, and Mexicans in Comparative Perspective. *Journal of Comparative Family Studies* 28 (1): 1–24.

Menjivar, Cecilia, Julie DeVanzo, Lisa R. Greenwell, and R. Burciaga Valdez. 1998. Remittance Behavior Among Salvadoran and Filipino Immigrants in Los Angeles. *International Migration Review* 32 (1): 97–127.

Meyers, Deborah, and Jennifer Yau. 2004. United States Immigration Statistics in 2003. *Migration Information Source*. http://www.migrationinformation.org/USfocus/display.cfm?id=263#3.

Mills, C. Wright. 1959. *The Sociological Imagination*. New York: Oxford University Press.

Moon, Seungsook. 2003. Immigration and Mothering: Case Studies from Two Generations of Korean Immigrant Women. *Gender and Society* 17 (6): 840–60.

Morgan, David, H. J. 2001. Family Sociology in from the Fringe: The Three "Economies" of Family Life. In *Developments in Sociology*. Edited by Robert G. Burgess and Anne Murcott. New York: Prentice Hall.

Myles, John, and Feng Hou. 2004. Changing Colours: Spatial Assimilation and New Racial Minority Immigrants. *Canadian Journal of Sociology/Cahiers Canadiens de Sociologie* 29 (1): 29–58.

Ng Chun Hung, Thomas Wong, Chu Yin-wah, and Anita Chan. 2009. Introduction. Doing Families in Hong Kong: Values, Relations and Strategies. *Transformations in Chinese Societies* 4: 3–16.

Ng, Michael. 2005. Rising Poverty on the Agenda for Tung's Address. *The Standard* (Hong Kong). January 10.

Nyiri, Pal. 2001. Expatriating is Patriotic? The Discourse on "New Migrants" in the People's Republic of China and Identity Construction Among Recent Migrants From the PRC. *Journal of Ethnic and Migration Studies* 27 (4): 635–53.

Omohundro, John T. 1981. *Chinese Merchant Families in Iloilo: Commerce and Kin in a Central Philippine City*. Quezon City: Ateneo de Manila University Press.

Ong, Aihwa. 1999. *Flexible Citizenship: The Cultural of Logics of Transnationality*. Durham, NC: Duke University Press.

Orellana, M. F., B. Thorne, A. Chee, and W. S. E. Lam. 2001. Transnational Childhoods: The Participation of Children in Processes of Family Migration. *Social Problems* 48 (4): 572–91.

Orrù, Marco, Nicole Woolsey Biggart, and Gary G. Hamilton. 1997. *Economic Organization of East Asian Capitalism*. Thousand Oaks, CA: Sage Publications.

Palloni, Alberto, Douglas S. Massey, Miguel Ceballos, Kristin Espinosa, and Michael Spittel. 2001. Social Capital and International Migration: A Test Using Information on Family Networks. *American Journal of Sociology* 106 (5): 1262–98.

Parreñas, Rhacel. 2005. Long Distance Intimacy: Class, Gender and Intergenerational Relations Between Mothers and Children in Filipino Transnational Families. *Global Networks* 5 (4): 317–36.

Parry, Jane, Rebecca Taylor, Lynne Pettinger, and Miriam Glucksmann. 2005. Confronting the Challenges of Work Today: New Horizons and Perspectives. *Sociological Review* 53 (s2): 1–18.

Parwani, Audrey. 2007. Warning as Income Gap Widens; Census Shows Rich-Poor Divide Growing; Expert Says it Will Worsen if Officials Don't Act. *South China Morning Post*. June 19.

Pearson, Veronica, and Sin-ping Ning. 1997. Family Care in Schizophrenia: An Undervalued Resource. In *Social Work Intervention in Health Care: The Hong Kong Scene*. Edited by Lai-wan Cecilia Chan and Nancy Rhind. Hong Kong: Hong Kong University Press.

Pepper, Suzanne. 2008. *Keeping Democracy At Bay: Hong Kong and the Challenge of Chinese Political Reform*. Boulder, CO: Rowan & Littlefield Publishers, Inc.

Pe-pua, R., C. Mitchell, R. Iredale, and S. Castles. 1996. *Astronaut Families and Parachute Children: The Cycle of Migration Between Hong Kong and Australia*. Canberra: AGPS.

Pessar, Patricia R., and Sarah J. Mahler. 2003. Transnational Migration: Bringing Gender in. *International Migration Review* 37 (3): 812–46.

Pettinger, Lynne. 2005. Friends, Relations and Colleagues: The Blurred Boundaries of the Workplace. *Sociological Review* 53 (s2): 37–55.

Pfaff, Steven, and Hyojoung Kim. 2003. Exit-Voice Dynamics in Collective Action: An Analysis of Emigration and Protest. *American Journal of Sociology* 109 (2): 410–44.

Piotrowski, Martin. 2006. The Effect of Social Networks at Origin Communities on Migration Remittances: Evidence from Nang Rong District. *European Journal of Population/Revue Europeenne de Demographie* 22 (1): 67–94.

Portes, Alejandro. 2001. Introduction: The Debates and Significance of Immigrant Transnationalism. *Global Networks* 1: 181–93.

Portes, Alejandro, and Jozsef Borocz. 1989. Contemporary Immigration: Theoretical Perspectives on Its Determinants and Modes of Incorporation. *International Migration Review* 27 (3): 606–30.

Post, David, and Suet-Ling Pong. 1998. The Waning Effect of Sibship Composition on School Attainment in Hong Kong. *Comparative Education Review* 42 (2): 99–117.

Presser, Harriet. 2003. Race-Ethnic and Gender Differences in Nonstandard Work Shifts. *Work and Occupations* 30 (4): 412–39.

Preston, Valerie, and Lucia Lo. 2000. Asian Theme Malls in Suburban Toronto: Land Use Conflict in Richmond Hill. *Canadian Geographer* 44 (2): 182–90.

Probyn, Elspeth. 2004. Everyday Shame. *Cultural Studies* 8 (2–3): 328–49.

Public Opinion Programme. 2009. "People's Trust in the HKSAR Government. People's Trust in the Beijing Central Government and People's Trust in the Taiwan Government—Combined Charts (7–12/1992–1–6/2009)." Hong Kong: University of Hong Kong. http://tinyurl.com/n8wjlu.

Pun, Ngai. 2005. *Made in China*. Hong Kong: Hong Kong University Press.

Ray, Bryan K., Halseth, Greg, and Benjamin Johnson. 1997. The Changing "Face" of the Suburbs: Issues of Ethnicity and Residential Change in Suburban Vancouver. *International Journal of Urban and Regional Research* 21 (1): 75–99.

Rodríguez-García, Dan. 2006. "Marriage Patterns and Discourses of Segregation and Assimilation Amongst Ethnic Groups: The Case of Chinese Ethnic Communities in Toronto, Canada." Paper read at Annual Meeting of North American Chinese Sociologists Association, Montréal, August 11.

Rosen, Sherry. 1976. *Mei Foo Sun Chuen: Middle Class Families in Transition*. Taipei: Orient Cultural Service.

Ryan, Louise. 2002. Sexualising Emigration: Discourses of Irish Female Emigration in the 1930s. *Women's Studies International Forum* 25 (1): 51–65.

Salaff, Janet. 1981. *Working Daughters of Hong Kong: Female Filial Piety or Power in the Family?* Cambridge: Cambridge University Press.

———. 2002. Women's Work in International Migration. In *Transforming Gender and Development in East Asia*. Edited by Esther Chow. London: Routledge.

Salaff, Janet, and Arent Greve. 2004. Can Chinese Women's Social Capital Migrate? *Women's Studies International Forum* 27 (2): 149–62.

———. 2006. Why Do Skilled Women and Men Emigrating from China to Canada Get Bad Jobs? In *Gender, Migration and Citizenship.* Edited by Evangelia Tastsoglou and Alexandra Dobrowolsky. London: Ashgate.

Salaff, Janet, Eric Fong, and Siu-lun Wong. 1999. Using Social Networks to Exit Hong Kong. In *Networks in the Global Village: Life in Contemporary Communities.* Edited by Barry Wellman. Boulder: Westview Press.

Salaff, Janet, Angela Shik, and Arent Greve. 2008. Like Sons and Daughters of Hong Kong: The Return of the Young Generation. *China Review* 8 (1): 31–57.

Saldaña, Johnny. 2003. *Longitudinal Qualitative Research: Analyzing Change Through Time.* Lanham, MD: AltaMira Press, Rowan & Littlefield.

Santos, Gonçalo Duro Dos. 2006. The Anthropology of Chinese Kinship: A Critical Overview. *European Journal of East Asian Studies* 5 (2): 275–333.

Sassen-Koob, Saskia. 1987. Issues of Core and Periphery: Labour Migration and Global Restructuring. In *Global Restructuring and Territorial Development.* Edited by J. Henderson and M. Castells. London: Sage.

Saxenian, AnnaLee, Yoko Motoyama, and Xiaohong Quan. 2002. *Local and Global Networks of Immigrant Professionals in Silicon Valley.* San Francisco: Public Policy Institute of California.

Sayer, Liana C., Anne H. Gauthier, and Frank F. Furstenburg. 2004. Educational Differences in Parents' Time With Children: Cross National Variations. *Journal of Marriage and Family* 66 (5): 1152–69.

Schmitz, Paul. 2006. "D'Agostino Supermarkets, From Pushcart to Product: Family and Ethnicity as Cultural Currency." Sociology, Boston University, Boston.

Scott, Ian. 1989. *Political Change and the Crisis of Legitimacy in Hong Kong.* Hong Kong: Oxford University Press.

———. 2003. The Disarticulation of Hong Kong's Post-Handover Political System. In *Hong Kong Government & Politics.* Edited by Sing Ming. Hong Kong: Oxford University Press.

Scott, W. Richard. 2001. *Institutions and Organizations.* 2nd ed. Thousand Oaks, CA: Sage Publications.

———. 2007. *Institutions and Organizations: Ideas and Interests.* 3rd ed. Newbury Park, CA: Sage Publications.

Shek, Daniel T. L. 2005. Perceived Parental Control and Parent-Child Relational Qualities in Chinese Adolescents in Hong Kong. *Sex Roles: A Journal of Research* 53 (9–10): 635–46.

Shuval, Judith T., and Elazar Leshem. 1998. The Sociology of Migration in Israel: A Critical View. In *Immigration to Israel: Sociological Perspectives.* Edited by Elazar Leshem and Judith T. Shuval. New Brunswick, NJ: Transaction.

Sinn, Elizabeth. 2004. Beyond Tianxia: The Zhongwai Xinwen Qiribao (Hong Kong 1871–72) and the Construction of a Transnational Chinese Community. *China Review* 4 (1): 89–122.

————. 2008. Lesson in Openness: Creating a Space of Flow in Hong Kong. In *Hong Kong Mobile: The Making of a Global Population*. Edited by Helen F. Siu and Agnes S. Ku. Hong Kong: Hong Kong University Press, 13–43.

Siu, Oi-ling, Phillips, David R., and Tat-wing Leung. 2004. Safety Climate and Safety Performance Among Construction Workers in Hong Kong: The Role of Psychological Strains as Mediators. *Accident Analysis and Prevention* 36 (3): 359–66.

Skeldon, Ronald. 1991. Emigration, Immigration and Fertility Decline: Demographic Integration or Disintegration? In *The Other Hong Kong Report, 1991*. Edited by Yun-wing Sung and Ming-kwan Lee. Hong Kong: Chinese University of Hong Kong.

————. 1994. Hong Kong in an International Migration System. In *Reluctant Exiles or Bold Pioneers: An Introduction to Migration From Hong Kong*. Edited by Ronald Skeldon. Hong Kong: Hong Kong University Press.

————. 1997. Hong Kong: Colonial City to Global City to Provincial City? *Cities* 14 (5): 265–71.

————. 2003. The Chinese Diaspora or the Migration of Chinese Peoples? In *The Chinese Diaspora: Space, Place, Mobility, and Identity*. Edited by L. J. C. Ma and C. Cartier. Lanham, Md.: Rowman and Littlefield.

Skeldon, Ronald, ed.1995. *Emigration From Hong Kong: Trends and Tendencies*. Hong Kong: Chinese University Press.

Smart, Alan. 2002. The Hong Kong/Pearl River Delta Urban Region: An Emerging Transnational Mode of Regulation or Just Muddling Through? In *The New Chinese City*. Edited by John Logan. Oxford: Blackwell.

————. 2003. Sharp Edges, Fuzzy Categories and Transborder Networks: Managing and Housing New Arrivals in Hong Kong. *Ethnic and Racial Studies* 26 (2): 218–33.

————. 2006. *The Shek Kip Mei Myth: Squatters, Fires and Colonial Rule in Hong Kong, 1950–1963*. Hong Kong: University of Hong Kong Press.

Smart, Josephine. 2004. Globalization and Modernity: A Case Study of Cognac Consumption in Hong Kong. *Anthropologica* 46 (2): 219–29.

Smelser, Neil J. 1995. *Problematics of Sociology: The Georg Simmel Lectures*. Berkeley: University of California.

So, Alvin Y. 1999. *Hong Kong's Embattled Democracy: A Societal Analysis*. Baltimore: Johns Hopkins University Press.

————. 2003. Cross-Border Families in Hong Kong: The Role of Social Class and Politics. *Critical Asian Studies* 35 (4): 515–34.

Song, Miri. 1999. *Helping Out: Children's Labor in Ethnic Businesses*. Philadelphia, PA: Temple University Press.

Stone, Elizabeth, Erica Gomez, Despina Hotzoglou, and Jane Y. Lipnitsky. 2005. Transnationalism as a Motif in Family Stories. *Family Process* 44 (4): 381–98.

Suarez-Orozco, Carola, and Desiree Baolian Qin. 2006. Gendered Perspectives in Psychology: Immigrant Origin Youth. *International Migration Review* 40 (1): 165–99.

Sun Wenbin, and Wong Siu-lun,. 2008. Is Hong Kong Entrepreneurship Declining?

In *Hong Kong Mobile: The Making of a Global Population*. Edited by Helen F. Siu and Agnes S. Ku. Hong Kong: Hong Kong University Press, 327–42.

Sung, Yun Wing. 1991. *The China Hong Kong Connection: The Key to China's Open Door Policy*. Cambridge: Cambridge University Press.

Swidler, Ann. 1986. Culture in Action: Symbols and Strategies. *American Sociological Review* 51 (2): 273–86.

Tam, Maria Siumi. 1997. Eating Metropolitaneity: Hong Kong Identity in Yumcha. *Australian Journal of Anthropology* 8: 291–306.

———. 2005. We-Women and They-Women: Imagining Mistresses Across the Hong Kong-China Border. In *Rethinking and Recasting Citizenship: Social Exclusion and Marginality in Chinese Societies*. Edited by May Tam, Hok-bun Ku, and Travis Kong. Hong Kong: Centre for Social Policy Studies, Hong Kong Polytechnic University.

Tam, Vicky C. W., and Kathryn D. Rettig. 1999. Decision Making of Mothers in Hong Kong Regarding the Occasional Use of Alternative Child-Care Arrangements. *Journal of Family and Economic Issues* 20 (2): 163–90.

Taylor, Peter J., D. R. F. Walker, and J. V. Beaverstock. 2002. Firms and Their Global Service Networks. In *Global Networks*. Edited by Saskia Sassen. New York: Routledge.

Tong, Chee Kiong. 2005. Feuds and Legacies: Conflict and Inheritance in Chinese Family Businesses. *International Sociology* 20 (1): 45–70.

Triadafilopoulos, Triadafilos. 2006. Family Immigration Policy in Comparative Perspective: Canada and the United States. *Canadian Issues* 3 (1): 30–33.

Tsang, Steve Yui-Sang. 2003. *A Modern History of Hong Kong*. New York: I.B. Tauris.

Turner, Matthew. 1995. 60's/90's: Dissolving the People. In *Hong Kong Sixties: Designing Identity*. Edited by Matthew Turner and Irene Ngan. Hong Kong: Hong Kong Arts Centre.

Van Hook, Jennifer, and Jennifer E. Glick. 2007. Immigration and Living Arrangements: Moving Beyond Economic Need Versus Acculturation. *Demography* 44 (2): 225–47.

Vincent, Carol, Annette Braun, and Stephen J. Ball. 2008. Childcare, Choice and Social Class: Caring for Young Children in the UK. *Critical Social Policy* 28 (1): 5–26.

Waldinger, Roger, and David Fitzgerald. 2004. Transnationalism in Question. *American Journal of Sociology* 109 (5): 1177–95.

Wang, Gungwu. 1989. Patterns of Chinese Migration in Historical Perspective. In *Observing Change in Asia: Essays in Honour of J. A. C. Mackie*. Edited by R. J. May and W. J. O'Mallen. Bathurst, Aus.: Crawford House.

Wang, Shuguang, and Lucia Lo. 2005. Chinese Immigrants in Canada: Their Changing Composition and Economic Performance. *International Migration* 43 (3): 35–71.

Waters, Johanna L. 2000. "The Geographies of Cultural Capital: International Education, Circular Migration and Family Strategies Between Canada and Hong

Kong." Unpublished Ph.D thesis. Vancouver: Department of Geography, University of British Columbia.

———. 2005. Transnational Family Strategies and Education in the Contemporary Chinese Diaspora. *Global Networks* 5 (4): 359–77.

Waters, Sarah. 2006. *The Night Watch*. London: Virago.

Watson, J. L. 1975. *Emigration and the Chinese Lineage: The Mans in Hong Kong and London*. Berkeley: University of California Press.

Watson, Rubie. 2004. "Families in China: Ties That Bind?" Presented at the Family Model in Chinese Art and Culture Conference. Princeton, NJ: Princeton University.

Wilmoth, Janet M. 2001. Immigrant Status, Living Arrangements, and Depressive Symptoms Among Middle-Aged and Older Adults. *Gerontologist* 41 (2): 228–39.

Witzleben, J. Lawrence. 1999. Hans Ebert: Cantopop and Mandapop in Pre-Postcolonial Hong Kong: Identity Negotiation in the Performances of Anita Mui Yim-Fong. *Popular Music* 18 (2): 241–58.

Wolf, Diane L. 1996. Situating Feminist Dilemmas in Field Work. In *Feminist Dilemmas in Fieldwork*. Edited by Diane L. Wolf. Boulder, CO: Westview Press.

Wolf, Margery. 1972. *Women and the Family in Rural Taiwan*. Stanford, CA: Stanford University Press.

Wong, Hung. 1999. "A Comparative Study of Marginal Workers in Britain and Hong Kong." Unpublished Ph.D. thesis. Warwick: Department of Sociology, University of Warwick.

Wong, Jum-sum, James. 2003. "The Rise and Decline of Cantopop: A Study of Hong Kong Popular Music (1949–1997)." Unpublished Ph.D. thesis. Hong Kong: Hong Kong University.

Wong, Lloyd L., and Michele Ng. 2002. The Emergence of Small Transnational Enterprise in Vancouver: The Case of Chinese Entrepreneur Immigrants. *International Journal of Urban and Regional Research* 26 (3): 508–30.

Wong, Martin. 2001. One in Six Gambling Addicts Suicidal: Survey. *South China Morning Post*. August 24.

Wong, Sam. 2007. *Exploring "Unseen" Social Capital in Community Participation: Everyday Lives of Poor Mainland Chinese Migrants in Hong Kong*. Amsterdam: Amsterdam University Press.

Wong, Siu-lun. 1985. The Chinese Family Firm: A Model. *British Journal of Sociology* 36 (1): 58–72.

———. 1988. *Emigrant Entrepreneurs: Shanghai Industrialists in Hong Kong*. Hong Kong: Oxford University Press.

———. 1995. Political Attitudes and Identity. In *Emigration From Hong Kong. Trends and Tendencies*. Edited by Ronald Skeldon. Hong Kong: Chinese University Press.

Wong, Siu-lun, and Janet Salaff. 1998. Network Capital: Emigration From Hong Kong. *British Journal of Sociology* 49 (3): 258–74.

Wong, Wai Ling. 2008. "Making Home: Three Generations of Chinese Immigrant Women in Hong Kong." Unpublished Ph.D thesis. Hong Kong: Sociology, University of Hong Kong.

Yi, Chin-chun, and Wen-yin Chien. 2006. Does Conjugal Disparity Affect Marital Relations? A Comparative Study of Taiwan, Shanghai and Hong Kong. *Current Sociology* 54 (2): 229–55.

Youngson, A. J. 1983. *China and Hong Kong: The Economic Nexus.* Hong Kong: Oxford University Press.

Zhou, Min. 1997. Segmented Assimilation: Issues, Controversies, and Recent Research on the New Second Generation. *International Migration Review* 31 (4): 975–1008.

INDEX

assimilation, integration, 2, 9, 58–59, 68–70, 74, 219; acculturation space, 68; melting-pot, 68; segmented assimilation theory, 3, 70–71

British empire, institutional carryover, 7, 151

cognitive-cultural aspects of institutional theory, 10–12, 25–28; Chinese heritage, 63, 103, 108, 125, 161; cognitive frames, 10–12, 101, 118, 124, 126, 217, 219; cultural tool kits, 11, 25–26; habitus (personal dispositions), 11

economy: civil service, 19, 21, 25, 81, 84, 105–6, 109, 111–12, 114, 115, 161; competence of Mainland workers, 38, 75, 78, 85, 92, 106, 218; construction industry, Hong Kong, 19, 22, 49–50, 105, 200–202, 206–8, 211; engineers, 8, 21, 30, 35–57; film, television industry, 59–60, 63, 67, 140, 147, 160–62; food services industry, Hong Kong, 22, 64, 93, 150, 126, 136, 149, 184, 187, 193; foreign domestic workers in Hong Kong, 23, 44, 113, 145–47; garment industry, Hong Kong, 104, 159, 162–66, 169, 176, 181, 202, 206; GDP, 22; hawking in Hong Kong, 60; Hong Kong integration with China, 20, 85, 166–67, 201; investment in Canada 6, 39, 40, 48, 50, 62, 63, 68, 74, 76, 77, 138; low-paid industries in Hong Kong, 20, 22, 43, 92, 146, 161–65, 185, 193, 192, 209;

machine-tool industries, Hong Kong, 74; manufacturing in Hong Kong, 19, 22, 180–81; North-South trade, 119–25, 130; property development, 63, 80, 81, 91; protective and security services 87, 92; semi-professionals in Hong Kong, 21; service economy, economic restructuring in Hong Kong 20, 21, 165, 194, 221; transportation industry, Hong Kong, 60, 73, 140–41, 169–70, 180, 191–92; unemployment and downward mobility, Hong Kong 171–72, 180–81; volunteer work, 94; women's employment, 22–23, 41–44, 66–67, 143, 147–49, 202; working hours, 111, 113

education, 19; adapting to schools abroad, 43, 53–56, 61; clan association school, 120, 122; English-language schooling, 7, 53, 81, 136, 161, 208; emigration and, 6–7, 26–27, 35, 41, 42, 45, 52–54, 61–62, 70, 84, 135–36, 142; expansion in Hong Kong, 19, 21, 43; gender and, 21, 153–54; school's overseas network, 7, 8, 61, 136, 198; social class and, 7, 38, 36,93, 104, 143, 151–54, 151,163, 181, 105, 211; studying abroad, 52–54, 56, 61–62, 65, 128, 135–36

emigrants, defined, 4

emigration styles; emigrant planners, 33–57; emigration as escapism, 105; family-tied emigrants, 135–55, 182; living a family-centered life abroad 68; preservation of British way of life, 81, 88

entrepreneurs, 13, 48, 49, 50, 58–79,

Janet W. Salaff is professor emerita of sociology at the University of Toronto and the author of *Working Daughters of Hong Kong: Filial Piety or Power in the Family?*

Siu-lun Wong is professor of sociology and director of the Centre for Asian Studies at the University of Hong Kong.

Arent Greve is professor of organization theory at the Norwegian School of Economics and Business Administration in Bergen, Norway.

Studies of World Migrations

The University of Illinois Press
is a founding member of the
Association of American University Presses.

———————————

Composed in 10/13 Sabon LT Std
at the University of Illinois Press
Manufactured by Thomson-Shore, Inc.

University of Illinois Press
1325 South Oak Street
Champaign, IL 61820-6903
www.press.uillinois.edu